COM ENT

Computers and Communication

Bob Steele · Jerry Wellington

Computers and Communication

Blackie

ISBN 0 216 91648 8
ISBN 0 216 919312 (Trade edition)

First published 1985
Reprinted 1986, 1987, 1988, 1990

© Bob Steele and Jerry Wellington

All rights reserved
No part of this publication may be reproduced,
stored in a retrieval system or transmitted,
in any form or by any means, electronic, mechanical,
photocopying, recording or otherwise, without
prior permission from the publisher

Illustrated by David Brogan

Published by Blackie and Son Limited
Bishopbriggs, Glasgow G64 2NZ
7 Leicester Place, London WC2H 7BP

Filmset by Tradespools Limited
Printed in Great Britain by
Bell and Bain Ltd, Glasgow

Preface

To the reader

This book tells you:
- what a computer is
- how computers developed from simple calculators
- what computers can do—and what they can't do
- how you can give orders to a computer
- how you can put data into a computer—and get information out again
- how computers are used to communicate information
- what 'information technology' is and how it affects you
- about the language used in computer books and magazines—bits, bytes, ROM, RAM, K, etc.
- what the main parts of a computer are called and the jobs they do
- how a computer does its arithmetic
- what computers are used for
- how computers have affected, and may affect, the society you live in

However, reading a book is not enough. To understand computers and computer programming fully you need to get your hands on one and obtain practical experience. You need to write your own programs and try them out. You will also need to visit offices, banks, police stations, libraries, shops, businesses, factories or any other place where computers are used, to see at *first hand* the jobs they can (and cannot) do. No book on computers can explain all their uses and possibilities. You will need to look out for newspaper stories, TV programmes, and magazine articles which show the ways in which computers are affecting the world you live in.

To the teacher

This book covers the topics common to all the GCSE Computer Studies courses in England and Wales. Many questions from past exam papers have been included to test knowledge and understanding of each topic. Further exam questions have been added at the end of the book for revision purposes.

Contents

Part 1: What is a Computer? — 1

1.1	What is a digital computer?	2
1.2	Digital computer systems	7
1.3	From the abacus to the computer	11
1.4	Computers in the 20th century	14
	Comprehension Extract	19
	Wordsearch	20

Part 2: Communicating with Computers — 21

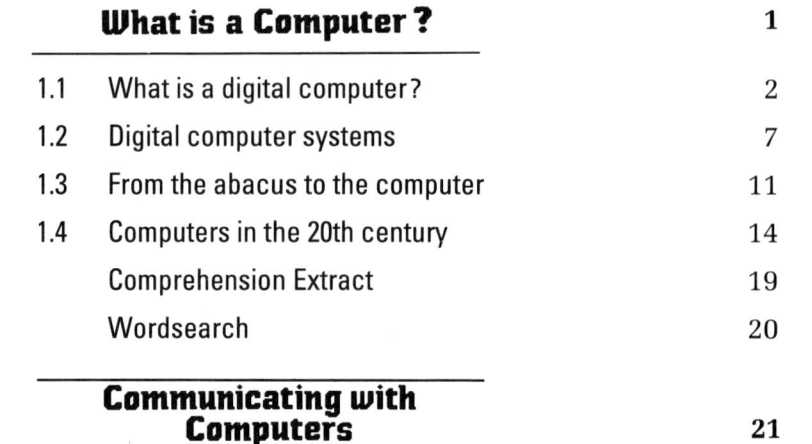

2.1	Putting data into a computer	22
2.2	Getting information back	29
2.3	Storing data	35
	Wordsearch	41

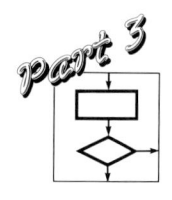

Part 3: Giving the Computer Instructions — 43

3.1	Principles of programming	44
3.2	Specifying the solution: flowcharts and algorithms	46
3.3	Breaking down problems: structured programming	52
3.4	Putting the program in a language for the computer	55
3.5	Types of programming language I: low-level	61
3.6	Types of programming language II: high-level	63
	Comprehension Extract	68
	Wordsearch	70

Part 4

Systems Software — 71

4.1	Getting the most out of a computer	72
4.2	Types of operating system	75
	Wordsearch	81
	CASE STUDY—CP/M	82

Part 5

Inside the Computer — 85

5.1	Representing data inside a computer	86
5.2	Representing whole numbers	91
5.3	Representing negative numbers	96
5.4	Representing fractions and real numbers	101
5.5	Computer logic	106
5.6	The heart of the computer: the central processing unit	118
5.7	Linking the inside of the computer to the outside world	125
5.8	Computer networks: linking computers together	130
	Comprehension Extract	134
	Wordsearch	135
	CASE STUDY—A washing machine controller	136

Part 6

Putting Computers to Work — 139

6.1	Computer-based systems	140
6.2	People who work with computers	143
6.3	Defining the system: systems analysis	146
6.4	Designing the system: systems design	150
6.5	Files in a system	160
	Wordsearch	168
	CASE STUDY—Hospital in-patient system	169
	CASE STUDY—Monitoring and controlling river levels	171

Part 7

Information Technology — 175

7.1	What is information technology	176
7.2	Information technology in action	182
	Wordsearch	189

Part 8

Into the Information Era — 191

8.1	A changing society	192
READER	Yesterday's tomorrows	196
8.2	More jobs or less?	198
READER	The computer revolution	202
8.3	Can computers save the woolly monkey?	205
READER	The man who has given up paper	210
8.4	Will big brother be watching you?	211
READER	The third industrial revolution	215
8.5	Can machines have minds?	217
READER	Machines with feelings	220
8.6	Towards the year 2000	222
Glossary		225
Further Questions		232
Acknowledgments		241
Index		243

Part 1

What is a Computer?

1.1 What is a digital computer?

This unit tells you what a digital computer is and explains some of the jobs it can do. It also tells you what computers use as their 'raw material': data.

Digital and analogue: what's the difference?

Suppose you stop somebody in the street, ask them for the time and '11.12' is the reply. You know that person is wearing a **digital** watch.

Just to be sure, you ask another passer-by. The reply comes back: 'Well ..., it's just before quarter past eleven.' That person has a watch with hands on it. It is an **analogue** watch.

Digital devices deal with *numbers* only. For example, a digital watch may tell you the time is '9.44'—an analogue watch tells you 'It's almost quarter to ten.' Readings on a digital device go in *jumps* from one number to the next, e.g. 9.44, 9.45, 9.46, 9.47 ... They do not give readings on a steadily rising, continuous scale.

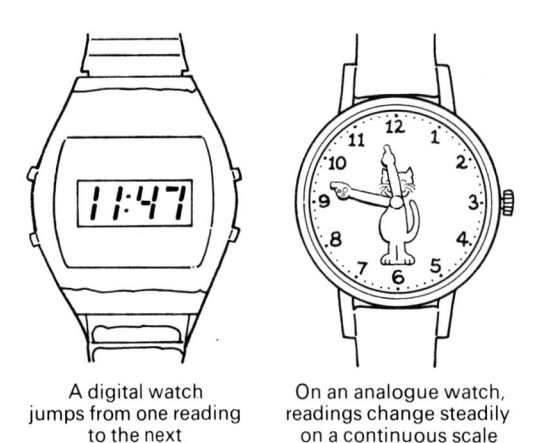

A digital watch jumps from one reading to the next

On an analogue watch, readings change steadily on a continuous scale

Fig. 1.1

Analogue devices measure something by comparing it with something else, called its 'analogue'. They give a reading anywhere between an upper and lower limit. These two features are common to all analogue devices. For example, a thermometer measures temperature by comparing how far mercury moves along a scale.

Here are some other examples of analogue devices.

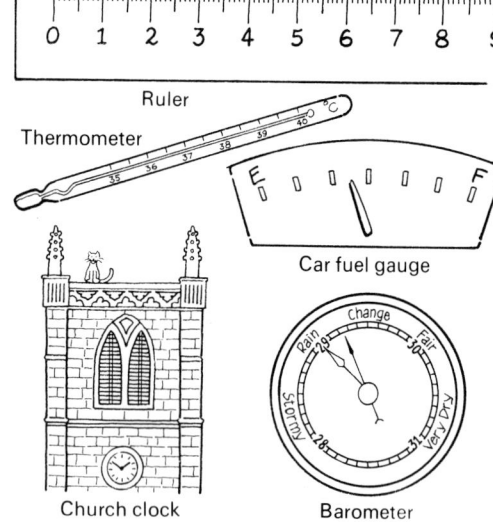

Fig. 1.2 Some analogue devices

Since digital computers can operate with numbers only, they cannot deal directly with information from an analogue device. Information must first be converted from analogue form (e.g. a reading on a scale) to digital form (i.e. a reading in the form of a number). This conversion is done by an **analogue-to-digital converter** or **digitizer**.

Some computers are analogue computers, but the rest of this book is about digital computers.

Information and data

The words 'information' and 'data' are sometimes given the same meaning, but there is an important difference between them. Look at this string of letters and numbers:

X K W 1 4 1 T.

It is just a string of symbols *until* you realize that it is a car registration number, then it starts to mean something. For example, 'XKW' tells you where the car comes from; 'T' tells you roughly how old it is.

A string of letters, numbers, and other symbols is called **data**. When you make sense of, or interpret, data it provides **information**.

A computer is often described as a machine that handles information. In fact, a computer can only deal with data.

Coding If you tell someone that you were born on the 7th July, 1970 then this information can be coded into data as: 07/07/70. There are several reasons for coding information into data:
- to make it easier to handle and communicate
- to make it shorter and more compact
- to make it exact and accurate
- machines can only handle data.

A Digital Computer

A **digital computer** is an **automatic**, **electronic**, **re-programmable**, **digital**, **data processor**. This is what most people nowadays mean when they talk about computers. So what is the meaning of each part of this definition?

automatic: A computer can work through, and carry out, a set of instructions *on its own*. This set of instructions is called a **program**.

re-programmable: The instructions given to a computer can be changed. It can be re-programmed to do a different job—either by changing an existing program or by giving it a completely new one.

electronic: There are no moving parts inside a computer—only tiny particles called **electrons** moving around in circuits. (This is one reason why they work so quickly.) A computer is just a vast collection of electric circuits and switches.

digital: Most computers deal with the figures 0 and 1. These are called **digits**.

data: A computer takes in data, changes it, then gives information *out* again. The data a computer takes in can be in the form of figures, letters, or punctuation marks, i.e. digital data ('data' is the Latin word for 'facts'). Inside a digital computer this is changed to a string of electrical pulses.

processor: A computer works on, changes, or processes, the data you give it. This is why it is called a processor. If the data put in is rubbish, the information got out will be rubbish. People who work with computers call this: 'Garbage In, Garbage Out' or GIGO for short.

All these ideas together make up the meaning of the word 'computer'.

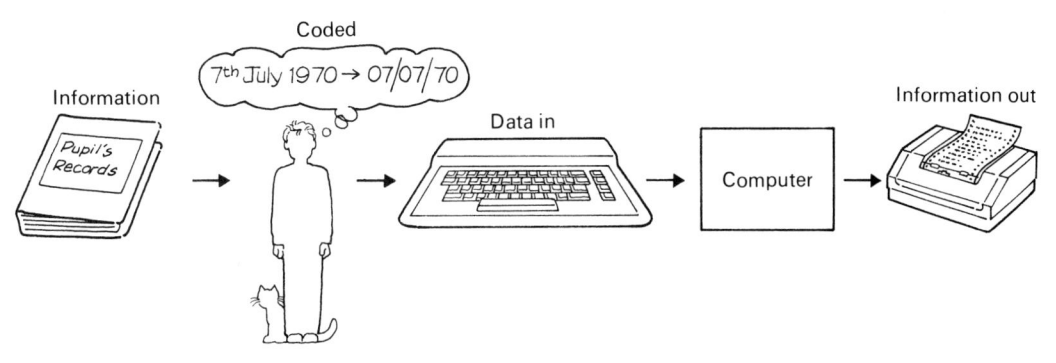

Fig. 1.3 A computer processes data

Little and large

There are three main sizes of digital computer: the **mainframe computer**, the **minicomputer** and the **microcomputer**.

The largest type, 'mainframes', are used by banks, insurance companies, universities and other big organizations which need a lot of computing power. They may cost over £1 million and need over 100 staff to operate and maintain them.

Minicomputers may cost several thousand pounds and need a staff of 5 or 10 people to operate them properly. They are often used by smaller businesses.

Microcomputers, or 'micros', started to develop in the 1970's. Nowadays you can buy a micro for less than £50 which has as much computing power as the original mainframes. They are used in homes, schools, and even small businesses.

A minicomputer

A mainframe computer and its operators

Using a microcomputer

	MAIN FRAME	MICRO
COST	Up to £1 000 000, or more	Less than £50, as much as £1000
SIZE	Housed in a large, air-conditioned room	Can sit on a desk; some can be carried in a brief case
USERS	Can support many users at once	Usually one user at a time
ACCURACY	Provide greater accuracy, e.g. for high precision maths	Accurate enough for most purposes
SPEED	Very fast operation	Slower, but fast enough for most purposes
MEMORY	Very large memory	Smaller memory, but increasing with new developments

The mainframe v. the micro

What can a computer do?

There are certain jobs that a computer can, and cannot, do. Computers *can*...
- follow and carry out a series of instructions (a program)
- work more quickly and tirelessly than your brain
- store data in their memory
- make simple decisions which they are programmed to make.

Computers *cannot*...
- do anything without a program of instructions written by a human
- think for themselves
- create symphonies, pop songs, novels, works of art or jokes
- judge a painting, poem, song or book to be good or bad
- feel hot, cold, irritable, tired or angry (which is just as well).

In other words, a computer can only do what a human being has programmed it to do in the first place.

The complex tasks which computers can perform can all be broken down into four basic jobs or operations:
- taking in and giving out data
- doing arithmetic (adding and subtracting)
- comparing items of data and making simple decisions
- moving data around inside the computer.

A skilful programmer can program a computer to do a complex task by gradually breaking it down into these four basic operations. (The way this is done, and how these tasks are carried out inside the machine are both explained in later units.)

Fig. 1.4 *Computers cannot lose their tempers!*

KEY POINTS

1. Digital devices only deal with quantities that go up in steps. Analogue devices deal with quantities that vary steadily and gradually.

2. A string of symbols may be data. Information is the meaning attached to those symbols by a person.

3. A digital computer is an automatic, electronic, re-programmable, digital, data processor.

4. There are three main sizes of computer: mainframe computer, minicomputer and microcomputer.

5. A computer can only do what it is programmed to do.

Questions

1 Copy out and complete these sentences:
   a) A _____ is an information processing device.
   b) Analogue and _____ are the two main types of electronic computer.
2 Why is a simple pocket calculator not a computer?
3 Write 'analogue' or 'digital', as appropriate, beside each of the following to indicate the mode of operation.
   a) A glass tube on the side of a fuel tank to indicate the amount of oil remaining
   b) A cricket scoreboard
   c) A weather vane
   d) A set of traffic lights
   e) A magnetic compass
   (SREB)
4 In Fig. 1.5 a digital computer is to receive signals from a furnace gauge. What is the unit, labelled 'Unit A', called? What job does it do?
   (SREB)
5 Explain the difference between information and data. Give two examples of data showing how it is interpreted to give information.
6* What is meant by saying that the mileometer of a car displays its results in a digital form, while the speedometer provides an analogue display?
   (OLE)

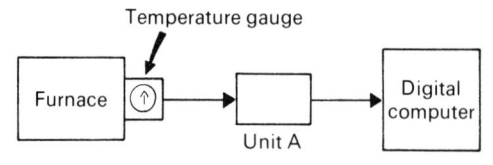

Fig. 1.5

*'O'-Level question

1.2 Digital computer systems

A digital computer system is made up of different parts connected together. This unit introduces you to some of the parts and the names given to them. All computer systems, from the smallest microcomputer to the largest mainframe, have these same basic components.

The main parts of a computer

One way of understanding how computers work is by comparing them with other machines, or even with people who do certain jobs.

You can compare a computer with an office clerk sitting at a desk. Information and instructions are given to the clerk. They reach his brain through his eyes and ears. These are his 'input devices'. All this information is converted into nerve impulses which travel to his brain. Some of the information, and the instructions on what to do with it, he remembers in his memory. Other parts of the information are handled and dealt with straight away. He may help his memory by jotting things down on his memo pad, for example: instructions or jobs to be carried out next day or next week. When the clerk has dealt with, or *processed*, the information from his 'in' tray according to the instructions given to him he can pass it along to his 'out' tray.

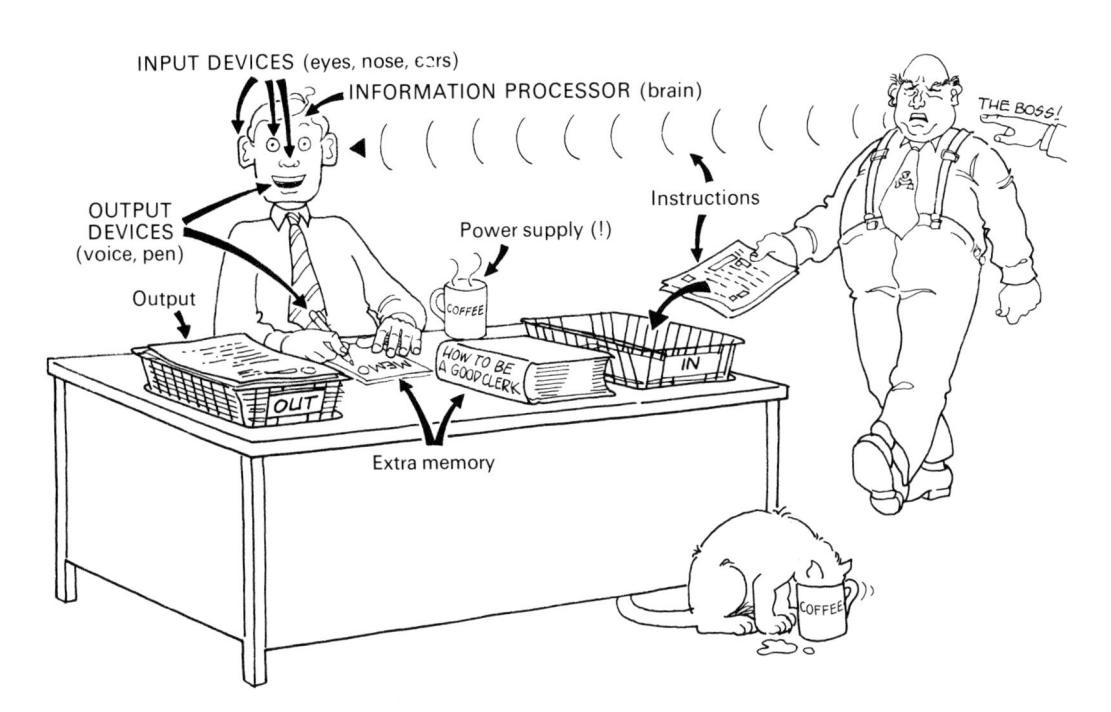

Fig. 1.6 *Comparing a computer with an office clerk*

	CLERK	COMPUTER
INPUT	1 Information supplied to him	1 Data fed in
	2 Instructions given on what to do with the information	2 Computer program given to process it
INPUT DEVICES	Eyes and ears convert messages to nerve impulses for the brain	Keyboard, paper-tape readers, etc. send electrical impulses to the central processing unit
THE 'BRAIN'	1 Holds information, remembers instructions (memory)	1 Memory: stores data, holds instructions
	2 Processes information, e.g. adds numbers, sorts into alphabetical order	2 Central processing unit takes instructions one at a time; processes data
OUTPUT DEVICES	1 Clerk writing on paper, e.g. results of a calculation	Printers, television screen, paper-tape puncher, etc.
	2 Clerk's voice	
OUTPUT	Information, e.g. a hand-written bill	Information, e.g. a computer print-out

Comparing an office clerk with a computer system

Like a computer, the imaginary clerk is an **information processor**. This table shows you how the job done by a computer system can be compared with the job of our office clerk.

This comparison may help you to understand the way in which a computer system works:

      input → process → output

However, don't take the comparison too seriously.

Inside the 'brain' of a computer

Memory The first part is the memory. This is made up of a set of 'pigeon holes' or **locations**. Each location can store a certain amount of data (just as a house has a certain number of rooms). Computers only deal with 1's and 0's—these are called **binary digits**, or **bits** for short. In some computers each location can hold 8 bits. Others can hold 12 bits and some can hold as many as 16, 24 or even 32 bits in each location.

Each location has an **address** so that data can be sent to it, and fetched from it.

This address is always given a number (like the number on the outside of a house), but the address number of each location must not be confused with the data inside the location, the **contents**.

8 bits in each location (the contents)

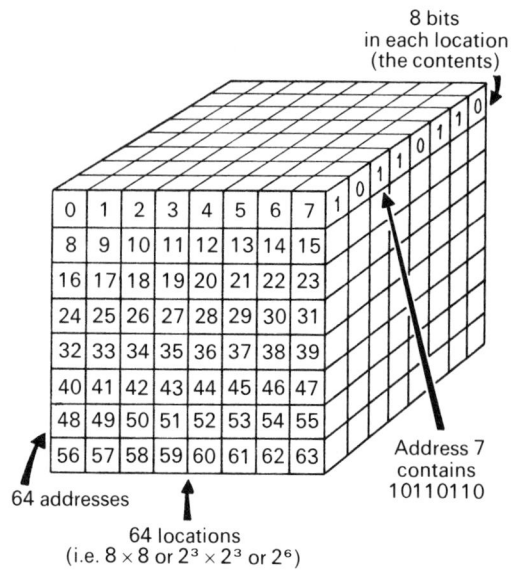

64 addresses

64 locations
(i.e. 8×8 or $2^3 \times 2^3$ or 2^6)

Address 7 contains 10110110

Fig. 1.7 A computer memory: locations and addresses

The memory inside the computer is often called the **main store** or **immediate access store**. To add to this, most computer systems have extra memory in their **backing store**. This contains data or instructions on **magnetic tape** or **magnetic disk** (for example) which can be loaded into the computer when needed. (Tapes and disks are discussed fully in Unit 2.3.) This extra memory is also called **long-term storage**, **mass storage** or **auxiliary storage**.

The part of a computer system which actually processes data is called the **Central Processing Unit** (CPU). This has two main parts: the **control unit** and the **arithmetic and logic unit**. The jobs done by these parts are explained in Unit 5.6.

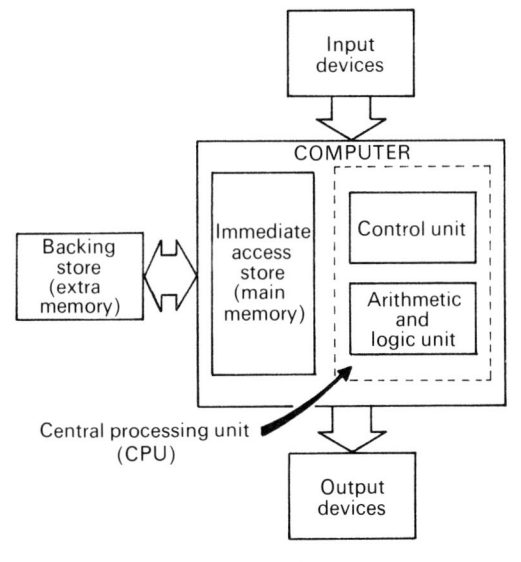

- the input and output devices
- the central processing unit
- the main memory
- the extra memory (auxiliary storage or backing store).

The input and output devices, and auxiliary storage, are outside the central processing unit. They are often called **peripherals** ('peripheral' = outward part).

Hardware—you can pick it up and fall over it

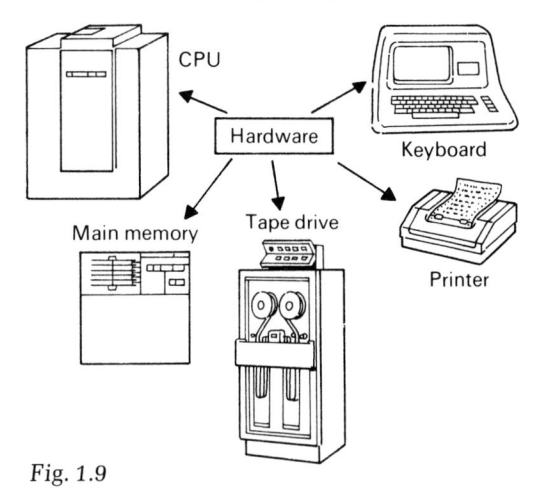

Fig. 1.9

Fig. 1.8 The main parts of a computer

What makes a 'computer system'?

A **system** is a mixture of parts working together. This section describes the different parts of a computer system which work together, as a whole, to make it do useful jobs.

Hardware This means the machinery itself, the parts you can actually trip over in a computer room. The hardware consists of:

Software The hardware alone is not enough to make a working computer system. Something is needed to operate and control the different parts. Besides this, the computer must be given instructions to make it do a useful job. These extras, which bring the hardware to life, are called **software**. Two types of software are needed: **systems software** and **applications software**.

'Systems software' is the name given to all the programs *inside* the computer which make it usable. One part of the systems software controls or 'drives' the different parts of the computer system. The other part 'translates' the **programming language** employed by the computer user (e.g. BASIC, PASCAL) into **machine code** which is a series of electrical pulses (see Unit 3.5).

The applications software for a computer is written to make the computer do certain tasks, or solve certain problems (i.e. to *apply* the computer). This is often written in a programming language best suited for certain jobs (e.g. FORTRAN for scientific work, COBOL for business uses). The systems software then has the job of translating this language when the computer system is used. The programs written to make use of the computer are called **applications programs**.

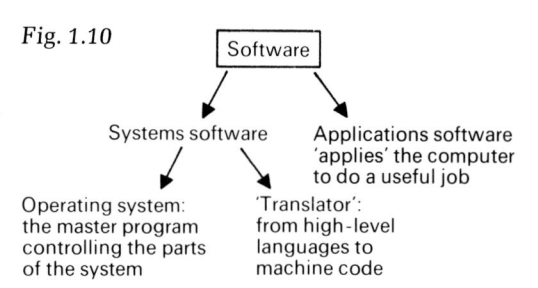

Fig. 1.10

Software
→ Systems software → Operating system: the master program controlling the parts of the system
→ Applications software 'applies' the computer to do a useful job → 'Translator': from high-level languages to machine code

---

KEY POINTS

1 Every computer system involves input, processing and output.

2 The central, or key, part of a computer system consists of a processing unit and a main, internal memory.

3 The processing unit consists of a control unit and an arithmetic and logic unit.

4 A computer system is made up of hardware and software.

5 The term 'hardware' refers to the actual physical parts or units which make up a computer system. 'Software' refers to the programs which operate and apply a computer system. Software puts hardware to work.

Questions

1 Briefly explain what each of these terms means:
mass storage   hardware
CPU   systems software
peripheral   applications software.

2 Draw and label a block diagram to show the four main hardware units that make up a computer system. Indicate the flow of data between the units.

3 A process is a sequence of actions carried out in a definite order. Here is a list of some processes that are done in everyday life:
  baking a cake
  washing clothes in a machine
  growing peas from seed
  playing a guitar
  cooking potatoes

For each of these processes write down:
a) the input, b) the output.
For two of them suggest what might be called:
a) the hardware, b) the software.

4 Go back and read the section where a clerk is compared with a computer. The section may help you to understand computers, but there are dangers in this comparison. Make a list of the important differences between a clerk and a computer.

1.3 From the abacus to the computer

You can get an idea of what computers are, and where they came from, by looking briefly at their history. Computers really developed from calculating devices, though nowadays they are much more versatile and sophisticated.

Calculating, from early times to the 19th century

The abacus The first calculators used beads that moved along wires or strings. You probably used one when you were about 6 months old without knowing it. Invented more than 400 years BC, it is called an **abacus**. The abacus was, and still is, widely used in eastern countries like China, Japan, Russia and India. It is a speedy and accurate way of adding and subtracting numbers. But it was never widely used in the Western World, and it was never quite good enough at multiplication and division.

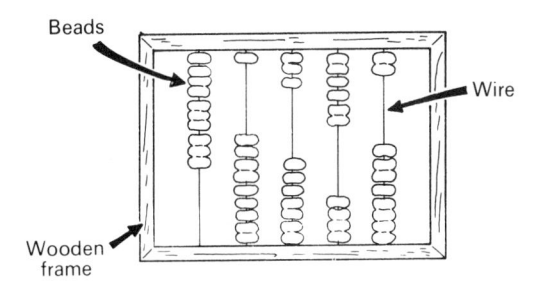

Fig. 1.11 An abacus

John Napier In 1617 a Scotsman called John Napier invented a new system for multiplying which would replace the abacus. He made a set of rods with numbers written on them: **Napier's bones**.

Napier also worked out the first set of logarithmic tables, or logs. It took many years, but once they were ready all multiplications and divisions could be done by adding and subtracting.

Pascal's adder and subtractor A Frenchman called Blaise Pascal made one of the first mechanical calculating machines in 1642. This used 'setting wheels' which could be turned to stand for a certain number. To add another number each setting wheel was turned the appropriate number of places.

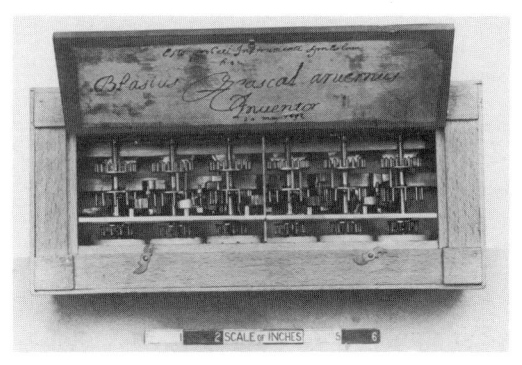

Pascal's calculating machine

Leibniz's machine Pascal's machine could only add and subtract. Multiplication had to be done by adding over and over again. In 1671 a German called Baron Gothfried Leibniz made a multiplying machine. But his invention never really spread because it was so hard for the engineers of the time to build. However, a design made in 1875 by F. J. Baldwin was used in mechanical calculators right up until the 1960's.

The machines of Pascal and Leibniz were certainly calculators, but by today's standards they were not computers. They all needed a human being to dial numbers or turn handles. It was a strange English genius who designed the world's first computer—a computer that was never completely built.

Babbage's engines: 100 years ahead of their time

Charles Babbage

Charles Babbage was born in Devon in 1792. At the age of 21 he had the idea of building a calculating machine which would operate *without* human intervention. Babbage was disgusted at the log tables used in his day, which were full of mistakes. He wanted to construct an engine that would calculate certain mathematical functions accurately and mechanically: the **difference engine**. Part of it was built but the engine was never finished. In 1832 Babbage lost interest in his idea because he had a new one: the **analytical engine**. This engine would have been the first automatic universal computer—it was designed to carry out any kind of calculation by following 'instructions' given to it. Babbage's analytical engine was never built, but it had all the features of a modern automatic general-purpose computer:

- a *store* (or memory) for holding numbers (Babbage's idea was to use columns of wheels. Each wheel could be set in any one of ten positions to stand for a number.)
- an *arithmetic unit*—this would carry out addition or subtraction of numbers in the store
  (Babbage called this the 'mill'.)
- a *control unit*—this would make the machine carry out its instructions in the right order
- an *input device*—this would feed numbers and instructions into the machine
- an *output device*—this would display the results of a calculation.

Why was the analytical engine never built? People have said that Babbage was 100 years ahead of his time. The engine needed very precise engineering for all its wheels, gears, rods and cogs. Engineers at the time were simply not capable of building it. Besides this, nobody saw any *need* to build the engine—what would they use it for?

Babbage's analytical engine

Babbage's ideas live on

The first program Babbage left no written description of his engine. Fortunately a lady called the Countess of Lovelace (1815–52) was one of his admirers. Lady Lovelace (the daughter of Lord Byron) made notes describing Babbage's engines in detail. She also wrote a list of instructions which would get the machine to carry out a calculation automatically. Lady Lovelace was the first computer programmer.

Lady Lovelace

Punched cards She wanted to have the instructions punched onto cards. The idea of **punched cards** had come from a Frenchman called Joseph Jacquard in 1801. He used them to control a weaving loom. The Jacquard loom could weave almost any pattern depending on the hundreds of cards that were used to control it. Babbage planned to use punched cards to control his analytical engine, but his idea was never tried in his own lifetime.

Hollerith's punched cards In the 19th century a census was held in the United States every 10 years to keep track of the growing population. Unfortunately the figures from the 1880 census were still being counted and sorted in 1887! The job would not be finished before the next census was due, in 1890. An engineer called Hermann Hollerith knew about Jacquard's loom and he suggested using similar punched cards to sort and count the census figures. A sorting machine was made, powered by electricity (the latest invention) and controlled by punched cards. Hollerith's machine sorted out the 1890 census in just six weeks.

Notice that the punched card was now being used in *two* ways: to give instructions, and *also* to store data. The present-day abilities of computers were beginning to develop.

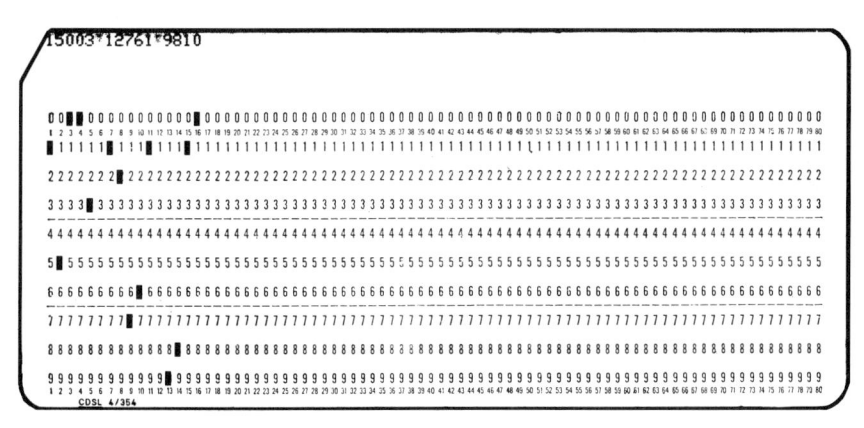

Fig. 1.12   A modern punched card

Questions

1 What were Babbage's two engines called? Which one is nearest to the modern idea of a computer? Explain why.
2 What was John Napier famous for?
3 Explain the difference between a calculator and a computer?
4 Make a simple time chart showing how calculators developed from 400 BC up until 1900.

13

1.4 Computers in the 20th century

The central processing unit of the world's first computer filled a room and used as much power as a steam engine. Thirty years later the same computing power could be built on a wafer of silicon as small as this:

☐

Unit 1.4 explains how computers have shrunk since 1944 and have spread from a few science laboratories into millions of front rooms.

Mechanical monsters

Charles Babbage first formed the idea of a fully automatic general-purpose calculator, or *computer*, in Cambridge, England in 1832. His idea finally became reality in Cambridge, Massachusetts, USA 112 years later. In 1937, Howard Aiken of Harvard University planned the **ASCC**: Automatic Sequence Controlled Calculator. It was finished in 1944—a mechanical monster over 16 metres long and nearly 3 metres high.

He claimed that it was the world's first computer. Like Babbage's analytical engine, numbers were stored by wheels in different positions—this machine had hundreds. Information was fed into the machine by punched cards.

More huge computers were built in 1937 and 1938. They were called **electromechanical computers** because they had both electrical *and* mechanical parts. When World War II broke out in 1939 there was a tremendous need for these machines (unlike Babbage's in 1832).

Faster and faster calculations were needed in tracking aeroplanes, cracking enemy codes, working out the path of missiles and shells, and computing the results of atomic reactions for the atom bomb project. Because of this need, computers developed much further from 1939 to 1945 than they had done in the previous 100 years.

The first electronic machines

In 1946 an electronic computer was built at the University of Pennsylvania. It was called **ENIAC**: Electronic Numerical Integrator and Calculator. This computer was built to calculate bombing and firing tables to help make bombs, shells and missiles more accurate. It was even bigger than the ASCC, occupying a space of 140 square metres and weighing 30 tonnes.

This computer used an earlier invention: the **valve**, or high-speed vacuum tube. ENIAC contained nearly 19 000 valves. Valves can operate far more quickly than cogs and wheels. ENIAC could do as many calculations in 1 *hour* as the ASCC could do in 1 *week*. In 1 second

ENIAC—the first electronic computer

ENIAC could perform 5000 additions or 300 multiplications. ENIAC made all mechanical calculators obsolete.

Stored program computers

The MANIAC A brilliant Hungarian mathematician, Dr. John von Neumann, had emigrated to America in 1930. He became involved in the building of the new hydrogen bomb. A faster and more powerful computer was needed to carry out all the necessary calculations. Von Neumann suggested two new ideas:
- using binary numbers, with only the digits 0 and 1, inside the computer (The electronic parts could be either 'on' or 'off'—these two positions could stand for the two binary digits.)
- storing a set of instructions inside the computer, i.e. *a stored program*.

The computer used for the H-bomb project was nicknamed **MANIAC**: Mathematical Analyser, Numerical Integrator and Computer. With MANIAC's help the new bomb was finished and tested by 1952.

EDSAC In fact, the first computer using von Neumann's ideas was built at Cambridge University in 1949. It was called the 'Electronic Delay Storage Automatic Calculator' or **EDSAC**.

Transistor machines

Computers which used valves were built right up until 1958, but they were huge and often unreliable. Some contained over 6000 valves and could become very hot. They also needed large amounts of electrical power—as much as 150 kilowatts (150 one-bar electric fires). By 1958 there were only about 60 computers in the whole of Britain.

However, in 1947 the **transistor** had been invented by an American called Shockley. This is a small piece of solid material which can do the same job as a valve, but it is smaller, needs less power and generates less heat. Computers using transistors were built from 1959 to 1964.

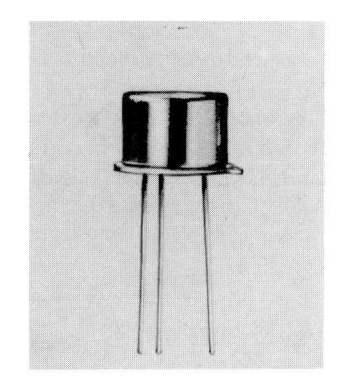

A transistor

Hundreds were made. These transistorized computers were far smaller, faster, cheaper and more reliable than the huge valve machines of the 1950's.

Miniature circuits

Another invention, in 1957, brought a new generation of computers (the **third generation**). Tiny electric circuits were printed onto a miniscule piece of material. Each circuit contained the equivalent of hundreds or even thousands of transistors. They were called **integrated circuits**. Computers were built with integrated circuits right through the 1960's and early 1970's. The first minicomputer was built in 1965.

The mini and the micro

The 1965 minicomputer was the first mass produced computer. 'Mini' just means 'small'. Some were small enough to go on a desk. Computers became more widely used in business, industry, offices and hospitals.

In the 1970's, **microprocessors** or **'chips'** arrived. A chip is just a tiny, thin wafer of silicon. Electric circuits can be 'printed' onto it. The circuit on a chip can do the controlling and calculating job at the heart of a computer. Chips became used in video games, pocket calculators, washing machines, cash registers and countless other devices. They may be smaller than a fingernail, but they can act as the control unit or 'brain' of larger machines.

In 1975, chips were first used inside computers. The microcomputer had arrived. Nowadays microcomputers are commonplace. The smallest will go into a carrier-bag, yet it is more powerful, faster and reliable than ENIAC, which occupied a whole room—and it only uses 10 watts of electrical power!

The first three generations

The development of electronic computers from 1940 to 1970 is often divided into three generations. In each of these generations the essential parts of the computer itself (the computer hardware) were made up of different electronic components (e.g. valves, transistors). In each generation the time for the computer to carry out an operation (e.g. addition) became less and less. This table shows those three generations.

The fourth and fifth Generations

The **fourth generation** of computers is with us already. These involve extremely complex electronic circuits, formed onto one tiny silicon chip. This is called **Very Large Scale Integration** (VLSI).

Countries like Britain, Japan and the USA are now planning the **fifth generation** of computers. These will be controlled by the human voice, and will respond to commands in our natural language. Future computers will be, in some ways, intelligent and capable of making decisions. They will have **artificial intelligence**.

You can read more about the fourth and fifth generations of computers in Part 8.

A complete microcomputer on a single chip

Magnification about ×15

GENER-ATION	DATES	MAIN ELECTRONIC PARTS	OPERATING SPEEDS MEASURED IN...
I FIRST	1944–1958	Valves (high-vacuum tubes)	Milliseconds (10^{-3} second)
II SECOND	1958–1964	Transistors	Microseconds (10^{-6} second)
III THIRD	1964–1969	Integrated circuits (IC's)	Nanoseconds (10^{-9} second)
LATE THIRD	1970–	'Chips' (microscopic IC's on silicon wafers)	Picoseconds (10^{-12} second)

The first three generations of computers

KEY POINTS in the development of computers

DATE	EVENT
450 BC	Abacus used in Greece and Egypt
1500 AD	Abacus called the soroban introduced to Japan
1614	John Napier calculated logarithmic tables
1617	Napier's bones
1632	Oughtred's slide rule
1642	Pascal's adding machine
1671	Leibniz's calculator
1805	Jacquard's loom controlled by punched cards
1822	Babbage's idea of the difference engine
1832	Babbage's idea of the analytical engine
1890	Hollerith sorted out the American census
1944	Harvard's mechanical monster, ASCC, built
1946	ENIAC—the first electronic computer
1947	Transistor invented
1949	EDSAC—the first stored-program computer
1951	UNIVAC—first commercial computer
1957	First integrated circuit
1965	First minicomputer
1975	First microcomputer

Questions

1.

```
    ○Ⓐ        ○       ○
                      ○
  ┬┬┬┼┬┬┬┼┬┬┬┼┬┬┬┼┬┬┬┼┬┬┬
  1780  1820  1860  1900  1940  1980
```

The diagram above illustrates a 'time-scale' upon which the arrows show the time when various events occurred in the history of computing. For example, A) indicates when Babbage constructed the first difference engine. Similarly record the following events by writing the appropriate letter in the circle.
B) Hollerith's invention of a tabulator
C) ENIAC became operational
D) Jacquard used punched cards to control a weaving loom
E) UNIVAC became operational
(YREB 1981)

2. In the following passage write the most appropriate words in the spaces provided.
First generation computers were developed in America about 1945 using _____ in their electronic circuits as active components. About the same time, John von Neumann and others proposed the _____ concept in which the sequence of instructions was held in the computer's store.
Second generation machines were available approximately 10 years later using _____ as the main electric component and had the advantage of increased _____ and _____.
In the 1960's, third generation computers using _____ were produced providing a reduction in _____ and laying the foundation for the silicon chip and accelerating the pace of the computer revolution.
(SREB)

3. What is meant by the 'three generations of electronic computers'?

4. Explain simply what a silicon chip is. What can a chip be used in?

5.*a) Since the ENIAC was built, two major advances in electronic devices have contributed to more rapid and efficient computing. Name the electronic devices responsible for these advances and state how each one contributed to the improvement.
b) What was von Neumann's major contribution to the development of computing?
(JMB)

6.*Describe the developments of computer hardware up to and including the present day. Include in your answer references to:
a) the work of Pascal, Babbage and Hollerith
b) the three generations of computers
c) present hardware developments.
(WJEC)

*'O'-Level question

? Comprehension Extract

9. What's Inside the Case?

The picture here shows what the inside of the ZX Spectrum looks like.

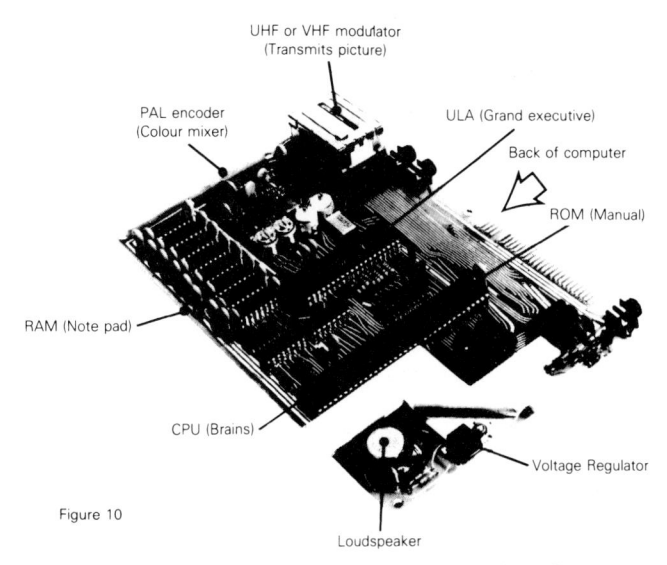

UHF or VHF modulator
(Transmits picture)

PAL encoder
(Colour mixer)

ULA (Grand executive)

Back of computer

ROM (Manual)

RAM (Note pad)

CPU (Brains)

Voltage Regulator

Figure 10

Loudspeaker

As you can see everything is named by a three letter abbreviation. The black rectangular pieces of plastic with lots of metal legs are the integrated circuits that actually do all the work. Inside each one is a ¼"×¼" square of silicon joined by wires to the metal legs. On that silicon chip are thousands of transistors that make up the electronic circuits that *are* the computer.

The brains behind the operation is the processor chip, often called the CPU (Central Processor Unit). This particular one is called a Z80A, which is a faster version of the popular Z80.

The processor controls the computer, does the arithmetic, looks at what keys have been pressed, decides what to do as a result, and in general decides what the computer should do. However, for all its cleverness, it could not do all this on its own. It knows nothing about BASIC or decimal point arithmetic, for example, and it has to get all its instructions from another chip, the ROM (Read Only Memory). The ROM contains a long list of instructions that make a computer program, telling the processor what to do under all foreseeable circumstances. This program is written not in BASIC, but in what is called Z80 machine code, and takes the form of a long sequence of numbers. There are altogether 16384 (16*1024) of these, which is why ZX Spectrum BASIC is sometimes called a 16K BASIC – 1K is 1024.

Although there are similar chips in other computers, this particular sequence of instructions is unique to the ZX Spectrum and was written specially for it.

The eight chips next to it are for the memory. This is RAM (Random Access Memory) and there are two other chips that work closely with them. RAM is where the processor stores information that it wants to keep, any BASIC programs, the variables, the picture for the television screen and various other items that keep track of the state of the computer.

The big chip is the ULA (Uncommitted Logic Array) chip. It really acts as the 'communications centre', making sure that everything the processor requires actually gets done; it also reads the memory to see what the television picture consists of and sends the appropriate signals to the TV interface.

The PAL encoder is a whole group of components that converts the logic chip's television output into a form suitable for colour televisions.

The regulator converts the slightly erratic voltage of the power supply to an absolutely constant five volts.

Questions

1. What do the letters ROM and RAM stand for?
2. Why is RAM called the 'note pad' and ROM the 'manual'?
3. How many is '1K'?
4. Why do you think the CPU is called the 'brains' of this microcomputer?

Wordsearch

Copy this grid into your workbook. In the grid you will find 9 words to do with the development of computers. Use the clues to help you.

1. An ancient counting frame, still used by some.
2. A set of instructions for a computer.
3. The man whose calculating engine was before its time.
4. The man who first used punched cards to store data.
5. The lady who is regarded as being the first programmer.
6. The first electronic computers had lots of these devices in their circuits.
7. Second generation computers used these instead of the devices described in 6.
8. This machine can be used to calculate, store and retrieve data under the control of a program.
9. A complete computer may be built on one of these tiny devices. When made out of potatoes you can eat them!

HISTORY WORDSEARCH

```
L  B  X  F  W C  X  R  O  M T  H  I    L  Q
O  A  C  U  P  Y  L  D  P  R  N  N  J   W E
W B  P  L  O  V  E  L  A  C  E  Q  R   T  K
G  B  M W N  E  Z  N  O  B  W G  S   M V
H  A  T  N  P  R  S  W E  R  E  C  O   C  X
T  G  T  C  H  I  M Q  J  V  J  C  H   E  L
N  E  M I  S  D  H  T  X  G  L  I  U   Z  U
H  T  A  T  R  O  O  C  V  A  B  A  C   U  S
B  H O  L  L  E  R  I  T  H  O  Z  V   D  M
A  R  L  U  C  O  T  J  L  Y  H  C  S   A  D
M Z  U  E  G  X  Z  U  O  Q  G  D  R   W J
B  G  U  A  X  R  B  Z  P  X  D  G  L   L  T
P  U  M S  I  A  X  O  Z  M O  C  I   S  M
B  G  C  B  Z  X  F  G  B  R  O  K  E   Y  N
Q  O  H  P  H  O  V  R  P  X  X  C  H   E  U
```

Part 2

Communicating with Computers

2.1 Putting data into a computer

Humans use words. Computers use electrical pulses. A device is needed so that humans can communicate with computers. Devices for putting data into computers are called input devices—this unit tells you about some of them and how they are used.

What are input devices?

2-state codes At the heart of every computer there are devices which can be *either* in one state *or* another. They are called **two-state devices**. Here are some two-state devices in everyday life.

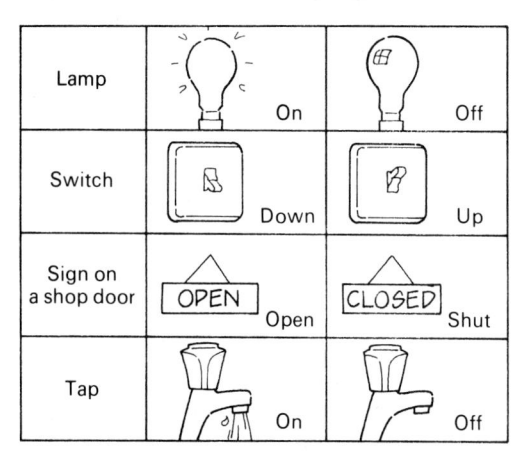

Lamp	On	Off
Switch	Down	Up
Sign on a shop door	OPEN — Open	CLOSED — Shut
Tap	On	Off

Fig. 2.1 Some everyday two-state devices

The two-state devices inside a computer are electronic. Think of their two states as:

Electrical pulse — 1   No electrical pulse — 0

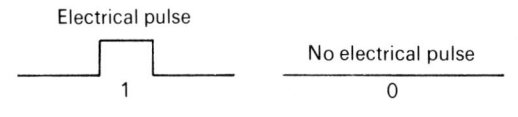

Fig. 2.2

The digits '1' and '0' are used to stand for the two states. Don't imagine that there are millions of 1's and 0's running around inside a computer, though. The only things moving are electrons.

Communicating When you communicate with somebody you convey information, for example:
'It's ten o'clock.'; 'They won 2—0.';
'See you at six.'
People use words and letters to communicate with each other, but to communicate with a computer these words and letters must first be changed into electrical pulses and signals. This is the job done by an **input device**—it enables a human being to communicate with a computer. The input device *translates* various messages into patterns of 'pulses' and 'no pulses', then *sends* them to the computer. The device may be right next to the computer, or hundreds of miles away.

To translate the electrical pulses from the computer back into a form that humans can understand an **output device** is needed (see Unit 2.2). The different patterns of 1's and 0's used to stand for, or represent, different items of data are explained in Unit 5.1.

Types of input device

The very first input devices were just switches. The 'inside' of a computer could be programmed just by turning vast arrays of switches on or off. This was not very convenient, to put it mildly, and it meant that only computer experts could use them. Nowadays there are a variety of input devices. Perhaps the most convenient of all is voice input.

There is an important distinction between the *medium* used for input (e.g.

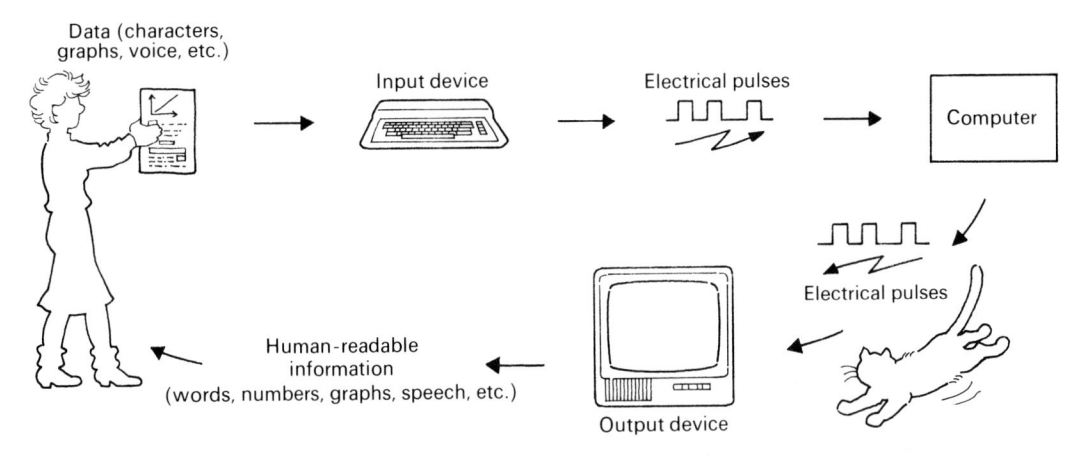

Fig. 2.3 *Communicating with the computer*

spoken word, letters on a keyboard) and the *device* used to convert and send electrical signals to the computer. Often, the more convenient the medium for humans (e.g. the spoken word), the more complicated the device needs to be.

MEDIUM	DEVICE
Punched card	Card reader
Paper tape	Paper-tape reader
Magnetic ink characters (MIC)	MIC reader
Optical characters (OC)	OC reader
Optical marks	Mark sense reader
Keyboard characters	Keyboard
Spoken word	Voice recognition device

At one time most data was input to a computer using punched card or paper tape. Nowadays there are dozens of different input devices for putting data into a computer. The rest of this unit tells you about some of the more common ones.

Keyboard devices

A keyboard can be used to enter data directly into a computer. It looks like a typewriter keyboard, with a Q-W-E-R-T-Y layout. But as well as the usual characters (A–Z, 0–9, punctuation keys, etc.) it may have **special function keys** which can be used to give direct commands to the computer. When each key is pressed a series of electrical signals is sent to the computer—different signals for each key.

As characters are typed in they may appear on a special display screen that looks like a TV screen. This is called a **Visual Display Unit** (VDU).

A visual display unit (VDU) and keyboard

Teletype Some keyboards are connected to a printer. The keyboard and printer together are called a **teletype** or **teletypewriter**.

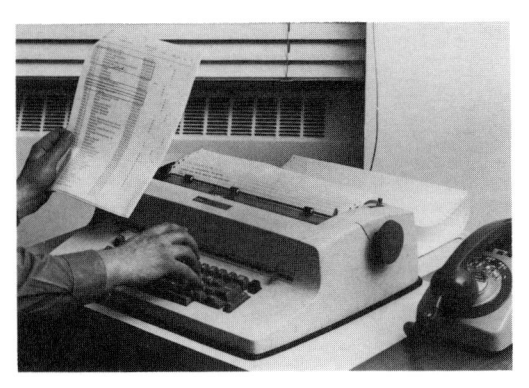

A teletype

Key-to-disk/key-to-tape Data can be typed directly from a keyboard onto magnetic tape. This can be used to store the data. This process is called **key-to-tape**. The same process can be used with magnetic disks—this is called **key-to-disk**. The tape or disk can later be used to input data at very high speed into the central processing unit of the computer.

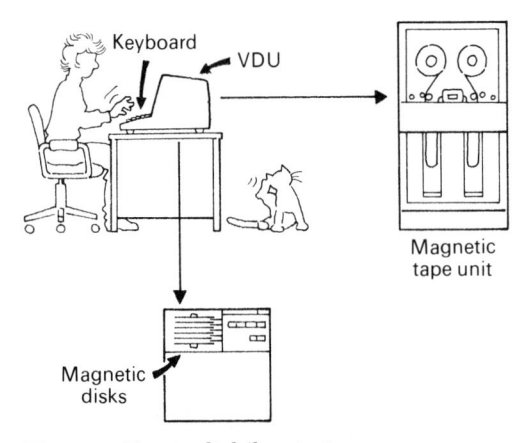

Fig. 2.4 Key-to-disk/key-to-tape

Hand-held terminals This is one type of keyboard which is likely to be used more and more in the future. It has fewer keys than a full keyboard device and can be carried around. It has no leads connected to it. The user keys-in the data and a small memory inside it stores the data. Later it can be linked via telephone (for example) to a computer, and the data transmitted to it.

A hand-held terminal

Document readers

Information is often in the form of written documents, that is, pieces of paper such as bills, forms, cheques, etc. In the past a human being was usually involved in transferring that information into data which a computer could then handle. Nowadays machines can 'read' documents directly and transfer the data straight into the computer. These machines are called **document readers**. There are various types:

Optical Character Readers (OCR) If special characters are used a machine can read printed documents directly. Two sets of characters, or **fonts**, can be recognized by OCR machines. These printed characters are scanned by a beam of light. Less light is reflected by the lines of the character than the white paper underneath. The reflected light is detected by the machine and the light pattern sends a certain electrical signal to the computer for each character.

Photo 1   Three generations of components used in the manufacture of computers — a thermionic valve (c.1950), a transistor (c.1960) and a microprocessor (c.1975).

Photo 2   A silicon wafer on which hundreds of individual 'chips' are produced. A wafer is about the size of the palm of your hand.

Photo 3   A 64K bit memory chip on a pen nib.

Photo 4 Telewriting is a development which enables users to 'write' electronically on a TV screen using a light pen. Their words or pictures can be sent instantly over the telephone and reproduced at the other end on a TV screen.

Photo 5 A 'mouse' is a device which can sometimes take the place of a keyboard. By moving it around on a flat surface the user controls the movement of the cursor on his/her VDU screen. The cursor can be moved very rapidly to any area of the screen, which is very useful when selecting an operation from a long list of possible options. 'Mice' can also be used in graphics to draw lines or 'paint' colours on the screen.

Photo 6 When the check-out assistant passes the box of tissues over this laser scanner, it converts the bar code on the package into a digital signal which is passed to the store's computer. The computer sends the price of the box of tissues to the cash register and also updates the stock total so that the manager knows when to order more tissues.

Fig. 2.5 Two OCR fonts

No machine can yet recognize handwriting because everyone writes in their own style, but many OCR machines can now read hand-written numbers if they follow a certain style. For example:

Fig. 2.6

Magnetic Ink Character Reader (MICR or MCR) Characters are printed, using a special font, in ink containing iron oxide. When the document is about to be read it is first passed through a magnetic field. This magnetizes the characters. Then they pass under a detection coil. The characters produce small electric currents in this coil—a particular pattern of electric currents is produced by each character. In this way the machine can detect or 'read' the characters that go through it. Even if the characters become dirty, or stamped over with a rubber stamp, the machine can still read them. This makes them very useful for cheques.

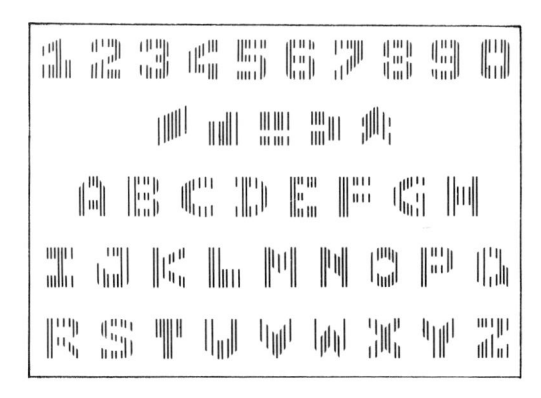

Fig. 2.7 A MICR font

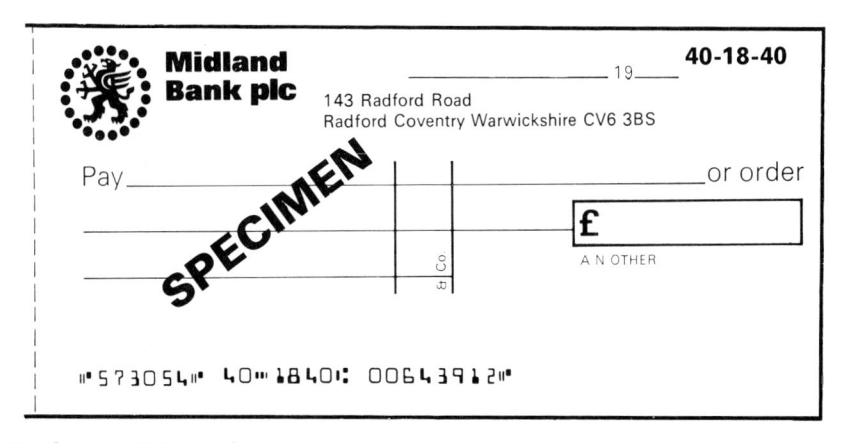

Fig. 2.8 Banks use MICR machines to process cheques quickly

Mark sense readers The document, form, or card is divided up so that a mark can be made in a certain position to stand for: yes/no; or A,B,C,D,E; or 1,2,3,4,5,6,7,8,9, and so on. A machine can detect a mark by 'seeing' how much light is reflected at different positions. If much less light is reflected in one position, for example, there must be a pencil mark there. The machine 'senses' the mark.

Fig. 2.9 *Multiple choice examination answer sheets are one example of a mark-sense document*

Badge readers

Small, oblong pieces of plastic can be used to carry data. These **badges** may hold data in the form of optical marks, magnetic marks, or punched holes. The badge is placed into a slot in the reader which then changes the data into electrical signals.

Badges and badge readers can be used to raise barriers at car parks, to check a person's identity, get money from a bank at a cash dispenser, clock on and off at a factory, or as cash credit cards.

Using an Autobank

Point-of-sale devices

More and more shops and supermarkets are using computers to keep a record of what they have sold and what is left in stock. A record can be made of a sale at the point where the goods are actually sold, for example, at the check-out. These devices which read the information and send it to a central computer are called **point-of-sale devices**.

Kimball tags This is just a small punched card. The tag gives details of the style, colour, size, etc. of an item, usually clothing. Sometimes cards are collected or batched together then read by a special machine each week. In other systems there is a card reader at the point of sale.

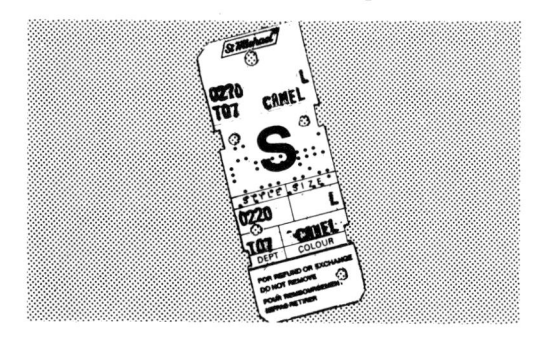

Fig. 2.10 *A Kimball tag*

Bar codes Each of the numbers 0–9 is represented by a series of bars of varying thickness and separations (there is no need for you to learn the code for each number). The codes are read by a **light pen**, or **bar-code reader**, which is linked to a computer. As the pen is stroked across the bars, a pattern of electrical signals is sent to the computer. Some bar codes can be read with a **laser scanner** which works in a similar way to the light pen.

Fig. 2.11 *Bar code*

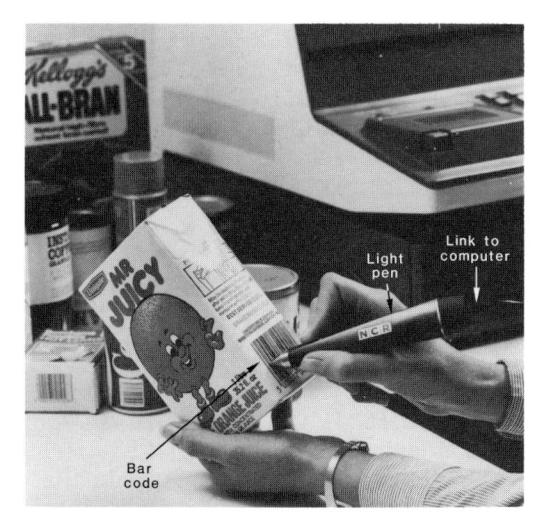

Reading a bar code with a light pen at a supermarket checkout

Kimball tags and bar codes are both used to send details of all sales transactions to a computer. These details can be stored on computer files to keep an accurate, up-to-date record of sales and stock levels. Notice that in both tags *and* bar code labels information about the goods is *coded*.

Voice input

It would be so easy if you could just speak to a computer to give it an instruction, or to tell it a number or an address to store in memory. In fact you *can*, but the amount you can say is very limited. The main problem is that everyone speaks differently. Even simple commands like 'on', 'off', 'up', 'down', 'right', or 'left' can be said in hundreds of different ways. Any voice-input system to a computer has to be 'trained' to recognize certain words. These are repeated over and over again until the system builds up a pattern of the sound. Then, when the system is being used, if a sound falls within this voice pattern the computer will respond to it. But if a person says the word wrongly, nothing will happen.

Voice-input systems are likely to be used more and more in the future especially where a user needs his or her hands free, or is disabled in some way.

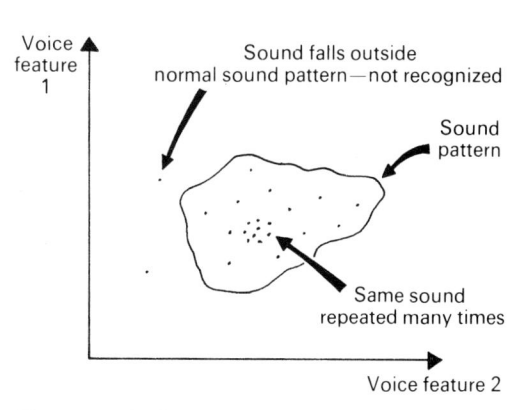

Fig. 2.12 Voice input

There are still many problems in training computers to recognize sounds—but some systems already have vocabularies of 200–300 words. Voices can be linked to a computer system by microphone, telephone or even radio transmission.

Other input devices

Many other devices have been created to send messages, signals and data to computers. **Joysticks** are often used in computer games. These can move objects on a VDU up, down, left or right. **Touch pads** are often used to send an electrical signal to a computer when they are pressed or even lightly touched. **Graphics tablets** can be used to transfer a map or drawing onto the screen of a VDU, or to store it in

A graphics tablet

the memory of a computer. A graphics tablet is a flat board which holds the map or drawing. A special pen, or stylus, can be moved over this board. This pen sends an electrical signal to the computer indicating its exact position on the board.

It is impossible to describe all the huge variety of input devices that are, and will be used, to enable people to communicate with computers. One thing is certain: the number and range of these devices will continue to grow.

Questions

1 Choose the correct answer from the choices A to D.
 a) Key-to-disk is a means of:
   A) unlocking disk storage
   B) protecting disks against theft
   C) preparing machine-readable data
   D) identifying programs on disks.
 b) Which of the following use magnetic ink character recognition extensively?
   A) library services
   B) banks
   C) local authority housing departments
   D) electricity boards
 c) The five main parts of a computer are:
   A) printer, VDU, CPU, backing store, power unit
   B) input device, output device, immediate access store, arithmetic unit, control unit
   C) input device, central processing unit, output device, modem, teletype
   D) acoustic coupler, mainframe, teletype, port, backing store.
 d) A console is a:
   A) A keyboard device for communicating with a computer
   B) desk-top computer
   C) person who works in data processing reception
   D) large television screen used for output.
 (NWREB)

2 a) List two ways in which a computer system linked to the cash tills of a supermarket may be used to the advantage of the store.
 b) Give one disadvantage to the supermarket.
 c) Give one advantage to the customer.
 (YREB 1982)

3*The use of point-of-sale devices is a method of computer recording the sales of goods as they are checked-out at a till.
 a) State two ways in which the identity of goods could be given to the point-of-sale device.
 b) State two purposes for which the information thus collected could be used.
 c) Give two ways in which this recorded information could be transferred to the computer.
 (JMB)

4 Here are some examples of source information which contain data in machine-readable form:
 a) cheque
 b) credit card
 c) mark sense card
 d) Kimball tag.
 For each of these examples explain the principles of operation, how the data is encoded and how it is read. What advantages does each method have over more traditional methods of capturing the same data?

5*a) Name three computer peripherals.
 b) State the functions of two of the peripherals named in part (a).
 (SUJB)

6*Explain the differences between the following input devices:
 a) mark sense reader
 b) OCR
 c) MICR.
 (SUJB)

*'O'-Level question

2.2 Getting information back

People put data into computers and computers send information back to people. You may be able to see this information on a screen, read it on paper or even hear it. The various devices which produce information in a form that is sensible to people are called output devices. This unit tells you about some of the many types available.

The earliest computers, in the 1940's, used lights as their output devices. These were arranged in patterns using 'on' to stand for a '1' and 'off' to stand for '0'. These binary patterns of 1's and 0's made sense to computer experts. But to ordinary people rows of lights, some on and some off, didn't mean much. Fortunately, printers were developed which could provide output that humans can read.

Different types of printer

Early printers were slow and noisy but they did provide output on paper, called **print-out** or **hard copy**, that people can make sense of and carry around. Nowadays there are many different types of printer. Some are **line printers**—these print a complete line in one process. The opposite of this type is the **serial printer**—these print one character after another along the line.

There is another way of comparing printers. Some are **impact printers**. These use a 'print head' in the shape of a character, which strikes a carbon ribbon onto a piece of paper. This makes the shape of the character, e.g. 'A', '9', '?', on the paper (just like a typewriter). You can guess that impact printers can be very noisy! With **non-impact printers** no mechanical heads or hammers are used. This makes them quieter, and often much faster. Their disadvantage, as you will see, is that special paper is often needed.

Line printers

The two main types of line printer are the **drum line printer** and the **chain line printer**:

Drum printers These use a drum or cylinder which has a *complete row* of each character across its surface. For each line to be printed the paper stops and the drum goes round once. When a character on the drum which has to be printed reaches the print position, a hammer

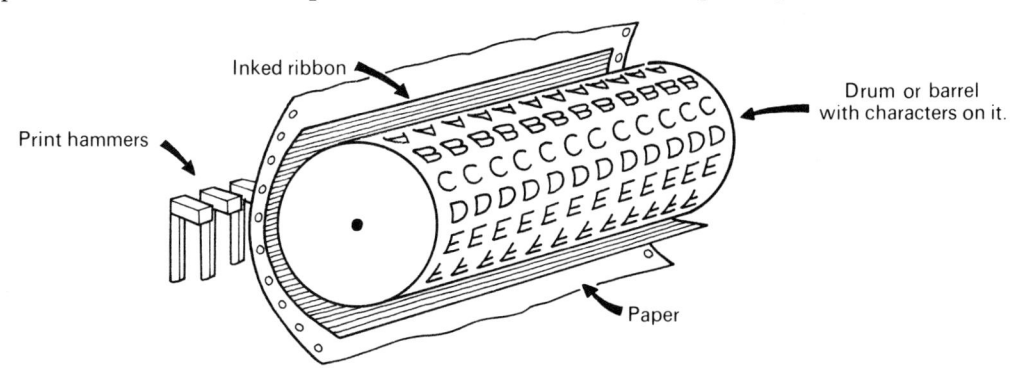

Fig. 2.13 A drum printer

bangs the paper and carbon against the character. All the A's on the line are printed first, then the B's, then the C's and so on until the whole line has been finished. For example, a line consisting of 'HELLO' will be printed in this order:

```
        E
      H E
      H E L L
      H E L L O
```

After the drum has gone right round once, the paper moves on to the next line. This may sound like a slow process, but in fact most drum printers can print 2000 lines in a minute! At this rate, this whole book could be printed in about 5 minutes. Drum printers are fast, but they are very noisy and very expensive. This means that only large businesses and organizations can usually afford them.

Chain printers These are cheaper but slightly slower line printers. They use a moving chain with characters on it which goes round and round *across* the paper. As each character reaches the position where it has to be printed a hammer strikes the paper and ribbon against it. Like the drum printer, each character on a line is printed in turn until the line is complete, then the paper is moved on.

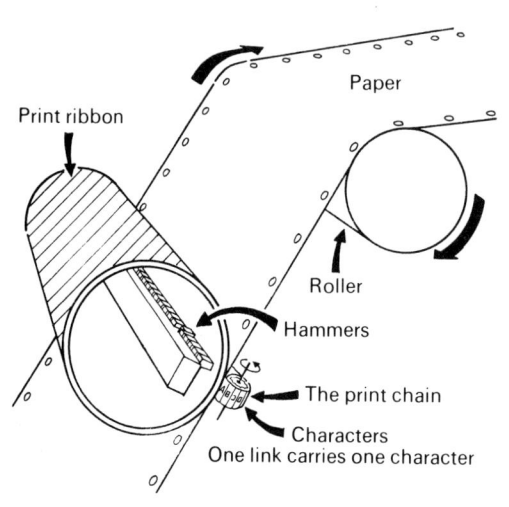

Fig. 2.14 A chain printer

Line printers use a long stream of paper that folds itself at the back of the machine. This is called **continuous stationery**. Separate sheets can be torn off.

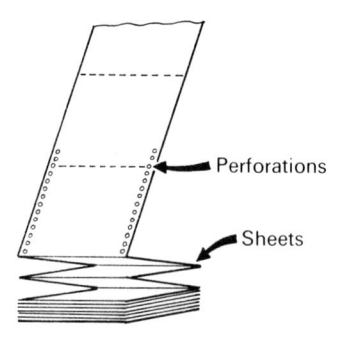

Fig. 2.15 Continuous stationery

Serial printers

Serial printers print *one character after another* along each line of output until the line is complete. They are often used on teletypewriter terminals. Serial printers are slower than line printers, but on a terminal this may not matter, because a human can only type about 10 characters per second onto a keyboard.

One common type is called a **daisy-wheel printer**. This uses a metal or plastic disk with spokes coming from it. At the end of each spoke (usually 96) is a different character.

Daisy-wheel printers give a high-quality output, so are often used with **word processors** (e.g. to print business letters, references, requests, etc.).

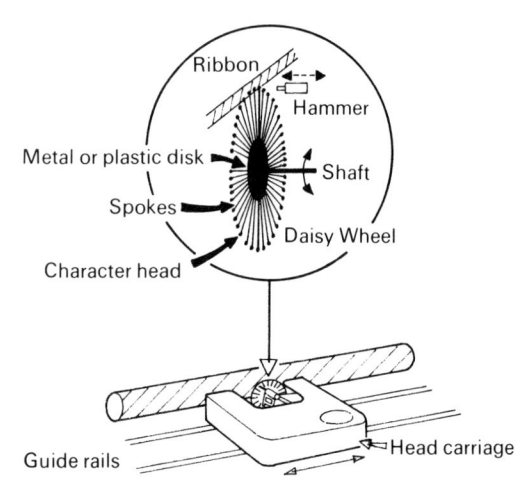

Fig. 2.16 Daisywheel printer mechanism

A second type of serial printer is the **dot-matrix printer**. This makes a character on paper by forming a pattern of tiny dots. This pattern is called a **matrix**. The print head is made up of many tiny needles which can produce the pattern of black dots on paper.

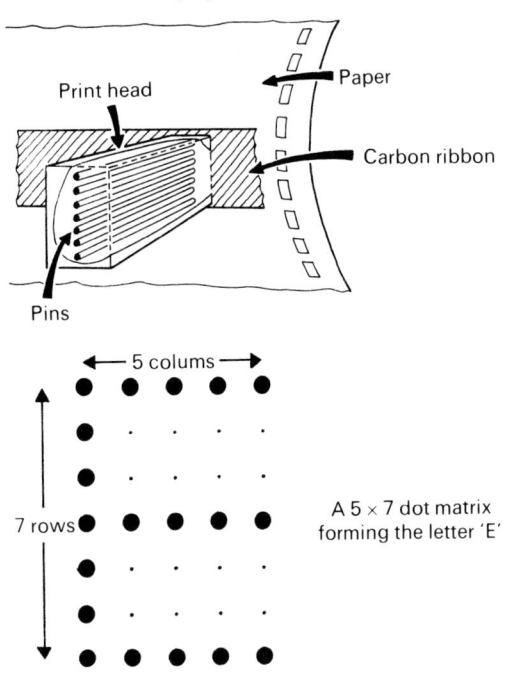

Fig. 2.17 Dot-matrix printing

Dot-matrix printers are faster than daisy-wheel printers, but the print quality is not so good. On some you can easily see the dots.

Non-impact printers

More and more printers are being developed which don't actually hammer a ribbon against a piece of paper. Non-impact printers are generally very fast, very quiet, but very expensive.
- **Thermal printers** use the effect of heat on specially sensitive paper to make characters from a pattern of dots (a dot matrix).
- **Ink-jet printers** actually squirt quick-drying ink onto the paper in the shape of the character to be printed. The ink-jet is electrically charged and can be deflected into the right pattern.
- **Laser printers** use the same technique as photocopiers. A carefully directed laser beam creates a pattern of electric charge onto a special drum in the printer. This charge attracts a special black powder to it. Then, the drum transfers this powder to the paper to give the printed output. Laser printers can print about 25 000 lines per minute—ten times faster than a drum line printer. They can even draw pictures, maps and graphs, of very high quality.

You can see that a wide range of printers are now available for giving hard copy output or print-out. Some are fast—some are slow. Some are cheap (less than £50 for some microcomputers)—some are very expensive, costing many thousands of pounds. Some give high-quality print—some produce poor quality. The person, or business, or organization that buys a printer often has to judge which one is most suitable in terms of: speed, expense and quality.

Computer Output Microfilm (COM)

Printed output produces large quantities of paper. Paper is expensive *and* it takes up a lot of space. To save money and space computer output can now be photographed onto **microfilm**. You have probably seen James Bond taking pictures of his enemies' secret documents onto microfilm. **Computer Output Microfilm (COM)** uses the same process. Printed output is reduced to a very, very small size. The microfilm can be read by a person by using a special reader which projects a readable image of the film onto a screen.

COM is ideal when huge amounts of information have to be stored, and space is limited. Microfilm is used in libraries, archives, and in keeping files in industry. Computer output on microfilm can now be produced directly from magnetic tapes, without the need for paper. This could save a lot of trees from from being chopped down!

Graphs, pictures and patterns

'A picture is worth a thousand words.' Output devices which can produce drawings, maps and pictures are becoming more and more common.

Graph plotters These simply use a pen moving across a piece of paper to produce graphs, drawings, maps or plans. They are usually slow, but very, very accurate which is what really matters. Two types of graph plotter are **drum plotters** and **flat-bed plotters**. With a drum plotter the paper is wrapped round a slowly moving drum, and the pen moves from side to side across the moving paper. The movements of both the pen and drum are controlled by the computer. Flat-bed plotters use a pen which can move in *two* directions across a piece of paper fixed to a flat bed. The movements of the pen are controlled by signals from a computer.

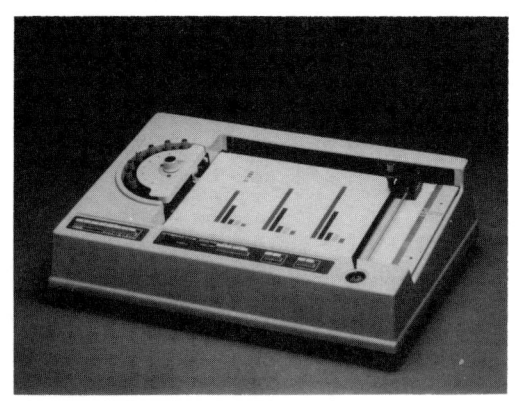

A flat-bed plotter

Visual display units A VDU looks like a television screen and works in a similar way. Indeed over a million television sets are probably used in Britain as VDU's to go with the microcomputers in people's homes. Output on a VDU has the advantage that it is displayed immediately, in front of a computer user—its disadvantage is that the output cannot be kept and carried away like a sheet of paper. However, most micros can be linked to a printer to provide hard copy of any display on the screen.

Characters are usually displayed on the screen using a dot matrix. A pattern of bright dots is used to make up letters, numbers and symbols.

Most VDU's can be used to display **graphics**, i.e. shapes, patterns and pictures. Using colour, computer graphics can be quite impressive especially when they are programmed to give the appearance of movement (animation). Some VDU screens use **low-resolution graphics** and use **blocks** of colour to make up patterns and pictures. Others use **high-resolution graphics**, forming pictures from much smaller points or **pixels** (picture cells).

A graphics display on a VDU

VDU's are now widely used for computer output in, for example: airline reservations, office work, word processing, and computer-aided design.

Light pens A person using a VDU can change the picture on the screen by using a light pen. When the light pen is pressed against the screen a signal is sent to the computer indicating exactly where the screen was pressed. The light pen can be used to draw more lines on the screen, or just to point to an item of interest. In fact, a light pen is an input device—it senses light on the VDU and sends a message *to* the computer. The screen itself is the output device.

Sounds, music and speech

Computers can be used to give output in the form of sound. Most microcomputers, for example, can easily be programmed to play simple tunes like 'Three Blind Mice', 'Jingle Bells' or 'Rule Britannia'. Computers are likely to be used more and more in the future to make musical sounds. Different notes and pieces of music can be put together to make new sounds. This is called **music synthesis**.

In a similar way the basic parts of human speech can be put together to make voice output. This is **speech synthesis**. By combining the very smallest parts of speech (called 'phonemes') a computer can be made to output spoken words. Speech synthesis chips can be added to some microcomputers.

Voice output could be useful in many areas. Some cars now use 'speech' chips to tell you to 'Fasten your seat belt.' or 'Put some petrol in.' One computer has been designed to read books to blind people by scanning printed words and producing voice output.

Computer output for computers?

Almost all the output mentioned so far is designed to make sense to *people*. However, many output devices are used which provide output that can later be used as input for another computer. Two that were widely used are the **card punch** and **paper-tape punch**. They both produce output, on punched card or paper tape, that can be used directly as input to another computer. Three newer examples are: bar-code label printers, printers of OCR fonts, and printers of MICR fonts. Just imagine the time when spoken output and voice input are widely used. Will computers start talking to each other?

Both the last two units have described input and output devices (i.e. peripherals). You can see that there is a wide range of both—they all have their uses in different places and circumstances.

Input and output—comparing speeds

INPUT DEVICES	APPROXIMATE SPEED (characters/second)
Keyboard	up to 10
Tape drive	50 000
Optical character reader	up to 2000
Disk drive	500 000
Paper-tape reader	1000
Punched-card reader	1000

MEDIUM	DEVICE
Printed word	Printers, e.g. drum-line, chain-line, daisy-wheel, matrix, laser
Punched card Paper tape	Card and tape punches
Graphs Pictures (graphics) Table Written word	VDU
Sound: voice or music	Speech synthesis and loudspeaker

OUTPUT DEVICES		APPROXIMATE SPEED (characters/second)
Line printers		800
Serial printers	Daisy wheel	up to 60
	Dot matrix	up to 200
Laser printer		30 000
Thermal printer		800
Electrostatic printer		3000
Electrosensitive printer		2000

Don't pay too much attention to the speeds quoted in the tables. They only give you a rough comparison, and within a few years the speeds of input and output devices will probably be much faster. The important thing to remember is how *slow* they are compared to the central processing unit which can deal with several million instructions per second.

Questions

1 Copy out and complete each of these statements.
   a) Barrel, chain and laser are all types of _____.
   b) Most VDU's consist of a keyboard and a _____.
   (NWREB)
   c) The letters COM as used in computing stand for _____.
   (SREB)
2 In which kind of peripheral device would you find a daisy wheel?
   (WMEB)
3 In a road traffic control application the flow of vehicles at a road junction is controlled by a computer.
   a) What input device, operated by the vehicles themselves, feeds information into a computer?
   b) What output device is used to tell drivers what they must do?
   (WMEB)
4*Explain briefly, with the aid of a diagram, how a chain printer operates.
   (AEB 1982)
5*Give three reasons why a VDU would be used in preference to a teleprinter for a classroom demonstration in a biology class of, say, river pollution.
   (London)
6*A great many printers are now available, ranging from small, slow devices to large, versatile, fast printers. Describe various types of printer which are now in use, giving an indication of their operating speeds and paying particular attention to:
   a) the different facilities which they provide
   b) typical applications for which they are appropriate.
   (Cambridge)
7*Teleprinters and visual display units are common input/output devices and are often used in schools and colleges. Explain, with reasons, which would be the most appropriate devices for the following educational applications:
   a) A computer assisted learning program which simulates the problems involved in motorway construction.
   b) The writing and testing of a typical student program to be submitted as coursework for an 'O'-Level computer studies course.
   (AEB)

*'O'-Level question

2.3 Storing data

Data can be put into a computer using input devices. Information can be given out by a computer through output devices. But in between input and output it may be necessary to store data. This data might be held for days, months, or even years in long-term or mass storage.

Permanent and temporary storage

A computer's internal memory is limited in size. Besides this it is only *temporary*—most internal memories lose their contents when the computer is switched off. However, large amounts of data can be stored *permanently* on backing store.

There are several reasons for using backing store to hold data.
- The internal memory of a computer is expensive and its capacity is limited.
- Internal memory is only used to store programs and data currently being processed by the CPU.
- Data, and programs, can be held for long periods on backing store then used when necessary.
- Data held on backing store can often be carried around or even sent through the post, i.e. it is portable.

Types of backing store

Various materials, or *media*, are used for backing store. The two most common (at present) are **magnetic tape** and **magnetic disk**. Magnetic drums and magnetic cards have been, and still are, used. New types of memory are described later.

All media used for mass storage have one thing in common. They use material which can either exist in one state or another, that is, they use a two-state code. One state can represent a '0'—the other can represent a '1'. With magnetic tapes each small area on the tape can be magnetized one way or the other. The same two states are used with magnetic disk.

Magnetic tape

Magnetic tape is made of plastic, with a coating of iron oxide that can be magnetized. It is just like the tape used for recording music. Sometimes it is longer lasting and of better quality—but many microcomputers use ordinary cassette tape.

Data is stored by using magnetized or non-magnetized spots arranged in tracks or lines across the width of the tape. Each line of spots is used to represent one item of data.

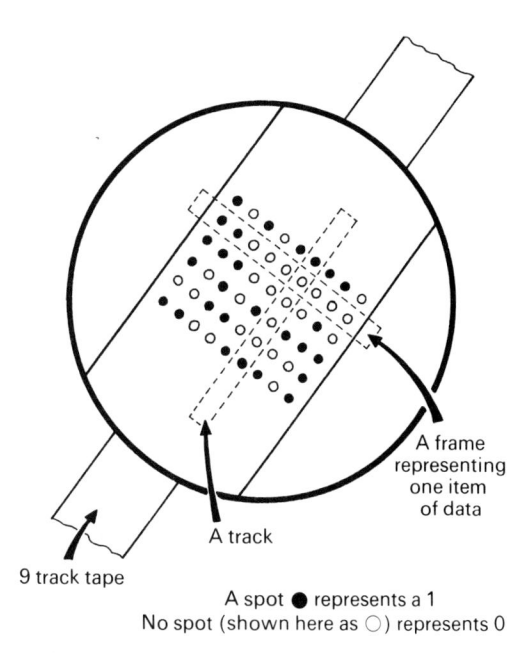

Fig. 2.18 Magnified 'view' of magnetic tape

A spot ● represents a 1
No spot (shown here as ○) represents 0

Data is stored in **blocks** along the tape, separated by gaps. These gaps allow for starting and stopping of the tape.

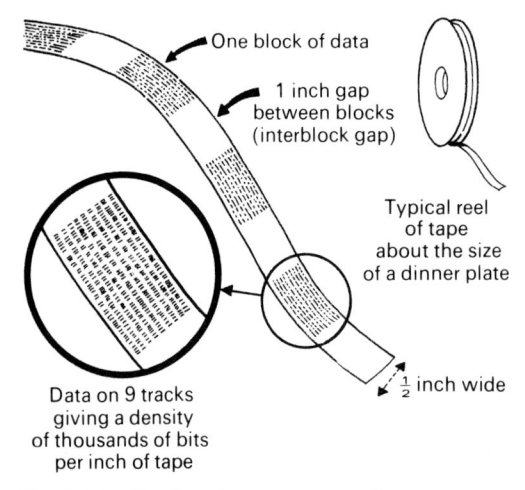

Fig. 2.19 Storing data on magnetic tape

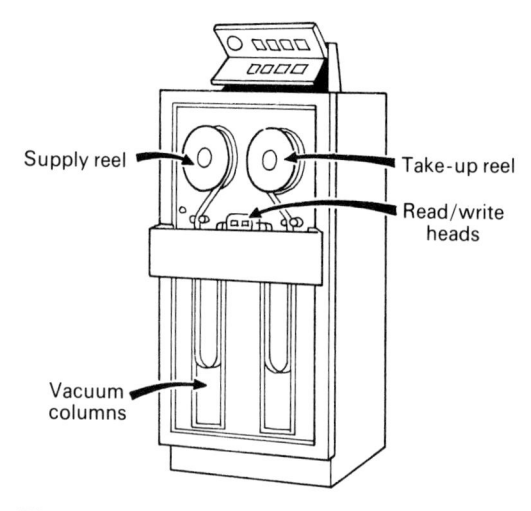

Fig. 2.20 Magnetic tape unit

Data can be fairly densely packed on modern tapes with as many as 7000 characters on 1 centimetre of tape. This means that as many as 50 million characters can be stored on a complete tape—as many characters as there are in several large books.

Tape drives and tape units

Sometimes data from backing store has to be transferred *to* the internal memory of a computer. At other times data has to be transferred *from* the computer's memory onto backing store. The device used to read from, or write to, magnetic tape is called a **tape unit** or **tape drive**.

Large tape drives run extremely quickly, with the tape moving at perhaps 250 centimetres per second. This is why the loops of tape are held in 'vacuum columns', to allow for the tremendous acceleration when the tape is starting or stopping.

The trouble with tape

Writing and reading speeds for large reel-tape systems are very fast, and data can be transferred at over 1 000 000 characters every second. Even so, it can take 5 minutes to read data from a long tape, or to write data to it. If the data you need is at the *end* of the tape the only way to get at, or *access* it, is to read right through the whole tape. This is called **serial access**. It means that data on a tape can only be reached in the order in which it is stored. The time taken to get to, or access, some data on the tape depends on how far it is along the tape from the read/write heads.

This problem is even worse with cassette tapes. Their read/write speed is about 5 centimetres per second. It can take as long as 45 minutes to read a whole tape.

This is one of the reasons why disks are better for mass storage. The data stored on a disk can be reached *directly*.

Magnetic disks

All magnetic disks are coated in a substance that can be magnetized. Small spots on the disk are magnetized in either one direction or the other; just like the spots on tape. These magnetized spots are arranged around the disk in circular tracks, like the tracks on an LP record. Each track contains the same number of

36

characters—this means that the characters are more densely packed on the inside tracks. The tracks are divided into **sectors** with gaps in each sector.

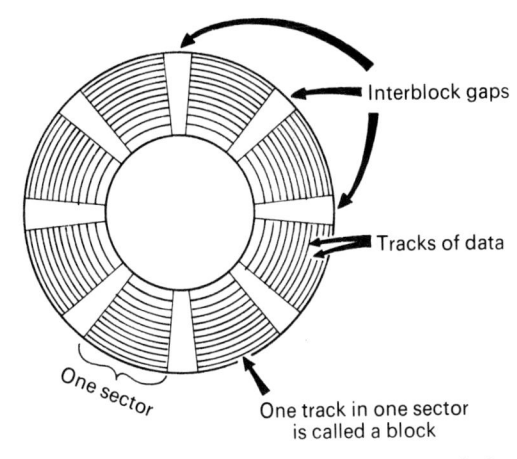

Fig. 2.21 How data is held on magnetic disk

There are two main types of disk: **hard** or **rigid** and **flexible** or **floppy**:

Rigid disks Rigid disks are made of metal. They are often used in packs of six, or usually ten, joined together by a shaft or spindle down the middle.

Data is written onto the disk with a **write head** and read from the disk with a **read head**. The single head unit is called a **read/write head**. Read/write heads can normally move in and out across the disk to reach, or access, the required track. This is called **direct access** or **random access**. The read/write heads can go directly to an empty track (to write on it) or an item of data (to read from it). There is no need to pass through any of the previous data first. This is the main advantage of disk compared with tape.

Floppy disks These are small, flexible plastic disks coated with a magnetic material. They were first used in the 1970's as backing store for microcomputers. Floppy disks must be kept in a protective sleeve with a small slot in it to allow the read/write heads to read their surface. Floppy disks are cheap, portable and also fast, when compared with most forms of magnetic tape. They are ideal for storing data and programs for microcomputers.

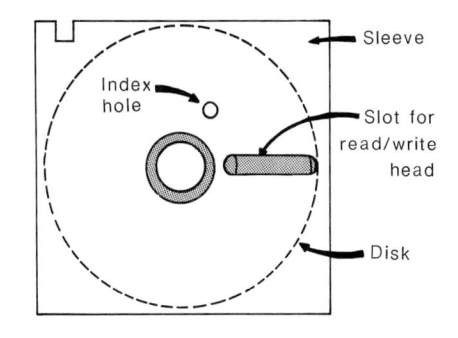

Fig. 2.23 A Floppy disk in its sleeve

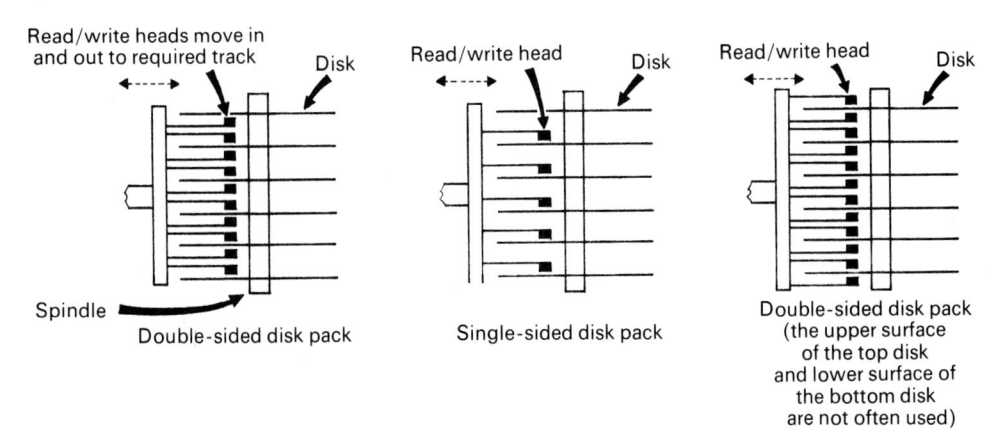

Fig. 2.22 Three kinds of magnetic disk pack

Magnetic disk drives

A disk drive, like a tape drive, is used to transfer data *from* the internal memory of a computer *to* the disk or to input data *from* the disk to the computer. In other words disk drives, and tape drives, are used as both input and output devices.

Disk drives are used to rotate a disk, or a pack of disks, at a very high speed—up to 40 revolutions in 1 second (over 90 miles per hour at the rim of the disk). Disk drives for floppy disks rotate more slowly (about 6 revolutions in 1 second). As the disks rotate the read/write heads move across the surface of the disk, but they don't actually touch the surface. They fly just above it, to save wear. But the flying heads are so close to the surface they will 'crash' into it if they meet dust, grit, a hair, or even a smudgy fingerprint.

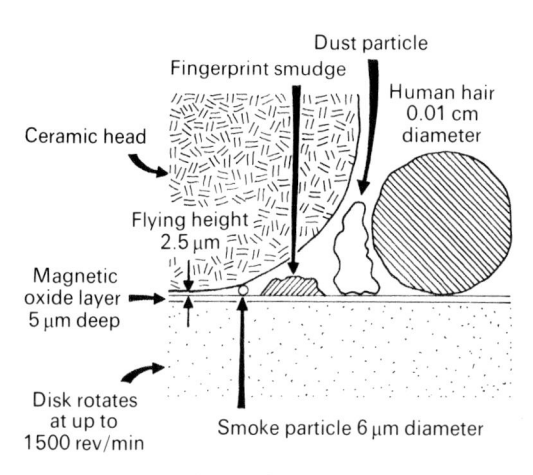

A Winchester disk drive

Fig. 2.24 *Particles that can cause a disk 'crash'*

Note: 1 μm = 1 micrometre = 1×10^{-6} m

Winchester disks Specially sealed units are now used to keep disks clean and free from dust. These units are called **Winchester disk drives**. They are fast, very reliable and gradually becoming cheaper. The read/write heads are designed to take off from and land on to the surface without damaging it.

Modern memory devices

Research is going on all the time to make memory devices that are faster and have larger memory capacity.

Optical disks are being developed to store data, rather like the video disks used to record television programs. These disks have holes 'burned' into their surface—the two states are either 'a hole' or 'not a hole'! The holes (or not-holes) can be detected by a laser beam passing across the disk. Far more data can be packed onto optical disks than magnetic disks.

Another type of mass storage uses magnetic spots or 'bubbles' which can move around on a silicon chip. These **magnetic bubble memories** will be far faster than disks, and certainly tapes. The two states used are the presence of a bubble and the absence of a bubble!

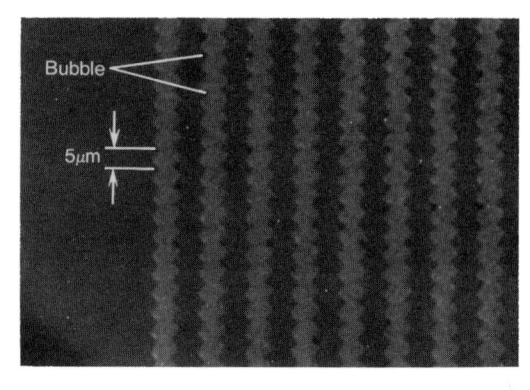

A magnified view of a magnetic bubble memory

Comparing different types of backing store

Just as with output and input devices, the various types of backing store are used to do different jobs. There are four main ways of comparing different types of mass storage.

Speed Magnetic tape is far slower than magnetic disk. Magnetic disks are becoming faster all the time, but they are still slower than optical disks and magnetic bubble memory.

Cost Magnetic tape is cheap. Disks are good value but more expensive, especially when you add the cost of the disk drive. Newer memory devices are expensive, but their cost is likely to come down.

Access Data stored on disk can be reached or accessed directly. This is often a great advantage, for example, when a bank needs information on a particular customer. Data stored on magnetic tape can only be accessed in the order in which it is stored. This may be suitable for some jobs, for example, for storing a complete mailing list where each and every letter has to be sent out in turn. However, serial access can be a big disadvantage.

Capacity The *amount* of data that can be stored is the fourth important factor. Size of memory is measured in **bytes**. Each byte is used to store one character of data (e.g. 'A', '9', '%' and so on). Memories can usually store thousands of bytes (kilobytes) or millions of bytes (megabytes):

1 kilobyte* = 1K bytes = 1024 bytes
= 2^{10} bytes

1 megabyte = 1M bytes = 1 000 000 bytes

So a 1 megabyte memory can store about 1 million characters of data. This table shows, roughly, the storage capacity of some different types of mass storage.

TYPE	CAPACITY (bytes)
Cassette tape	200K
Floppy disk	500K
Winchester disk	40M
Large reel of tape	125M
Disk packs	1000M
Future devices (e.g. optical disks)	250 000M?

Storage capacity of some types of mass storage

Don't try to remember these figures. They are only approximate and most of them are improving all the time.

*kilo normally indicates 1000. In computing it means 2^{10}, i.e. 1024.

Questions

1 Copy out and complete these statements:
 a) Magnetic tape may be used only for serial access to data; magnetic disks may be used for either _____ access or _____ access.
 b) When data is stored on magnetic tape it is split into units known as _____.
 (Cambridge)
 c) The time taken to retrieve data from a storage device is known as _____.
 (SREB)

2 a) The diagram below shows a short piece of magnetic tape. Copy the diagram and indicate the way in which a number of individual characters can be represented on the magnetic tape.

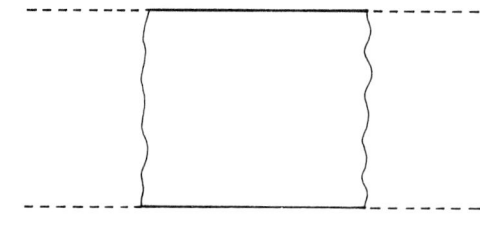

Fig. 2.24

 b) The diagram below shows a longer length of magnetic tape. Copy the diagram and show the layout of data within a file on the length of magnetic tape.

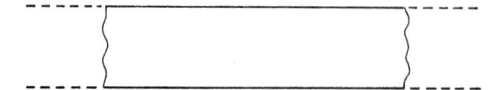

Fig. 2.25

3* Briefly explain what is meant by:
 a) backing store
 b) serial access
 c) floppy disk.
 (SUJB)

4 Explain, with the aid of diagrams, how information can be stored using:
 a) magnetic tape
 b) magnetic disk.

5* a) Explain the terms serial (sequential) access and random (direct) access.
 b) Describe how information is organized on a magnetic disk pack.
 c) State two factors which govern the number of characters that can be stored on a magnetic disk.
 d) What factors affect the access time of a disk?
 e) How many surfaces would be used of a magnetic disk-pack that has six disks? Give reasons in your answer.
 (OLE)

6 Read the following passage carefully and then answer the questions below:
 'The computer installed in a commercial organization was described as having 256K words of store running under ASAS II operating system with four disk units, two magnetic tape units, a VDU, a teletype, two fast card readers and a line printer.'
 a) What does '256K words of store' mean?
 b) What backing store facilities does the installation have?
 c) How is most of the information entered into this computer?
 d) How many output devices are listed?

*'O'-Level question

Wordsearch

Copy the grid below into your workbook. Then use the clues to find 10 words which appeared in Part II.
1. This produces 'hard copy'.
2. A word meaning 'on the outside'.
3. Used in an aeroplane and as an input device.
4. A direct access storage medium.
5. A serial access storage medium.
6. Used by James Bond and as computer output.
7. You touch this with your fingertips.
8. Much more than a byte!
9. The opposite of stiff.
10. At the end of the line.

PERIPHERALS WORDSEARCH

```
P N E M R X C S A I O V K G O
R N N Y O W I L C Y G R I A H
E R T E R M I N A L H U G W U
K F B M F C I U D T L Z Z L U
Q J O Y S T I C K A W Z P X C
D S I P T G K C R L D M C P C
X L A T R K F E W O Q V V C Q
W E P K A I H B Y L F C M U G
F Z S L M P N L Y B L I D N D
E I Y C I O U T U H O V L H N
D N Y R Q T R A E T P A A M B
X Z E E X W H P B R P P R L D
D P G B X C Y E J V Y D R D L
A U D U N Y C F C W C Y P F N
O P A S A O M E G A B Y T E Q
```

41

Part 3

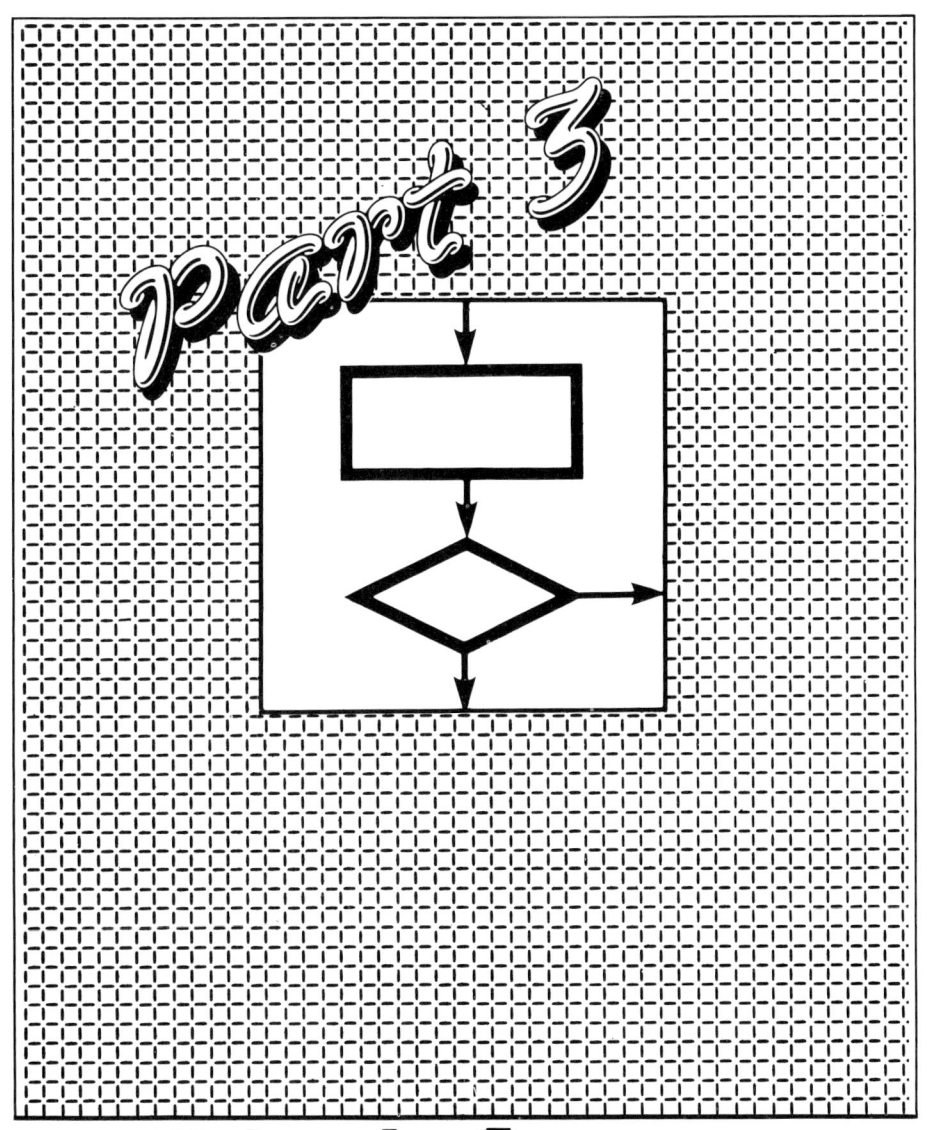

Giving the Computer Instructions

3.1 Principles of programming

All computers consist of hardware and software. Software consists of programs and programs have to be written by people. How do we set about writing programs?

What is a program?

Remember that the digital computer consists of a central processing unit and a high-speed storage area. The CPU will execute (carry out) instructions taken from the memory *one at a time*. These instructions are part of a **program**, a very precise set of instructions. If each instruction is correct *and* the instructions are in the right order, then the computer will do the right thing. The task of the **programmer** is to get each instruction right, *and* to get them in the right order.

Saying what you mean and meaning what you say—algorithms

If you make a cake or mend a puncture, the chances are you will follow a recipe or a set of instructions. You start with step one and work through each step until you finish at the last step. The name used to describe a sequence of steps for a computer to follow is '**algorithm**'.

Usually, instructions are written in our language—English. But sometimes using English to describe how to do something can be very difficult and confusing. Sometimes it is easier to use another notation. For example, imagine knitting without a knitting pattern.

Fig. 3.2 Knitting instructions

Another example is algebra. The +, −, ×, ÷, ( ), etc. all make it easier to do algebra. You may not think so, but try doing algebra in English!

To knit or do algebra you have to learn the notations. You have to be able to read a knitting pattern or understand the algebraic symbols.

Fig. 3.1 Baking a cake—an everyday algorithm

```
      INTEGER LIST(100),VALUE,POSTN,ERROR
      READ(3,1) LENGTH
      READ(3,2) (LIST(ICOL),ICOL=1,LENGTH)
      READ(3,1) NUMTST
      DO 10 K=1,NUMTST
         READ(3,1)VALUE
         CALL BISECH(LIST,LENGTH,VALUE,POSTN,ERROR)
         WRITE(2,3) (LIST(ICOL),ICOL=1,LENGTH)
    3    FORMAT(1H0,15HLIST UNDER TEST/20I4)
         WRITE(2,11) VALUE,POSTN,ERROR
   11    FORMAT(1H0,5HVALUE,3X,5HPOSTN,3X,5HERROR/3(I5,3X))
   10 CONTINUE
    1 FORMAT(I2)
    2 FORMAT(20I2)
      STOP
      END
```

Fig. 3.3 Part of a FORTRAN program

Computer programs can be very complicated and computer languages can be difficult for us to understand, so it helps to describe what you want your program to do *before* you write it. You first write an algorithm. The algorithm can then be used to write the program using whatever programming language you wish.

What can go wrong?

Lists of instructions can be wrong in the following ways:

- an instruction could be wrong
- all the instructions could be right, but in the wrong order
- an instruction could be wrong *and* in the wrong order.

Take a look at the recipe example. Getting things right for the computer is so important because it can only do what it is told—no more, no less. Do not forget, a computer has no more sense than a light switch.

The next unit describes how you can write algorithms for your computer programs.

KEY POINTS

The task of programming involves the following steps:
1 working out and writing down the sequence of steps needed in English (the algorithm)
2 converting the algorithm to the programming language required
3 putting the program into the computer and getting it to work

---

Questions

1 Complete this sentence.
   _____ is the word used to describe a set of instructions.
2 An algorithm is a computer program. True or false?
3 Write down four examples of sets of instructions you have seen.
4 What are the two things that could be wrong with a set of instructions?
5 One activity which is very difficult to explain in English is how to tie a knot. What method would you use?

45

3.2 Specifying the solution: flowcharts and algorithms

In the previous unit you met the idea of an algorithm—a set of instructions from which you can write a program. This unit describes how algorithms may be written.

Basic elements

An algorithm states what the program should do and the order in which it should be done. The steps can be written down in English and the order can be shown by a **flowchart** or by *structuring* the English language instructions. Algorithms can be built from three basic structures: **sequence**, **selection** and **repetition**.

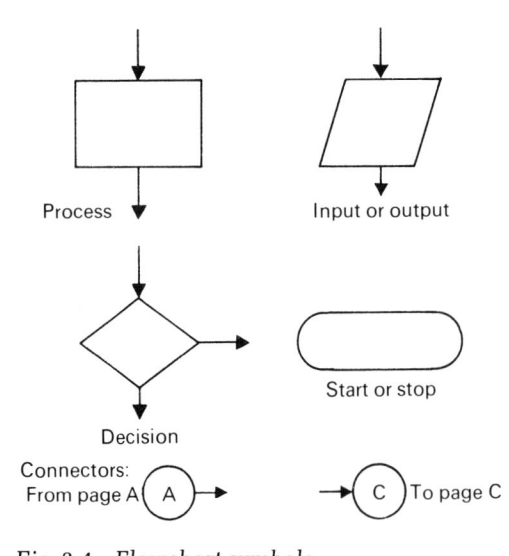

Fig. 3.4 Flowchart symbols

(Process, Input or output, Decision, Start or stop, Connectors: From page A, To page C)

Sequence

The simplest algorithm is a single sequence of instructions. You, or the computer, start with step 1, followed by step 2 and so on. This is shown as follows:

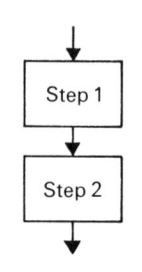

Fig. 3.5 The boxes contain a description of the step. The arrows indicate the sequence

(Step 1 → Step 2)

Selection

IF ... THEN Often, it is necessary to make a choice of what to do next. For example, when playing *Snap!*:
IF your next card is the same as the card on the table THEN shout 'Snap!'
This illustrates the idea that a *condition* is tested. If the condition is *true* then you do one thing. If the condition is *not true*, you continue with the next step in sequence.

    IF ‹condition› THEN ‹action›

Testing a condition is the same as asking a question. The answer to the question must be either 'yes' or 'no'. The answer cannot be 'maybe'. This is shown as follows:

IF the cards are the same THEN shout 'Snap!'

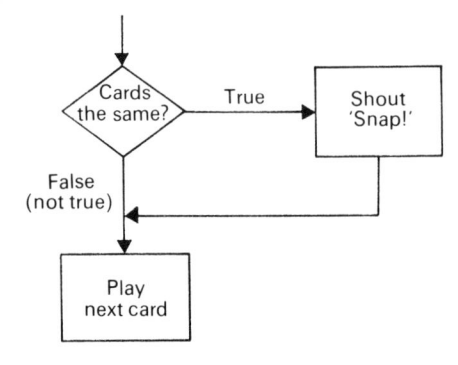

Fig. 3.6

IF ... THEN ... ELSE Sometimes you may have to do one thing if the condition is *true* and another thing if the condition is *not true*. To show this you draw a diagram almost the same as for IF ... THEN.

The ELSE means do what follows if the condition is not true. For example, a flowchart and algorithm for choosing a hard- or soft-centre chocolate could be:

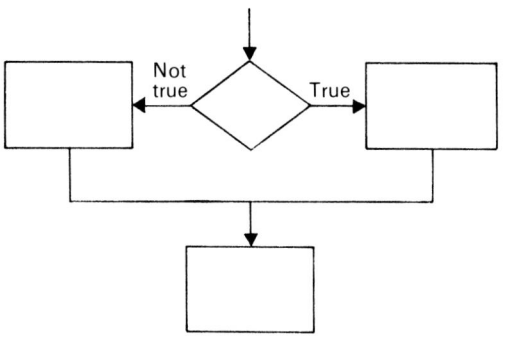

Fig. 3.7 IF ... THEN ... ELSE flowchart

Can you see the difference between this diagram and Fig. 3.6? There is one extra box shown. If you follow the arrows you will see that you do one thing or you do the other. This is written as:

```
IF <condition> THEN <action 1>
               ELSE <action 2>
```

Fig. 3.8 Testing a condition

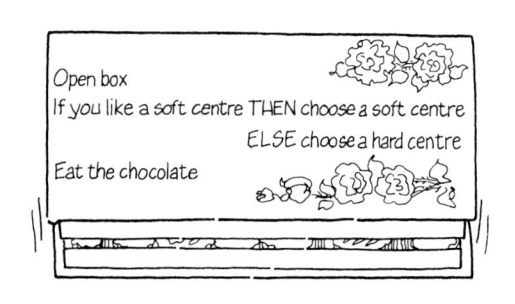

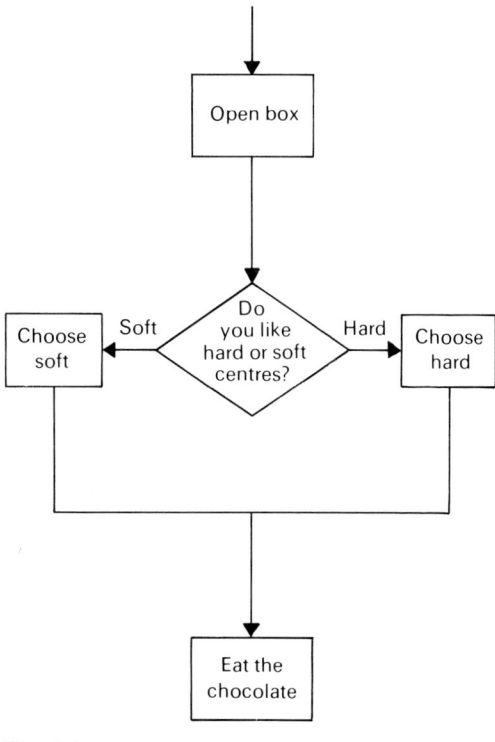

Fig. 3.9

In either case the algorithm goes on to tell you to 'Eat the chocolate'.

Repetition

Computers are often used because they are good at doing the same thing over and over again. This is repetition. For instance, adding a lot of numbers together. Perhaps you find this boring. A computer can do this easily, but you have to tell it how. To show repetition in an algorithm proceed as follows:

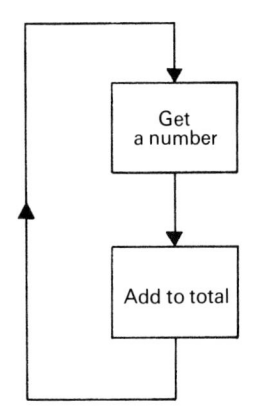

Fig. 3.10

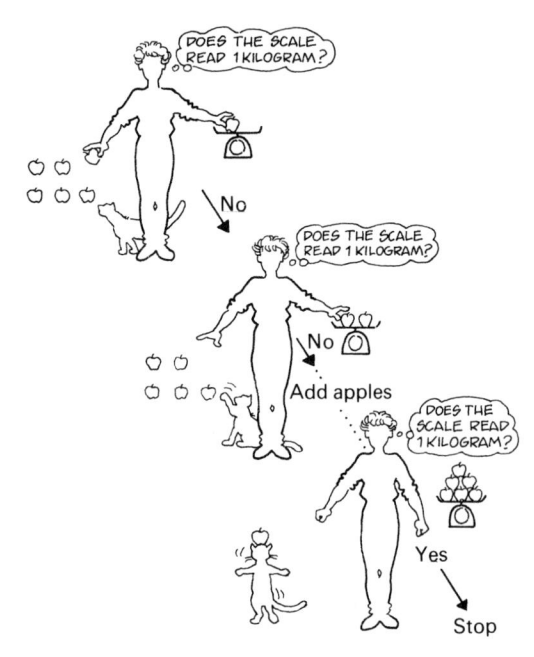

Fig. 3.11 Repetition—measuring a kilo of apples. An apple is added until the scales read 1 kilogram

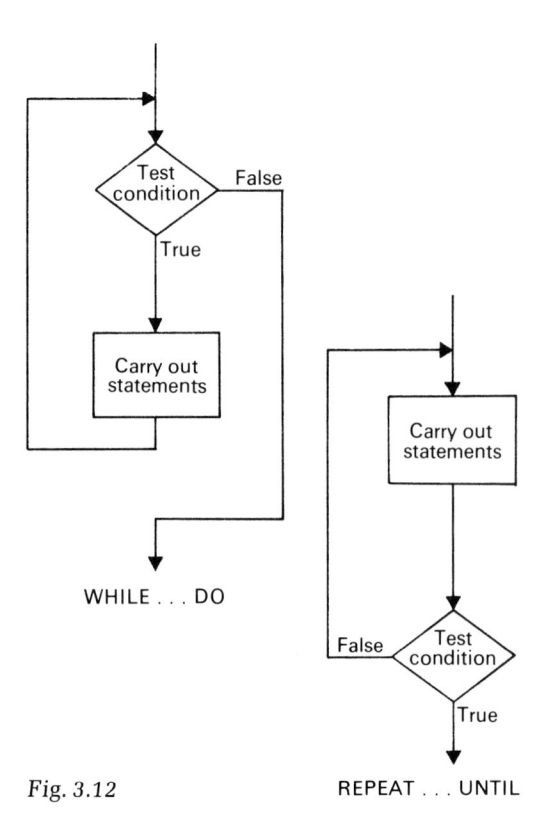

You now have an arrow pointing backwards. If you follow the arrows you will find that 'Get a number' and 'Add to total' are repeated.

The problem with this algorithm is that it will carry on 'getting' and 'adding' forever, unless someone switches the computer off. In most cases you need to state how long the repetition should last. This is done by testing a condition. When the condition changes from 'true' to 'false' or from 'false' to 'true', the repetition may be halted.

WHILE ... DO and REPEAT ... UNTIL Two ways you can show repetition, including the testing of a condition, are by using:

```
WHILE...DO  or  REPEAT...UNTIL
```

With 'WHILE ‹condition› DO' actions the actions will be repeated *while* the condition is true. With 'REPEAT ‹actions› UNTIL ‹condition›', the actions will be repeated *until* a condition becomes true. These are shown as follows:

Fig. 3.12

Let's have a look at two ways of writing the algorithm for reading and adding a set of numbers. Imagine that our computer can read the numbers, but don't worry how. When the computer reads a value of 999 or more it should stop reading. This final value should not be added to the total. An item of data used in this way is often called a **rogue value**. For example:

    1 5 16 3 4 56 999

1 Using WHILE ... DO.

2 Using REPEAT ... UNTIL

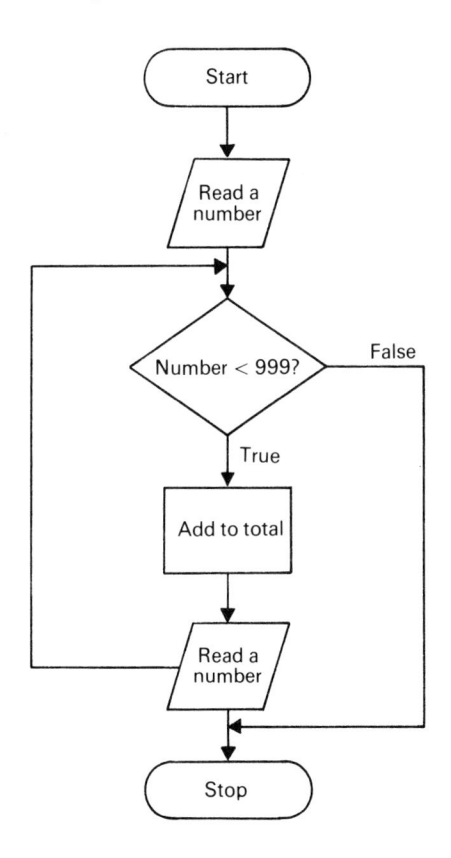

```
Start
Read a number
WHILE number < 999 DO
    ⎡Add number to total
    ⎣Read a number
Stop
```

Fig. 3.13

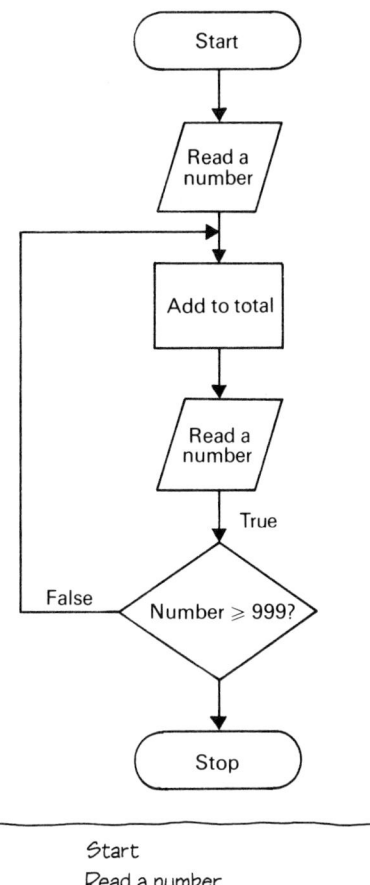

```
Start
Read a number
REPEAT
    ⎡Add number to total
    ⎣Read a number
UNTIL number ≥ 999
Stop
```

Fig. 3.14

The parts enclosed by the single bracket are repeated. A WHILE loop tests the condition *before* carrying out the actions. A REPEAT loop carries out the actions and *then* tests the condition. Notice that 'actions' may mean only one action.

Writing your algorithms

By using the basic blocks just described you should be able to write algorithms for most problems. This may seem tedious—but things do have to be spelt out very carefully for a computer. Remember that at this stage you have not written a program. You are describing what you want the program to do.

Have a go at writing algorithms for some other problems. Here are a few examples for you to try.
1 Read a set of numbers and total them. Stop adding when a negative number is read.
2 Read a set of 1's and 0's, one digit at a time. Write the word BLACK for a 1, WHITE for a 0.
3 Read a number. Multiply the number by itself until the result is more than 1 million.
4 Try your answer for Example 3 with the number 1 or zero or a negative number. If it doesn't work, alter it so that it does.

You will find that there are two major jobs in writing algorithms:
- thinking out a solution in simple logical steps
- testing your solution with different data to prove it always works.

The final step

You should test your algorithm by '**dry-running**' it. This means you should pretend to be a computer running your algorithm. Follow each step exactly, using sensible and non-sensible input. 'Sensible input' means values which you expect to be input. 'Non-sensible' means values which you would not expect, but *could* be input by mistake.

Keep asking yourself 'What happens if?' Don't forget that as a computer, you can only do exactly as you are told by the algorithm. For example, if your program contains a divide statement, it would not be sensible for it to divide by zero, because dividing by zero is not mathematically possible.

Write down any results. Correct the algorithm where necessary. When you are happy with your algorithm you can begin to write your program.

The next unit takes a look at a way of making algorithm writing easier.

KEY POINTS

1 Algorithms may be built from three basic structures:
- sequence
- selection
- repetition

2 A sequence is a simple list of things to do.

3 Selection involves testing a condition and choosing to do one thing or another.

4 Repetition means repeating a set of statements until a condition changes.

5 You should always test your algorithm by trying sensible and non-sensible data and seeing what happens. This is called dry-running.

Questions

1 Fill in the blanks:
   a) An algorithm states the _____ and _____ of a program.
   b) Algorithms can be built from 3 basic structures. These are: _____, _____ and _____.
2 Sketch the flowcharting symbol which denotes processing.
   (EMREB 1983)
3 A part of a computer program repeated a number of times is called:
   a) a counter
   b) repetition
   c) nest
   d) loop
   e) routine.
   (EMREB 1983)
4 The name given to testing an algorithm using 'sensible' and 'non-sensible' data is _____.
5 Sketch the pieces of flowchart which show IF ... THEN and IF ... THEN ... ELSE.
6 The flowchart below shows a simplified way to use a telephone. Put in the appropriate boxes and lines with 'yes' or 'no' labels.

BEGIN

LIFT UP RECEIVER

AND DIAL NUMBER

IS IT RINGING?

IS IT ANSWERED?   PUT DOWN RECEIVER

TALK   END

HAVE YOU FINISHED?
(SWEB 1983)

3.3 Breaking down problems: structured programming

'Divide and conquer' is an often used phrase. It means that if you tackle small parts of a large job one at a time then you will get the large job done more easily. This approach can be used in computer programming. It is called structured programming.

What is structured programming?

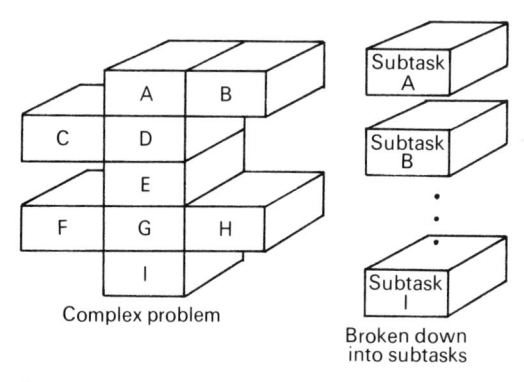

Fig. 3.15

Complex problem — Broken down into subtasks

The easiest way to approach any job is to break it down into a set of smaller tasks, or sub-tasks. Each of the smaller tasks may then involve some even smaller tasks. These, in turn, may involve smaller tasks, and so on. This is true in lots of things we do, and it is true in programming. Each small task or sub-task may consist of a simpler set of statements. A set of sub-tasks may then be used to make another task. This process can continue until you have built the complete program. If you think about building bricks, either toy or real, then you can see how this works. The simplest unit is a brick. Combining the bricks together gives a building. The sort of building it is depends on how the bricks are combined.

It is difficult to imagine a whole building just by looking at a brick. It is easier to imagine a room. Given a room it is easier to imagine a set of rooms making a house. The basic building bricks of an algorithm are **statements**. The bigger units are called: **sub-tasks** or **sub-routines** or **procedures** or **sub-programs** or **modules**. The exact name used does not matter. The important thing is to realize why you use it.

Why use structured programming?

Let's take a non-programming example—going on holiday. Some of the things you do when you go on holiday are:

    Get tickets
    Pack cases
    Travel to destination
    Unpack cases
    Enjoy holiday
    Pack cases
    Travel home
    Unpack cases

Each of these tasks sounds straightforward and the sequence seems all right. However, each activity is in fact quite complex and may well need more explanation or instructions. For instance, 'Get tickets' may involve the steps:

    Obtain cash
    Get bus to station
    Consult timetable

and so on. The point is that these steps are important for 'Get tickets', but they are not important to 'Going on holiday', as long as the right tickets are obtained.

Notice that 'Pack cases' and 'Unpack cases' are repeated. This is another common occurrence. The same activity is often done more than once. It would be very tedious to state all the steps in 'Pack cases' each time we use it.

These are the major benefits of using sub-tasks:
- they allow the overall task to be stated simply
- each sub-task may be written and tested separately
- a sub-task may be used more than once.

How to do it

When writing algorithms you should try to identify the sub-tasks. These should be small enough to understand and test quickly. As with the 'Going on holiday' example you can write these down as a list. You may then write down the separate set of steps for each sub-task. As you do this you might find a step is more complicated than you first thought. You should make such steps into another sub-task, and so on.

If you use a flowchart then use this symbol to signify a step as a sub-task:

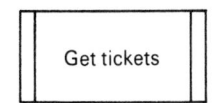

Fig. 3.16 Symbol to represent a sub-task

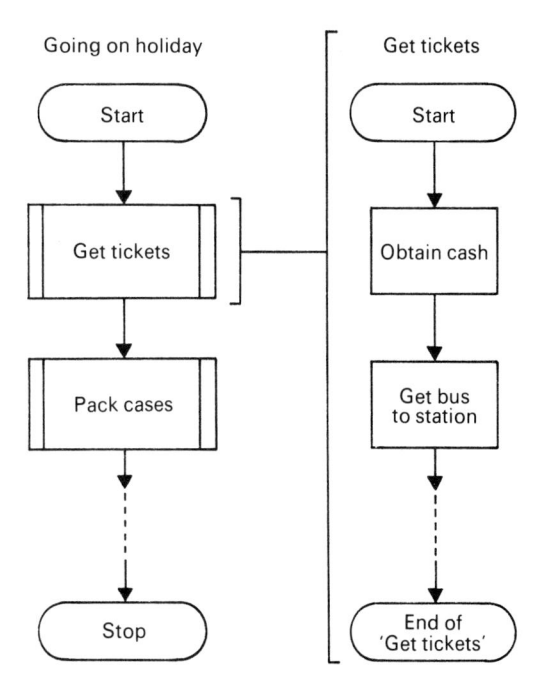

Fig. 3.17 One statement can mean a lot of actions

Don't forget an algorithm is the basic plan of what you want the program to do. You have still to write your program in a programming language. The next unit shows you how to do this.

KEY POINTS

1. Solving problems is made simpler by breaking them down into smaller chunks. These chunks are often called sub-tasks.

2. Each sub-task may be written and tested independently of others.

3. The same sub-task may be used more than once in the same algorithm.

4. Algorithms written in this way are easier to understand and should prove more reliable.

5. The algorithm is the plan of the program. The next step is to write the program in a programming language.

Questions

1. A set of statements to be obeyed several times, written only once and called when required is a:
   a) loop
   b) nested loop
   c) routine
   d) subroutine
   e) part program.
   (EMREB 1983)

2. The rule for crossing a busy road may be expressed as:
   'Stop at the kerb, look right, look left. If the road is clear look right again and then cross the road if it is still clear.'
   Represent these instructions in the form of a flowchart which will go back to the beginning of the sequence if the road is not clear.
   (YHREB 1983)

3.*Explain briefly the advantages of using subroutines when writing programs in a high-level language.
   (London 1983)

4.*Draw a flowchart to outline the scoring for one player in a new game of darts. The method of scoring is:
   a) A player starts with a score of 650.
   b) Two players take turns to have a 'go'. (A 'go' involves throwing one dart.)
   c) The score for each 'go' is deducted from the current total.
   d) The game is over when a player's 'go' reduces the total to exactly zero.
   (NOTE: If the score for a 'go' reduces the total below zero then that score is ignored.)
   (WJEC 1983)

*'O'-Level question

3.4 Putting the program in a language for the computer

Working out the solution to a problem is done by writing an algorithm. Unfortunately, computers can't read English or flowcharts—yet. To get the computer to solve your problem you still have to put a program into a programming language, or code.

Some programming languages

There are hundreds of programming languages available. For each programming language there are often several versions or dialects. Luckily, most programming languages are easier to learn than natural languages like English or French. Amongst the most commonly used ones are BASIC, COBOL, FORTRAN and PASCAL. This book does not try to teach you any particular language. But for any language you are going to use, you need to know how to get from algorithm to program.

Elements of programming languages

Every language has in it:
- references to data—values input to the computer and stored in the computer's memory (e.g. 'Number of tins of beans in stock' or 'Price per tin')
- statements—actions on the data (e.g. ADD, SUBTRACT, etc.)

Data items How you refer to an item of data varies from language to language. For example, the item 'Price per tin' might be referred to as: 'PRICE-PER-TIN' in COBOL and 'PRICE' in FORTRAN. This is because COBOL allows long names, including hyphens. FORTRAN allows six letters or digits.

Statements Actions on data include:
- addition, subtraction, multiplication, etc.
- comparisons—is one item equal to, greater than, less than another?
- input or output.

Let's take an example to illustrate the same action in BASIC and COBOL. An algorithm states:
'Add the number of tins of beans received to the number of tins in stock.'

In COBOL this may look like:
ADD NO-OF-TINS-RECEIVED TO NO-OF-TINS-IN-STOCK

In BASIC:
2000   LET Y = Y + X

If you imagine the contents of the data items as follows:

Before
NO-OF-TINS-IN-STOCK or Y |100|

NO-OF-TINS-RECEIVED or X |50|

After
NO-OF-TINS-IN-STOCK or Y |150|

NO-OF-TINS-RECEIVED or X |50|

You can see that in both cases the names refer to locations or boxes. These are often called **variables** because the contents of the boxes may vary. The *contents* of these boxes are added and the result left in one of the boxes. The action is exactly the same although the code looks very different. The algorithm details the procedure in English.

Here is the same statement in PASCAL:

NO-OF-TINS-IN-STOCK:= NO-OF-TINS-IN-STOCK + NO-OF-TINS-RECEIVED

In PASCAL ':=' means 'becomes' or 'takes the value.' The '=' sign is reserved for comparisons, e.g. IF NAME = "FRED" ...

Sequence, selection and repetition in code

Sequence A sequence of steps in an algorithm should convert directly into a sequence of program statements. But, as in an algorithm, a statement might be a reference to a sub-task. (The previous unit explains what a sub-task is.)

A reference to a sub-task might be as follows.
In BASIC:
      1000   GOSUB 2000
In COBOL:
      PERFORM ADD-ROUTINE.
or
      CALL ADD-ROUTINE.
In PASCAL:
      ADD-ROUTINE;
In FORTRAN:
      CALL ADDRTE

In each case these refer to a block of more program steps.

Selection Remember, selection looks like:

```
IF <condition> THEN <statements>
```

or

```
IF <condition> THEN <statement 1>
               ELSE <statement 2>
```

What do these look like in code? Again, it depends on the language. Let's take the 'Tin of beans in stock' example. This time we will extend the problem to include a condition test. Imagine that the storage space for tins of beans allows a maximum of 100 tins. If a total of more than 100 tins are received then the extras are sent back. The algorithm for this might say:

```
Add the no. of tins received to no. in stock
IF the no. in stock is more than 100
THEN subtract 100 from no. in stock and
     print resulting no. of tins to be sent back
```

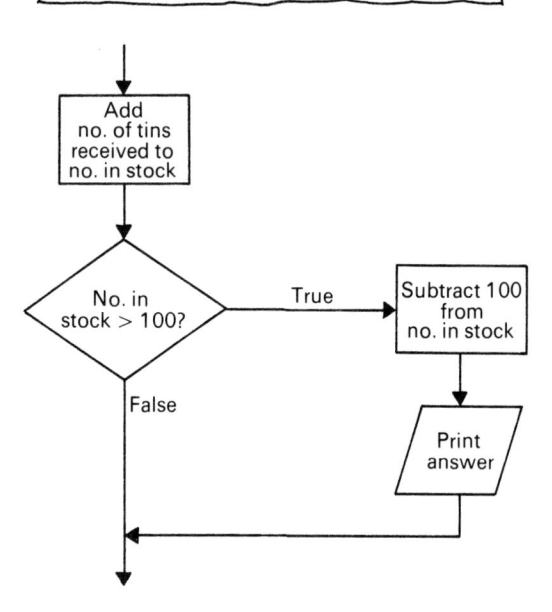

Fig. 3.18 Flowchart and algorithm to maintain stock level

In BASIC this may look like:

```
100  REM X holds no. of tins in stock
200  REM Y holds no. of tins received
300  REM Z holds no. of tins to be returned
400  LET X = X + Y
500  IF X < 101 THEN GO TO 800
600  LET Z = X - 100
700  PRINT Z
800     .
```

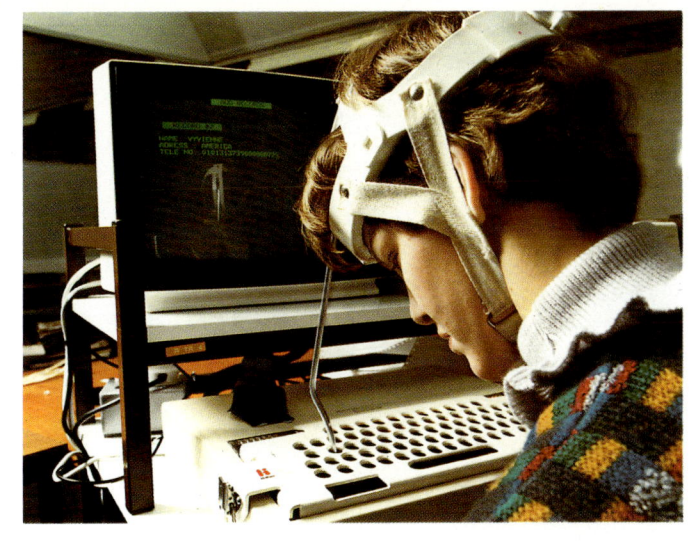

Photo 7   A physically disabled person is often at a disadvantage educationally. The physical problems involved in just taking notes are a considerable barrier to achievement. In the past, typewriters have gone part of the way to overcome these difficulties, but a typewriter cannot produce graphs, do calculations, allow text to be edited or provide control for electrical appliances. A microcomputer, however, can.

Photo 8   This computer system — known as a 'home work unit' — allows disabled people to work from home.

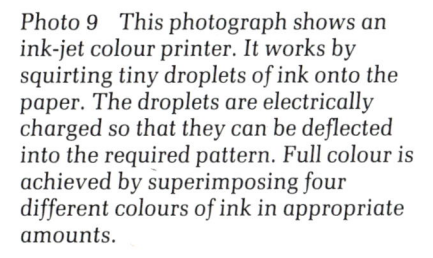

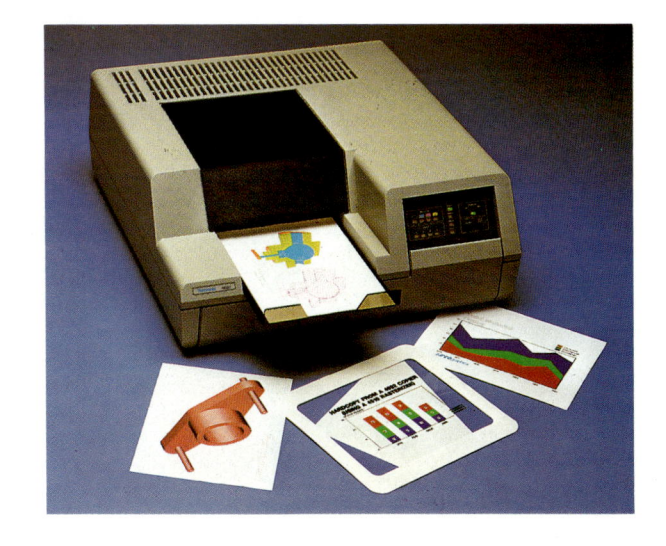

Photo 9   This photograph shows an ink-jet colour printer. It works by squirting tiny droplets of ink onto the paper. The droplets are electrically charged so that they can be deflected into the required pattern. Full colour is achieved by superimposing four different colours of ink in appropriate amounts.

Photo 10   These magnetic disk units are being used as the backing store to a mainframe computer. The main advantage gained by using magnetic disks instead of magnetic tape is that it is possible to go directly to an item of data without having to go through previously stored data first.

Photo 11   Here are two computer graphics which you can try for yourself if you have access to a BBC microcomputer.
(See 'Creative Graphics on the BBC Microcomputer' by John Cowie published by Acornsoft).

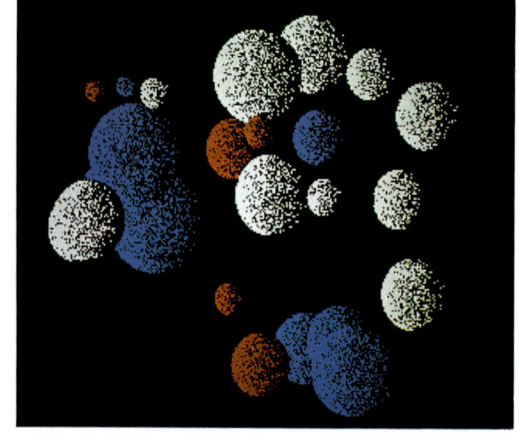

In COBOL:

```
        ADD NO-OF-TINS-RECEIVED TO NO-OF-TINS-IN-STOCK.
        IF NO-OF-TINS-IN-STOCK IS GREATER THAN 100
        THEN SUBTRACT 100 FROM NO-OF-TINS-IN-STOCK
            GIVING NO-RETURNED
            DISPLAY NO-RETURNED.
```

In PASCAL:

```
NO-OF-TINS-IN-STOCK := NO-OF-TINS-IN-STOCK + NO-OF-TINS-RECEIVED;
IF NO-OF-TINS-IN-STOCK > 100 THEN
    BEGIN
        NO-RETURNED := NO-OF-TINS-IN-STOCK - 100;
        WRITELN (NO-RETURNED)
    END
```

Repetition To remind you, repetition is shown in an algorithm as:

```
| WHILE ‹condition is true› DO ‹something› |
```

or

```
| REPEAT ‹something› UNTIL ‹condition is true› |
```

Here is an example to illustrate how this appears in a program. The program is to input a series of numbers and add them to a total. As soon as the total gets to more than 100 the program should output the total and stop.
The algorithm states:

```
Start
Set total to zero
WHILE total < 101 DO
    ⎡Input a number
    ⎣Add number to total
Print total
Stop
```

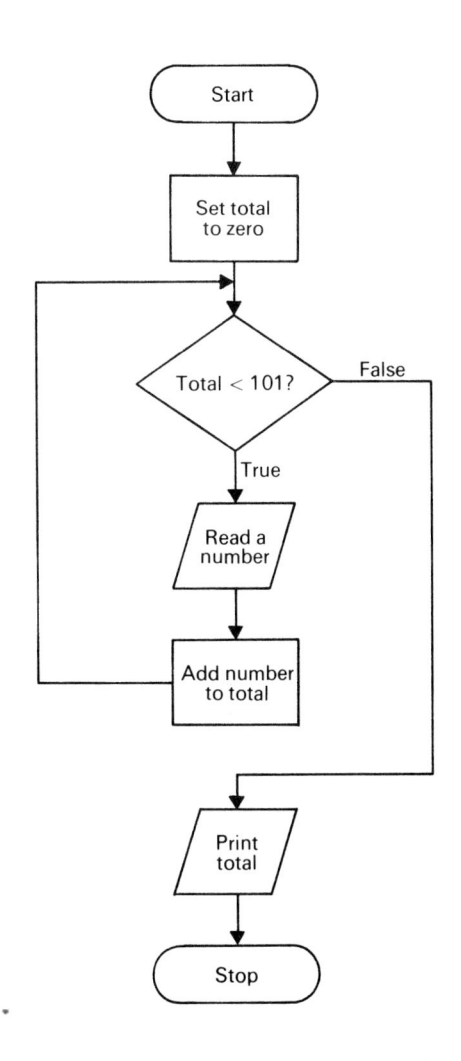

Fig. 3.19 *WHILE ... DO flowchart and algorithm*

It could also state:

```
Start
Set total to zero
REPEAT
    ⌈Input a number
    ⌊Add number to total
UNTIL  total > 100
Output total
Stop
```

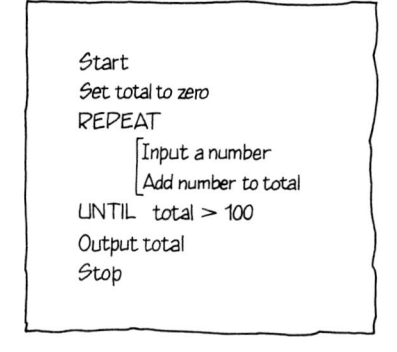

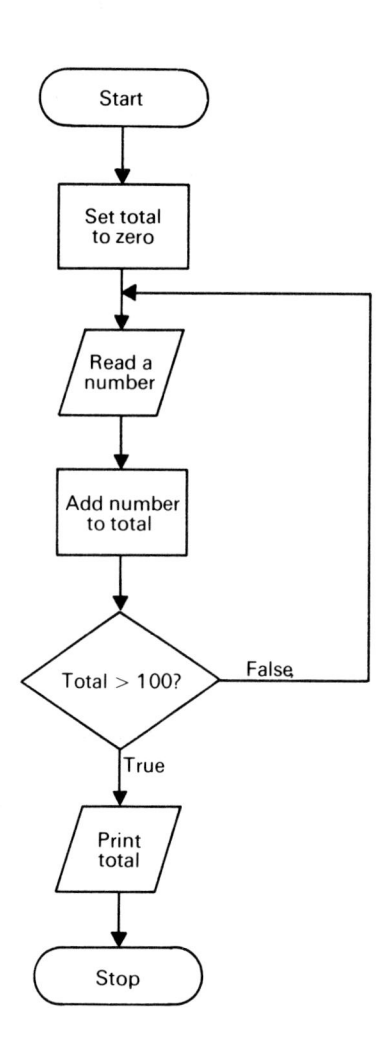

Fig. 3.20 REPEAT ... UNTIL flowchart and algorithm

In BASIC this might look like:

```
100   REM T holds total, N holds numbers to add
200   REM zeroise totals
300   REM
400   LET T = 0
500   REM
600   REM while total < 101 do
700   REM       input and add numbers
800   IF T > 100 GO TO 1300
900       INPUT N
1000      LET T = T + N
1100      GO TO 800
1200  REM
1300  REM print total and stop
1400  REM
1500  PRINT T
1600  STOP
```

In COBOL:

```
          MOVE ZEROS TO TOTAL.
       NEXT-ADD.
          IF TOTAL > 100 GO TO PRINT-AND-STOP.
              ACCEPT VALUE.
              ADD VALUE TO TOTAL.
              GO TO NEXT-ADD.
       PRINT-AND-STOP.
              DISPLAY TOTAL.
              STOP RUN.
```

In PASCAL:

```
       BEGIN
          TOTAL := 0;
          WHILE TOTAL < 101 DO
          BEGIN
              READLN (VALUE);
              TOTAL := TOTAL + VALUE
          END;
          WRITELN (TOTAL)
       END
```

Notice that in all these examples the total is first set to zero. This is because the initial content of a variable is not known. The memory location to which it refers could start with any value in it. It is safest to set a totalling variable initially to zero.

Writing clear programs

You can see that in the BASIC example the code looks very different to the algorithm. The COBOL code looks similar and the PASCAL code looks almost identical. This is no accident. PASCAL is a newer language than the other two and has been designed to make converting algorithms easier.

In the other examples you often have to use GOTO statements. These are often necessary when converting IF ... THEN and WHILE ... DO into code. This problem can be solved by using sub-tasks in some cases. Most books on programming will show you how to do this.

Other factors which will help you to understand a program are:
- using comments to explain what a section of code is doing
- using meaningful names for data items (e.g. TOTAL for accumulator).

Try the examples you have seen here, using your own data. See if you can dry-run them. The program should produce the same results as the algorithm.

> **KEY POINTS**
>
> 1 Lots of programming languages are available. BASIC, COBOL, FORTRAN and PASCAL are often used.
>
> 2 Languages may look very different to each other, but they all do the same thing.
>
> 3 Programming languages all refer to data and act on data.
>
> 4 All programs have sequence, most have selection and repetition.
>
> 5 Most languages allow you to specify sub-tasks.
>
> 6 Comments and meaningful data names help you to understand a program.

Questions

1 Complete this sentence. A memory location holding a data item is often called a _____.
2 A remark, or comment, statement used in a program gives:
   a) the line number
   b) information about the program
   c) decisions in the program
   d) error messages
   e) instructions to the computer.
   (EMREB 1983)
3 Name 3 types of statements found in most programs.
4 Write down examples of references to sub-tasks in COBOL, BASIC and PASCAL.
5 The following flowchart is designed to work out the average of one set of three numbers.
   a) Draw a flowchart that will work out the average of each of four sets of three numbers.
   b) Dry-run your flowchart with the following four sets of three numbers:
   1, 4, 4   2, 3, 7   6, 3, 9   5, 5, 2
   (EMREB 1983)
6 Rework Question 5 showing the original flowchart as a subroutine.

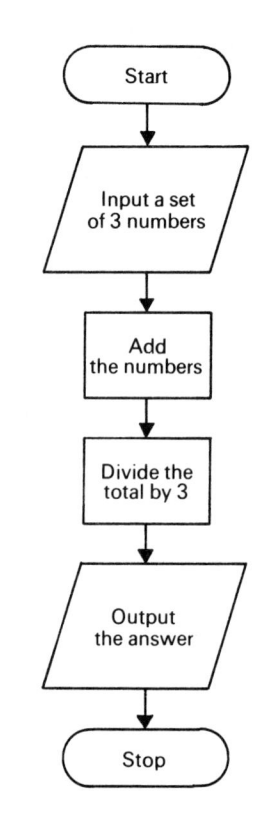

Fig. 3.21

Flowchart:
Start → Input a set of 3 numbers → Add the numbers → Divide the total by 3 → Output the answer → Stop

3.5 Types of programming language I: low-level

There are many programming languages available. Languages are also classified as either low-level or high-level. The next two units describe the differences between high-level and low-level programming languages.

Process and data

The computer memory holds data and programs. The program processes the data. To be able to do this the program has to know the *address* of the data item required. The addresses of locations of data items are included in the program instructions. The *contents* of these locations are then processed. A process might be to add, subtract, or print.

Machine code

When your program is running on a computer, the instructions will contain two main items. The first part will be a code to tell the computer what to do—the **operation code**. The second part will often be one or more addresses. These are called **operands**. Since the computer can 'understand' only 1's and 0's this will be a string of binary digits. This is called **machine code** because this is what actually runs on the machine.

All computers can be programmed in machine code. However, as you can imagine, writing programs in machine code is very tedious and difficult to do.

The next stage—assembly language

When they were first invented, the only way to program computers was in machine code. Luckily, a way was found to make programming easier. This is to write the program using short simple words to stand for the machine code instructions. These words are often called **mnemonics** ('mnemonic' = memory aid) and the program is said to be written in **assembly language**. For example, ADD may be used for 10111011.

The other main advantage of assembly language is that instead of having to mention the memory address of data you can give a data item a name. For example, to add two data items together, you can write:

ADD   VAL 1, VAL 2

'VAL 1' and 'VAL 2' are names given by the programmer to memory addresses.

When writing programs it is often necessary to **branch** or **jump** to an instruction. As with data items, the address of a program instruction needs to be known. An instruction address is often called a **label**.

```
SUBTR:
        DEC     IY
        DEC     IY
        LD      H,(IY+0)
        LD      L,(IY+0)
        LD      D,(IY+2)
        LD      E,(IY+3)
        SBC     HL,DE
        LD      (IY+0),H
        LD      (IY+1),L
        JP      PO,SUBTR1
        LD      H,(IX+2)
        LD      L,(IX+3)
        LD      (LINENO),HL
        CALL    RANGET
SUBTR1:
        JP      NEXT2
```

Fig. 3.22 Assembly level code (Z 80)

The assembly process

The programmer writes the code in assembly language. The assembly language is different for each type of computer.

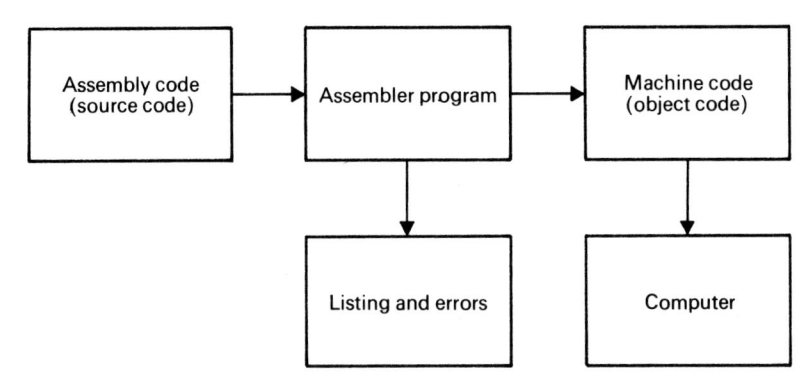

```
┌──────────────┐     ┌──────────────┐     ┌──────────────┐
│ Assembly code│────▶│  Assembler   │────▶│ Machine code │
│ (source code)│     │   program    │     │ (object code)│
└──────────────┘     └──────┬───────┘     └──────┬───────┘
                            │                    │
                            ▼                    ▼
                     ┌──────────────┐     ┌──────────────┐
                     │  Listing and │     │   Computer   │
                     │    errors    │     │              │
                     └──────────────┘     └──────────────┘
```

Fig. 3.23 Converting assembly language code into machine code

Different makes of computer have different instruction sets in their machine code.

The assembly code is then used as input to an **assembler**. An assembler is a program which translates the assembly language into machine code. The input code is often called **source code**. The assembler checks that the correct codes and formats have been used. It will also check for errors like giving the same name to a data item address and a program instruction address.

If there are no errors in the code the assembler will then create an output file, often called **object code**. The object code is the machine code which will run on the computer. The assembler also has to replace address names with actual addresses in memory.

ADVANTAGES	DISADVANTAGES
Easier than machine code programming	It is low-level, that is, nearer to the 'level' of the machine than to a human being
The programmer can take full advantage of the machine's instruction set	A knowledge of machine hardware is required
The timing of code can be very exact. This is useful in real-time programming	Each machine's assembly code is different. Programs are not portable to other machines

Advantages and disadvantages of assembly-level programming

Advantages and disadvantages of assembly-level programming

Around 1950 there was a lot of discussion about the development of programming languages. One group of people thought that it was best to continue using assembly-level code. Their argument was that programming was easy and low-level programming would make best use of the machines.

Another group thought that programming should be made easier for human beings. The argument for making programming easier won the day. High-level languages began to be invented in the early 1950's, as the next unit explains.

3.6 Types of programming language II: high-level

High-level languages

High-level programming languages are languages which are designed to be easy for people to use. Assembly code is high-level when compared to machine code. However, it is usually accepted that 'high-level language' means a language which is designed for solving particular types of problems.

High-level languages should not be concerned with the computer, but with problems. They are often called **problem-oriented languages**.

Development of high-level languages

The first major high-level language to be developed was **FORTRAN** (FORmula TRANslation). This was developed for use by mathematicians, scientists and engineers. FORTRAN code looks very much like algebra.

Computers are not used just for science and engineering problems, but in business also. In 1960 a language was designed for use in business. This was **COBOL** (COmmon Business Oriented Language). This language looks more like English. It is designed for writing programs for business applications.

ALGOL (ALGOrithmic Language) was designed in 1957–1962. This language was designed for expressing algorithms. It has never been used as much as FORTRAN and COBOL but PASCAL owes a lot of its features to ALGOL.

BASIC (Beginner's All-purpose Symbolic Instruction Code) is based on FORTRAN but it has been designed for use on microcomputers.

There are several hundred high-level languages available now. Some are better for certain types of applications. Although there are many high-level languages, they all have these features in common:

- they are designed to be easy to use
- they are portable, i.e. they can be used on more than one type of computer
- programs written in them need translation into machine code before they can be run
- they cannot use the computer as flexibly as a low-level language.

These features are very general. Ease of use is not easy to define. Some people find a language easier to use than other people. Most high-level languages are not truly portable. For example, a COBOL program written for an IBM computer cannot be run on an ICL computer. However, if you know the COBOL language for one computer you should be able to quickly learn the differences required for another.

Translation

A high-level language is used to write a program in more human terms. The computer has to run programs in machine code. Between the high-level language and the machine code translation has to take place. In the last unit we saw that an assembler is used to translate assembly code into machine code. There are two main methods of translating high-level code into machine code: **compilation** and **interpretation**.

Compilation With this method a **compiler** takes *all* your program code and translates it in one go. As in the case of an assembler, the input code is called **source code**, the output is called **object code**. Each line of high-level code will generate many lines of low-level code.

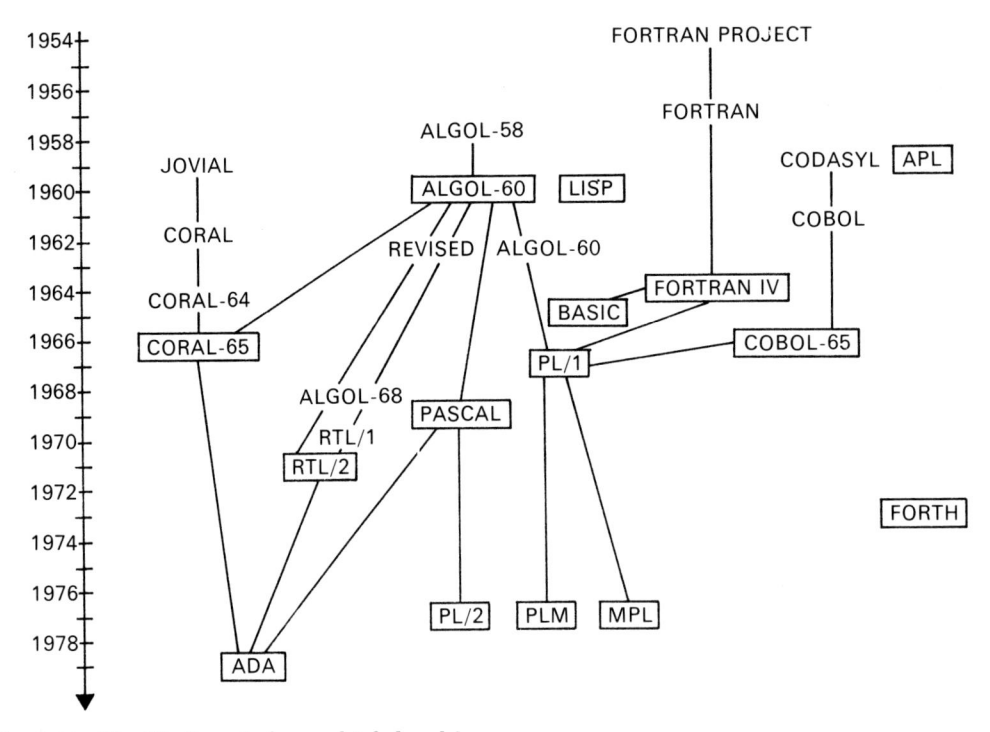

Fig. 3.24 The 'Pedigree' of some high-level languages

For example, in COBOL:
    ADD VALUE TO TOTAL.
may generate (shown in assembly code)
    LD   4, TOTAL
    ADD 4, VALUE
    STO 4, TOTAL
Once compiled, with no errors, the **object program** may be run on the computer.

Interpretation An **interpreter** translates each line of code and runs it straight away.

Compilers and interpreters are themselves programs. They are part of the software which is provided with the computer, called systems software. (Systems software is covered in Part 4.)

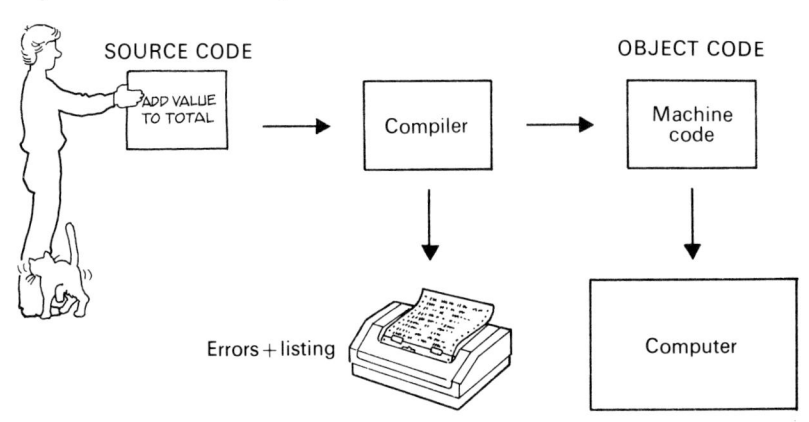

Fig. 3.25 Compilation

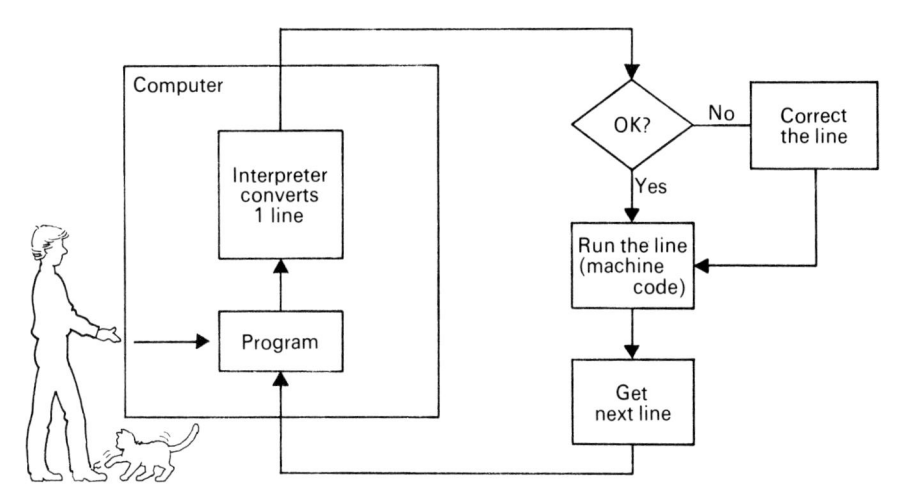

Fig. 3.26 Interpretation

Advantages and disadvantages of compilers and interpreters

	ADVANTAGES	DISADVANTAGES
COMPILATION	Object program runs on its own Programs usually run faster Less memory space needed to run the program	Whole program needs to be compiled again when one error is found
INTERPRETATION	A line in error can be corrected and run again	Programs run more slowly More space needed to store the interpreter when the program is running

Comparison of compilers and interpreters

Sometimes an interpreter may be used when testing the program being written. When the program has no errors a compiler can produce the final object code.

Another method is to compile source code into a 'shorthand' version of the original code. A lot of the errors may be detected and the code simplified. The simplified and shortened code can then be input to an interpreter. This makes interpretation easier and faster. In this way the disadvantages of using an interpreter are reduced.

KEY POINTS of high and low-level languages

1. There are two general levels of computer programming languages: low-level and high-level.

2. The lowest level of programming language is machine code, the code which actually runs on the computer. Machine code instructions are made up of numbers only.

3. Assembly-level languages use a simple 'mnemonic' code in place of the numbers in machine code. They also allow for references to memory locations by name. Assembly-level language is regarded as being low-level.

4. High-level programming languages are designed to make programming easier. Examples of high-level languages are FORTRAN, BASIC, COBOL and PASCAL.

5. An assembly-level language program will run only on the particular model of computer for which it was written. High-level programming languages are designed to be used on many different makes of computer.

6. Before they run on a computer, programs are translated into machine code. Assembly-level language programs are translated by an assembler, high-level language programs are translated by either a compiler or an interpreter.

7. One line of assembly-level code usually translates into one machine code instruction. One line of high-level code translates into several machine code instructions.

Questions

1. An instruction that can be recognized and used without translation is written in:
   a) assembly code
   b) machine code
   c) PASCAL
   d) COBOL
   e) BASIC.
   (EMREB 1983)

2. Name two examples of high-level languages other than BASIC.
   (NWREB 1983)

3. Give an example of a mnemonic and explain its meaning.
   (NWREB 1983)

4. Complete the sentences below.
   a) The input to a compiler is a source program written in _____ level language.
   b) The input to an assembler is a source program written in _____ level language.
   c) The output from a compiler or an assembler is known as the _____ program.
   (SREB 1983)

5*a) Define (i) computer program, (ii) high-level language.
   b) Compare the relative merits of using a compiler for: (i) development and (ii) the regular running of high-level language programs.
   (London 1983, part)

6. a) Most programs are now written in high-level languages. Give two reasons why low-level languages are still used.
   b) (i) A number of high-level languages have been standardized. Explain why it has been considered desirable to do this.
   (ii) Account for the fact that there are no similar standards for assembly languages.
   (Cambridge 1983)

7. State the two main functions of a compiler.
   (EMREB 1983)

*'O'-Level question

Comprehension Extract

Computer, watch your language

You have to be careful what you say to a computer. But there must be an easier way of saying it, argues Douglas Bell

A computer program instructs a computer to carry out a specific task. Just as a knitting pattern or a piece of music are expressed in a particular notation, so a program is expressed in terms of a programming language. Like the English language there are rules of grammar and a program must be meticulously correct. There are hundreds of programming languages, but only a few are well-known and widely used. The most-used language, Cobol, is used in commercial applications of computers like printing a payroll or keeping records of stock. FORTRAN is a language used widely by engineers and scientists to carry out calculations. The language BASIC, purportedly easy to learn and use, has recently enjoyed a comeback because of its widespread availability on microcomputers.

A few years ago the Americans sent a space vehicle to look at Venus. When it was near to its destination, a computer, trying to alter the trajectory of the space ship, executed the FORTRAN statement: DO 3 I = 1.3.

The programmer's intention was one thing, and the statement as written means something else. But regrettably the statement should have a comma rather than a full stop. The computer, as an automaton, took the strict interpretation and sent the Venus probe off to oblivion, at a cost of several billion dollars.

In 1979 five nuclear reactors in the US were closed down. A bug had been found in a program used to perform calculations to aid the design of the cooling systems. Many heart pacemakers are today controlled by microcomputer (some are programmable after implantation). But would you be willing to write the program for your own? I wouldn't.

I do not suggest that all problems would be solved simply by the use of better programming languages. But human life is increasingly dependent on programs that work properly. We should therefore take very care to use the best techniques we can in order to avoid failures.

Expressiveness is the ability of the language to describe exactly what we want to do in a precise, clear way. The evidence suggests that we can test a program until we are blue in the face; it will still have bugs in it. So it's better to try to ensure that in constructing the program we have got it right.

Consider the common situation in which we want a program to do something repetitively, but the number of repetitions is not fixed. Examples are: 1. input and process a set of numbers until some special number indicates the end. 2. perform a numerical computation iteratively until the error is less than a set amount. 3. search a table such as a telephone directory until a required item is found.

Although this sort of processing is extremely common, neither BASIC nor FORTRAN provide language features designed specifically to express it. What we have to do is use IF and GOTO statements to express what we want. In my telephone directory I am advised to start finding the telephone number I want by following the instruction: Find the surname (surnames are in alphabetical order). Few programming languages have this sort of expressive power. But FORTRAN and BASIC both make a meal of it. The sort of thing we have to do is like this: Step 1: if this surname is the one we seek then go to the next step, otherwise look at the next entry—go to step 1. Next step:

The available features of BASIC and FORTRAN completely distort the programmer's intent, in this situation as in others. What we would like to do is to express our intention in directly meaningful terms, something like: repeat: look at the next entry until the surname is the one we seek.

After a program has been written on paper it is entered into a computer via some suitable device like a typewriter. Then, before the program is obeyed, a sophisticated program called a compiler translates it from whatever language it is written in into the instructions that the computer can obey. As the translation takes place, the compiler checks the program for errors. It would be highly desirable if the compiler, when translating our program could (politely) inform us of the bugs—and not just the grammatical errors. Language design is moving firmly in this direction.

A recipe normally starts with a list of the ingredients, and we don't expect to meet an unexpected ingredient half way through. If we do, we would suspect that something is wrong with the recipe. Similarly in a program, if the language requires us to name all the items we need at the start, then the compiler can check that we haven't inadvertently mis-spelled a name later on. Unfortunately FORTRAN and BASIC don't carry out this sort of checking.

Another way in which a compiler can be provided with adequate information to enable it to check a program is if we distinguish carefully between different types of data. For example, a bus number, my annual salary, and the distance from Sheffield to London are all numbers. But we are not likely to want to add a bus number to a salary or compare a distance with the value of pi. However FORTRAN and BASIC both allow this to go on freely.

Such faults could be exposed automatically by the compiler if the language did not allow us to freely "mix" data of different "types", but instead forced us to spell out exactly what we want to do.

Writing programs is a delight: it is creative and interesting. But using real examples, I have tried to convey my fears of disasters that may in the future be caused by computer system failures. I do not allege that BASIC or FORTRAN has been or will be the villain. But there are weaknesses in these languages.

I don't believe that the ultimate language is available. Nor do I claim that, by itself, good language design can lead to reliable programs. But I do assert that there are "better" languages than BASIC or FORTRAN. I recognise that there are many other factors that affect the reliability of a computer system. But we should seize on every technique we can to improve reliability, and that includes good programming languages.

Douglas Bell is of the Department of Computer Studies, Sheffield City Polytechnic.

The Guardian 22nd January 1981

Questions

1. What is the job of a compiler?
2. What are program bugs and how are they found?
3. What is meant by 'types' of data in a programming language?
4. Why does the author argue that 'data typing' is desirable in a programming language?
5. What is the main argument expressed by the author in the article? Do you agree or disagree with the argument?

Wordsearch

Copy this grid into your workbook. In the grid you will find 8 words all to do with programming languages. Use the clues to help you.

1. This piece of software translates low-level code into machine code.
2. This software translates a complete program written in high-level code into machine code.
3. This software does the same as 2, but just one line at a time.
4. A language for business applications.
5. A language for scientific and mathematical applications.
6. With this language it is easy to draw pictures using a turtle!
7. This language is more structured than most and sounds French.
8. The most popular language for microcomputers.

PROGRAMMING LANGUAGES WORDSEARCH

```
B Z G S F Z R V O W P Z T W C
I A A I U Z H I D V I T O Q O
T W S P A S C A L U N O S W B
C T S I K U O I H R T O X K O
M Q E O C O F M D O E U A L L
E N M C G F O R D P R D G L A
W C B O M R R N A Y P N A D P
C O L C P J T Z A X R P D R I
P M E B U E R B N Q E Q T Y G
X P R Q Z H A A X V T E B X E
Z I Z D A L N Q K W E B Y P R
X L P U U W J H A K R X Q Q S
T E K H T N N C A O Z R V K A
Y R B H C K L N U X F I X S M
W K Q V F L V T K K X G K V X
```

Part 4

Systems Software

4.1 Getting the most out of a computer

You cannot use a computer without having programs. But even when you have a program you still need some more software to help it run. This software is called an operating system.

What is an operating system?

To make use of a computer you need three things. You need hardware and you need a program to run on the computer (software), but you also need something to help your program to run on the hardware. This 'something' is more software called **systems software** or an **operating system**. The operating system stays in the computer all the time it is switched on.

microcomputer is usually used by one person at a time, a large mainframe computer is used by several people at the same time.

Jobs done by the operating system

Here is a list of some of the jobs done by all operating systems. They:
- load programs and data into immediate access store
- store programs and data on backing store
- list programs or data on a VDU screen or printer
- communicate with a computer user or program
- allow for changes to programs or data files.

Fig. 4.1 The operating system

Little and large

The size and complexity of the operating system depends on the size of the computer. The simplest operating systems are on microcomputers, the most complex on large, shared computers. This is because small computers have less hardware to organize, large computers have more. A

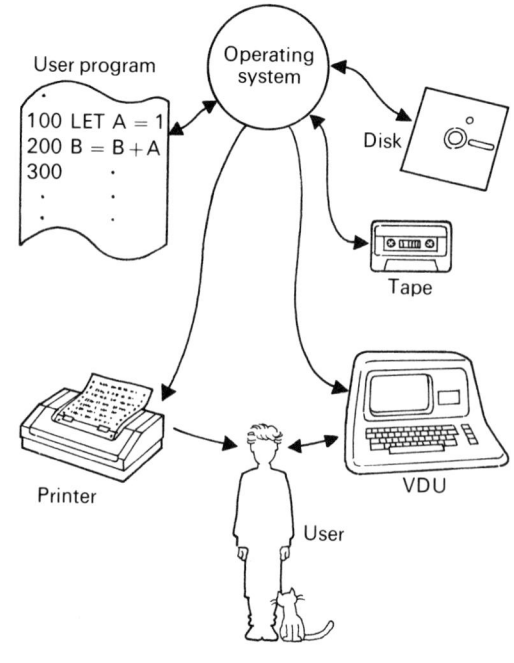

Fig. 4.2 The operating system handles communication between the parts of the computer and the user

The user can communicate with the computer through the operating system. It takes care of fetching data from disk, tape, terminal, etc. Also, the loading of the user's program into the computer's memory is done by the operating system. Some instructions are given to the operating system directly by the user, some by programs running in the machine.

Command language

The user gives instructions to the operating system by means of a **command language**. This looks like another programming language, but instead of having instructions like 'LET A = A + B' as in BASIC, the command language has instructions 'LOAD STARWARS' or 'LIST STARWARS'. You may also need to 'tell' the machine to store your program on disk or tape. These simple commands will be taken by the operating system and it will carry out the tasks for you.

COMMAND	ACTION
LOAD	Load a program from disk or tape into memory
RUN	Start the program that is in memory
SAVE	Store the program in memory on disk or tape

Operating system commands

The operating system and your program

As well as communicating directly with the user, the operating system also helps applications programs to run. An example of this is the INPUT instruction in a BASIC program. INPUT means 'Fetch a number or some letters from the keyboard.' This actually gives an instruction to the operating system, which fetches what is required and then passes it to the program.

PRINT, GET and PUT are also BASIC instructions which set the operating system off on its tasks of transferring data between the user's program and VDU, printer and disk. As you can see, the operating system has quite a lot to do.

Loading the operating system

The operating system is software, it is a program. It has to be in the computer's immediate access memory all the time it is switched on. How does it get there?

There are two main ways of loading the operating system into memory. These are by:
- using ROM (Read Only Memory)
- bootstrapping.

Operating system in ROM If the operating system is small, for example, on a microcomputer, it may be possible to store it on a ROM chip. When the computer is switched on this sets the operating system running. You may then give com-

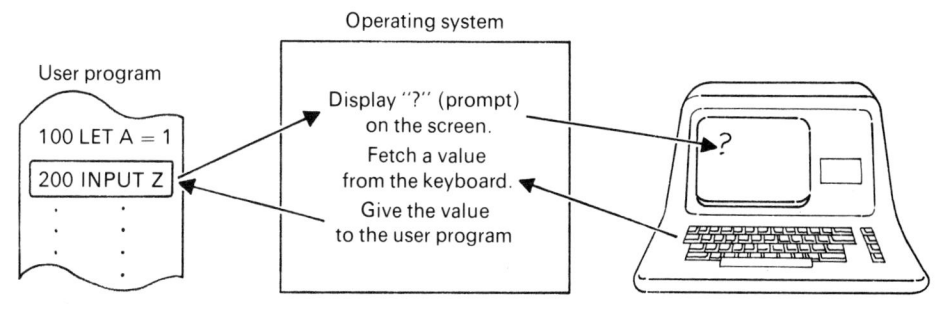

Fig. 4.3   *The role of the operating system in inputting a value*

73

mands to the operating system, using the command language mentioned above. On many small microcomputers this also gives access to the BASIC programming language. With these machines you are usually limited to writing applications programs in the one language.

The machine will usually display a 'response' such as:

BASIC >

or >

on the screen which means it is waiting for a command. Two examples are the BBC and the Sinclair Spectrum microcomputers.

Bootstrapping the operating system For larger machines, the operating system is usually too large to store on a chip. (Although changing chip technology means that this may not always be true.) This means that it has to be stored on disk or tape and loaded into immediate access store when the computer is switched on.

The problem is that it is usually the operating system's job to fetch things from disk or tape. One way around this problem is to do as follows:

- have a small program stored in a particular place on a disk
- have a very small program stored in ROM which reads the small program from the disk into RAM and sets it running
- this program may then read the large operating system from the disk and store it in RAM and set it running.

This process is called **bootstrapping**, from the old saying: 'Pull yourself up by your own bootstraps.' The idea is that you have a very small program reading a bigger program and so on.

KEY POINTS

1 An operating system is software which makes the computer more usable. It helps users communicate with the computer and helps application programs to run.

2 Users communicate by means of a command language. It is stored in the machine all the time the machine is switched on.

3 Small operating systems may be stored permanently in ROM. Larger operating systems have to be read from disk or tape by a process called bootstrapping.

Questions

1 Fill in the blanks.
 a) The software which controls the loading and running of programs is called _____.
 (SREB 1980)
 b) A user communicates with the operating system by means of _____.

2 Describe the process of bootstrapping an operating system.

3 Why does the operating system have to be stored in the computer all the time it is switched on?

4 Give the meaning of the term operating system and give an example of a task for which it could be used.
 (YREB 1981)

4.2 Types of operating system

Ever since computers were first used, people have tried to get more work out of them. Computers cost money, and time means money in the business world. This is why hardware and software developments have aimed at making the most of the available computer time.

The early days (1950–1960's era)

The early commercial computers were very expensive and did not have much systems software with them. To use them, people would load the program they wanted to run in the computer's main memory and put their data in the input device. The program and data were usually on punched cards or punched tape. Often there would be a computer operator to do this. Once the program was loaded and the data ready for input the operator would press the 'go' button. The computer would run the program which would read the data and produce the output on a printer. The happy user would then walk away with the output, ready to let the next person in the queue use the computer.

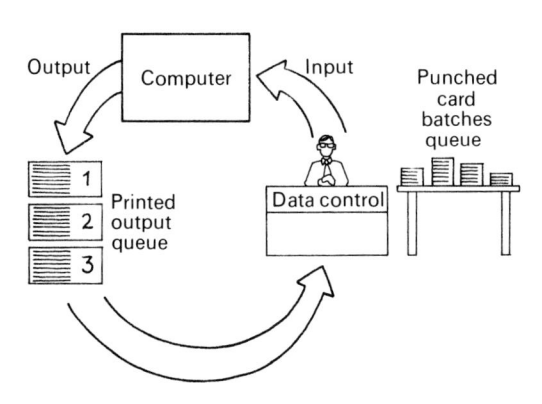

Fig. 4.4 The batch processing system

Batch processing (1960's–1970's era)

Batching With the early method, the computer spent a lot of time doing nothing because it had to wait for the operator to put the next job in and press 'go'. Time means money, so changes were made to save time. This was done by **batching** jobs together. Instead of the operator putting in a program and the data one job at a time, a set of jobs were put in a stack in the input device along with instructions to the computer about how to run each of the jobs.

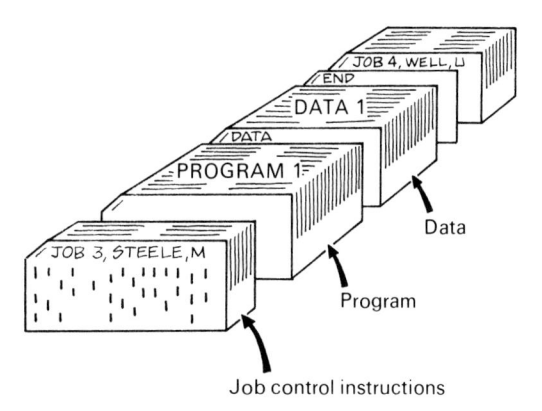

Fig. 4.5 A batch of jobs with job control instructions

Job Control Language (JCL) These instructions were addressed to the operating system, which would then run the programs in the right sequence. The instructions to the operating system were, for example, the program name, the name of the data, etc. These instructions were, and still are, called **job commands** and are written in **Job Control Language** (JCL). Job control language is the name for instructions given to the operating system. JCL can look very much like a programming language.

Data control clerks Batch processing speeds things up by reducing CPU waiting time. This means that a lot more input and output is processed. The danger is that all this input and output could become mixed up, so extra people are required to make sure things are kept in order. These people are often called **data control clerks**. Their job is to keep control of the data—to make sure the input gets passed to the machine in the right order, and that the output is passed back to the right person.

Off-line processing with batch input/output

Although batch processing increased the amount of actual work done by the computer (through-put), there was still a major problem. The computer still had to stop after each job before reading the next one in. It also had to stop to print the output. Remember that the CPU runs at an extremely high speed when compared with an input or output device. To make more efficient use of the CPU the input and output times had to be reduced. The answer to this problem was to **off-line** the input and output. 'Off-line' means to input the programs, data and instructions to a fast storage device, such as magnetic disk, and save them. Then when the computer is ready to run a particular job it can get all the input it needs at higher speed from the disk.

It can also do the same with the output. Instead of sending the output data direct to the printer, it can go on to a fast disk for printing later. This is often called **spooling**. Each job running sends its output to a disk. When the computer is less busy, the operating system prints the output on a printer. This helps to spread the workload by doing slow printing work at off-peak times.

Of course, things could get into a real mess if this was not done properly. It is the job of the operating system to keep track of all the inputs and outputs and to make sure they all get processed at the right time.

Scheduling Having all the data and instructions off-line means that the jobs do not have to be run in the same sequence as they were input. This means that the jobs can be input in *any* order, and the operating system can run them in the *best* order. For example, one job may be more important than another, but happens to get input by the operator at a later time. If the instructions (in JCL) on the more important job say 'urgent', the computer could be made to run this first. This is known as **scheduling**. In this way more important jobs can be run more quickly than others by giving them higher priority.

Multiprogramming— doing more than one job at once

Even with batch and off-line processing the CPU can still spend a lot of time doing nothing. This is because each time it has to read from or write to a peripheral, it has to stop doing anything else. Even a disk drive is very slow compared with the CPU. Because of this, a lot of processing time is lost. The answer is to have more than one program running at the same time. This is known as **multiprogramming**.

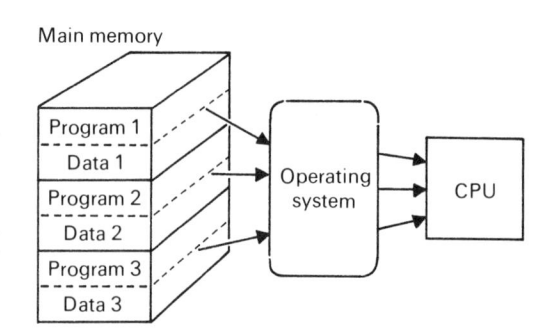

Fig. 4.6 *The operating system 'switches' the CPU between programs sharing the main memory*

With multiprogramming the immediate access memory of the computer may hold more than one program at once. Each program will need to use the CPU to process its instructions. Each program may at some time need to read some data from a disk or print on a printer. The operating system will allow each program a certain amount of time in the CPU on a **round-robin** basis. That is, one program runs for a few milliseconds and is then stopped. Another program starts to run, and so on. When a program has finished, it drops out of the round robin and a new one is included. If a program needs to read or write some data, the operating system stops including that program in the round robin. When the program has finished reading or writing it will be included in the round robin again. This may occur with any of the jobs. With this arrangement very little CPU time is wasted in waiting for programs to input or output.

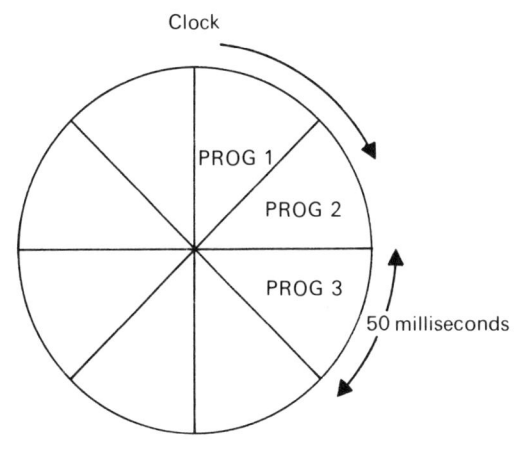

Fig. 4.7 The 'round-robin' clock—each program gets a fixed time slice

Distributed computing— the rise of the terminal

On-line processing On-line processing means that the person wishing to use the computer has a direct link to it. This link is usually through a VDU or teletype terminal connected by wires. Having a direct link can save a lot of time because you can tell the computer what you want it to do yourself. You tell the computer what to do by means of JCL via the terminal. The operating system may still schedule its work.

A typical large modern computer will run batch jobs and on-line jobs all at the same time. The operating system should attempt to give on-line users a quick service as well as getting all the batch work done.

Interactive processing Having on-line access to a computer means that you can do more than just tell the computer to run a job. You can also input data while your program is running. At the same time the computer can produce its results on the VDU screen or teletype. This is called **interactive processing** and has become very popular. It means you can have a dialogue or conversation with the computer. The dialogue may take several forms. Two examples are:

- question and answer
  (You ask the computer a question using the keyboard. It gives you the answer on the screen. The computer may then ask you a question and so on.)

(a) Question and answer

- forms filling
  (The computer displays a screen which looks like a form with blanks to be filled in. You fill in the blanks.)

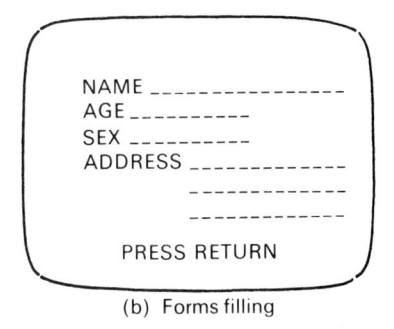

(b) Forms filling

Fig. 4.8 Two types of interactive dialogue styles

Multi-access Many terminals can be connected to the computer. These can all be in use at the same time. Each user is connected on-line. This arrangement is often referred to as an **on-line, multi-access system**.

Real-time computing

Real-time means the time as we know it, which seems obvious. So why have a special name for computing in real-time? Well, as you saw earlier, a lot of processing is done according to schedules which make best use of the CPU's time. No account of the time of day is taken.

With real-time computing the time by the clock becomes the most important factor. Let us take an example—controlling a lunar module landing on the moon. A computer on board might be controlling the descent rate by firing retro rockets. The exact timing and duration of each firing needs to be very exact. Fire for too long and off you go into space again. Fire for not long enough and you smash to pieces on the surface. If the program controlling this were stopped for a while and another one run, the results would be disastrous.

The example illustrates the main features of real-time computing:
- the actual time taken by the program instructions is very important
- the commonest applications are in control systems
- there is no attempt to make the best use of the *computer's* time, just the *real* time.

The present day (1984–future)

Large mainframe computers are still used but mini- and microcomputers have taken a lot of their work. The spread of minis and micros has also meant that a lot of new work is done on computers. Batch processing still has its place for jobs requiring large volumes of data, but interactive processing is by far the most popular mode of working. Magnetic tape and disks have largely replaced punched card and paper tape for batch input.

Linking micros to mainframes Increasingly, the micro and mini are being linked to mainframe computers. This means that your terminal can be a microcomputer with a VDU. You can do some processing at your micro and also use the power of the big computer when required. This arrangement is sometimes referred to as an 'intelligent terminal', as opposed to a 'dumb terminal'.

In business this means that someone at a desk can do their personal computing without 'disturbing' the mainframe. The mainframe could have a large database. The micro user can obtain and send information from, and to, the database. Also, if the program is too big to run on the micro, it could be run on the big machine.

This way of working is also useful for home computing and is seen as a way of passing programs and information around. The units on communications and social implications also discuss this development.

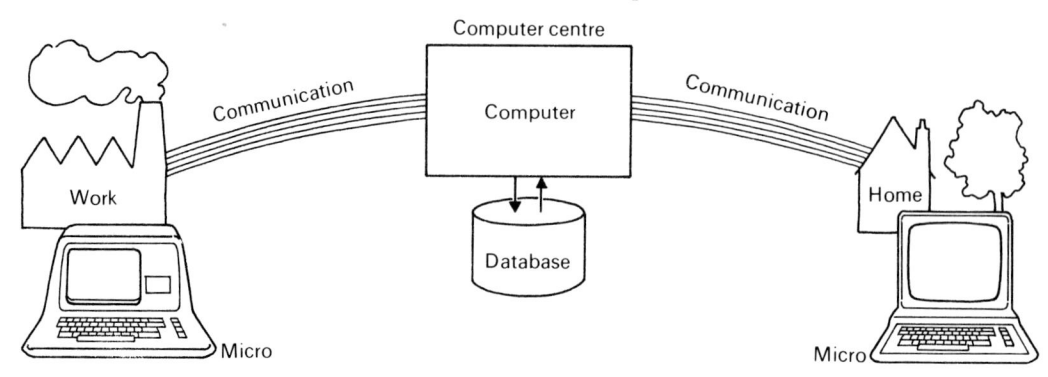

Fig. 4.9 *Sharing data using micros at home and work*

It is interesting to realize that today's personal microcomputer is similar to the computers of the early days. The micro will run your job when you want without scheduling. It does have limitations of speed and data storage capacity, but today's micro fits in a briefcase; the early equivalents filled a large room.

KEY POINTS

1 The early commercial computers ran one job at a time.

2 Batch processing was introduced to increase the amount of work done by reducing waiting times between jobs.

3 Data control clerks are needed to handle all the input and output. They batch input jobs and data together and send the outputs back to the right people.

4 Job control language (JCL) is needed to instruct the operating system.

5 Off-line processing was introduced and the operating system began to schedule work.

6 Multi-programming means sharing the CPU between jobs, saving yet more time.

7 On-line working gives you direct access to the computer and allows for interactive programming. Several people may do this at the same time, giving multi-access.

8 Micros are increasingly being linked to large machines.

Questions

1. Complete these sentences.
   a) A collection of programs and data ready for processing by a computer is known as _____.
   (SREB)
   b) _____ means having several programs in memory at the same time and running each for a small space of time in sequence.
   c) The process by which the operating system decides which job to run next from the input batch is called _____.

2. What is meant by real-time computing?

3. For which of the following computer applications is real-time not essential?
   a) guided missile control
   b) traffic control
   c) intensive care monitoring
   d) patients records
   (NWREB)

4.*Explain the difference between the on-line and batch processing modes of operation.
   (SUJB)

5. What is meant by interactive computing?

6. Why is interactive computing a popular way of using the computer?

7. For which applications are remote terminal systems and batch processing systems most suited?

8. This diagram shows a computer controlling a number of terminals. This type of system is often known as an on-line, multi-access system.

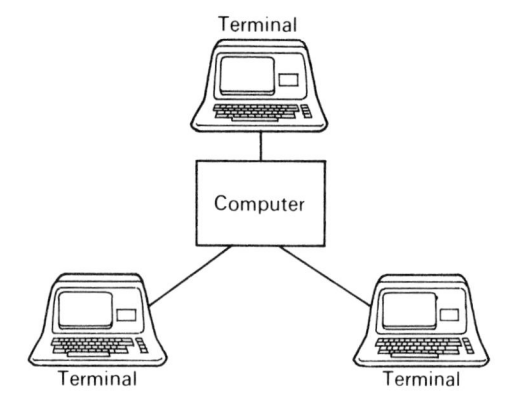

Fig. 4.10

   a) Explain what is meant by on-line working.
   b) Explain what is meant by a multi-access system.
   c) Explain what is meant by a job queue.
   d) Explain what is meant by a time slice.
   e) Name three different types of job where such a computer could be used.
   (SREB)

*'O'-Level question

Wordsearch

Copy this grid into your workbook. In the grid you will find 8 words to do with operating systems. Use the clues to help you find them.

1. The operating system is often loaded into the computer by means of a _____ program.
2. A computer system which is being used to control a process such as landing a lunar module on the moon is said to be operating in _____.
3. This word is used to describe the process of outputing data to a disk to be printed later.
4. _____ processing produces the output when the computer is ready.
5. _____ processing provides the answers straight away.
6. An _____ system allows users to 'converse' with the computer.
7. With this type of system a data controller inputs job control instructions and data to the computer.
8. An off-line operating system will try to increase the total work done by _____ the jobs done by the computer.

SYSTEMS SOFTWARE
WORDSEARCH

```
H S X K E B P Y X O N L I N E
Q L I Y C O J Z E J D D F S E
O L L S F O Y E G P E B P M T
C S O T X T Y N P V U G I G O
X C V A N S J X I C N T R O E
G H G S W T J T C I L P Q N H
C E U A I R C R L A A C I F A
M D U A G A Q O E W E L J K B
O U H C R P O R W I F R I U E
F L C E B P Y I W F B A T C H
Y I T A S L J K O D U T K I M
O N U C M Q E G R I E B V G E
I G A O L M E H H H U M N R Q
H J N T X H R Q H G U C I L K
J S O A Z C O W Z Z A D R S O
```

Case Study — CP/M

CP/M (Control Program for Microcomputers) is an operating system originally developed for 8-bit microcomputers. It first became available in 1975 and is now one of the world's two most popular operating systems, UNIX being the other.

To allow CP/M to run on different computers the software is split into two parts: the *variant* part and the *invariant* part. The invariant part contains the standard CP/M software and is written in a high-level programming language called PL/M. The variant part is written in the assembly language of the particular computer for which it is intended. The variant part contains the code for driving input and output devices for the particular computer.

Structure of CP/M

CP/M contains 3 major parts:
- Console Command Processor (CCP)
- the Basic Input/Output System (BIOS)
- the Basic Disk Operating System (BDOS).

CCP interprets commands entered by the user and issues responses to the user. The CCP 'calls' BIOS or BDOS to perform actual input and output from peripherals. Each of these 3 parts contains variant and invariant code.

The disk-handling software (BDOS) is separate from the basic input/output software (BIOS) because disks are far more complicated than other peripherals. BIOS and BDOS are also used by applications programs to handle peripherals. The person writing programs for the computer doesn't have to worry about how to handle the peripherals because CP/M does the job for him.

How main memory is used

Once the operating system is loaded into **Random Access Memory** (RAM) it stays there. User programs also have to be

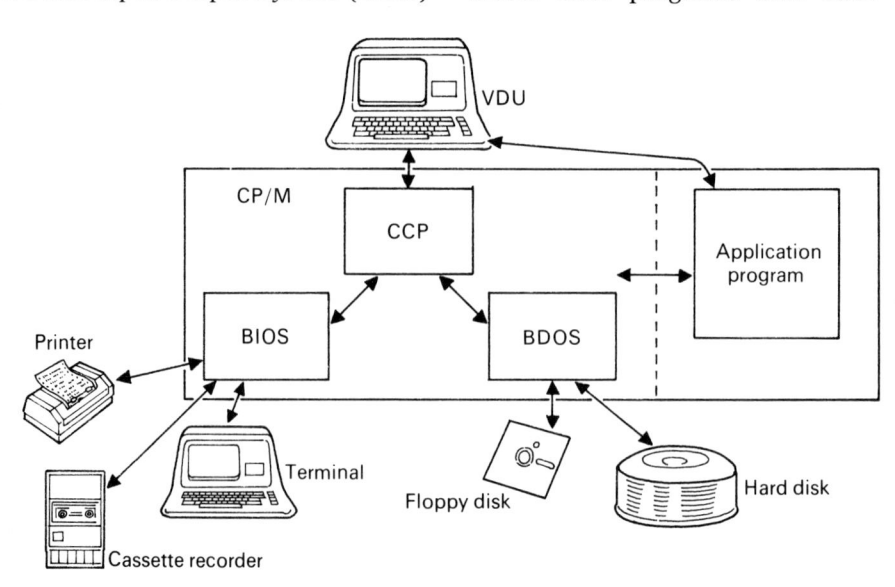

Fig. 4.11 The structure of CP/M

loaded into memory. The diagram shows how the memory is shared by CP/M and user programs.

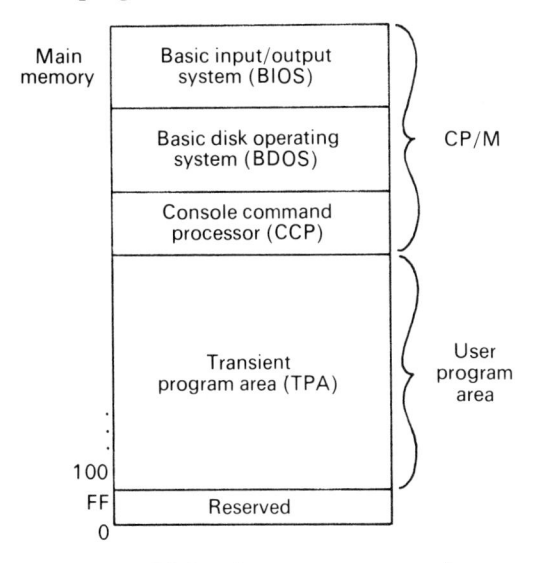

Fig. 4.12 CP/M and user program area in memory

CODE	CP/M COMMAND
ASM	Assemble a program
DIR	Display a list of the names of the files stored on the disk
ED	Edit a file, i.e. add new lines, change lines, delete lines, etc
ERA	Erase a file from the disk
PIP	Copy a file
REN	Rename a file
TYPE	Display the contents of a file

CP/M commands

Using CP/M

CCP reads lines entered by the user at the VDU. It checks that the line is valid and then calls BIOS or BDOS to carry out what is required.

If you want to run a program you have written, you type in the program name. If the program is stored on disk then BDOS will load the program from disk into memory. CCP will then set the program running.

Each of the commands in the list below are programs provided with CP/M. They each carry out a special task. A common task not shown in the list is to compile or interpret a program. The commands for these depend on the compiler or interpreter being used.

Other versions of CP/M

CP/M is a single-user operating system. This means that only one program may be running at any time.

MP/M is a version which allows **multi-tasking**. Using MP/M several programs may run at the same time. The memory is shared between the programs.

CP/NET is a version which manages a **local area network** of microcomputers. CP/NET is useful in 'Office of the future' applications. Individual work-stations may be networked together and may share a common set of files.

CP/M is available on many different machines, for example, Research Machines 380Z, Apple, Tandy TRS-80, IBM-PC. This means that there is a lot of applications software available to run with CP/M. The CP/M operating system is likely to be the most popular microcomputer operating system for some years to come.

Part 5

Inside the Computer

5.1 Representing data inside a computer

You already know that computers only 'understand' 0's and 1's. Their code is a two-state code; on (1) or off (0). So any piece of data that you put into a computer becomes a collection of 1's and 0's. This unit tells you how different patterns of 1's and 0's are used to stand for, or represent, data.

Binary representation: what's the problem?

The electronic circuits of a computer can only be in two different states. The two digits '1' and '0' can be used to stand for these two states. For this reason all the data inside a computer has to be represented by patterns of 1's and 0's. These are called **binary patterns**. The representation of data by 1's and 0's is called **binary representation**.

What sort of data will these binary patterns need to represent? Binary patterns will be needed to stand for:
   numbers: small ones and large ones, positive and negative numbers, whole numbers and fractions
   letters: all the letters of our alphabet (including capitals), punctuation marks, addition and subtraction, brackets, special signs and so on
   control codes: to clear the screen, or move the cursor on the VDU
   program instructions
   addresses: of memory locations which hold data and instructions.
All these items have to be represented by their own unique pattern of 1's and 0's. The ingenious methods used to do this are explained in this unit, and the three that follow it.

The idea of a binary word

Bit patterns Using just the binary digits 1 and 0 you can make four different patterns:

| 0 | 0 | | 0 | 1 | | 1 | 0 | | 1 | 1 |

With 3 bits you can make 8 binary patterns:

0	0	0		0	0	1
0	1	0		0	1	1
1	0	0		1	0	1
1	1	0		1	1	1

Each of the 7 colours of the rainbow could be given its own binary code by using 3 bits as shown in the table.

COLOUR	BINARY CODE
Red	0 0 1
Orange	0 1 0
Yellow	0 1 1
Green	1 0 0
Blue	1 0 1
Indigo	1 1 0
Violet	1 1 1

But suppose you wanted a code for 15 different colours. You would need 4 bits to make enough patterns so that each colour had its own *unique* code. This is the first rule to remember: the more items of data you need to represent, the more bits you need. For example, with 4 bits there can be 2^4 or 16 distinct patterns;

86

THE POWERS OF 2											
2^{10}	2^9	2^8	2^7	2^6	2^5	2^4	2^3	2^2	2^1	2^0
1024	512	256	128	64	32	16	8	4	2	1

with 5 bits, 32 patterns; with 6 bits, 64 patterns and so on (have a look at the 'Powers of 2' table).

Bytes A group of bits, arranged in a binary pattern is called a **byte**. Usually 8 bits are used. How many different patterns could you make with 8 bits? The answer is 256 or 2^8. Each one of these patterns can be used to stand for a different number, letter of the alphabet, or symbol. For example:

| 0 | 1 | 0 | 0 | 0 | 0 | 1 | 1 |

could be used to stand for the character 'C'

| 0 | 0 | 1 | 1 | 0 | 0 | 1 | 1 |

could be used to stand for the character '3'

| 0 | 0 | 1 | 0 | 0 | 0 | 0 | 1 |

could be used to stand for the character '!'

Each pattern of 1's and 0's is called a **code**. Letters, numbers and symbols (like '!', '%' and ';') are called **characters**. Different computers use different codes for characters. The next section will show you some of these **character codes**.

Words These codes are used inside the computer. But they don't just float around. They all have a 'home' to go to, and each 'home' has its own address. The 'home' which stores these patterns of 1's and 0's is called a **location** or **store**. The collection of 1's and 0's inside the location is called a **binary word**. These words are often 8 bits long, i.e. the same length as a byte, but the large, mainframe computers use word lengths of 16, 24, 32 or even 48 bits.

Character codes

Characters are the things you see on the keyboard of a microcomputer. They may be letters of the alphabet—these are called **alphabetic characters**. They may be a number from 0 to 9—these are **numeric characters**. Data which contains a mixture of these characters is called **alphanumeric** data. Characters may be symbols like '%', ';', '£' or '$'—these are called **special characters**. When you press the keys on the keyboard of a micro each character you press is 'changed' into a pattern of 1's and 0's inside the computer. Each character must have its *own* pattern or code.

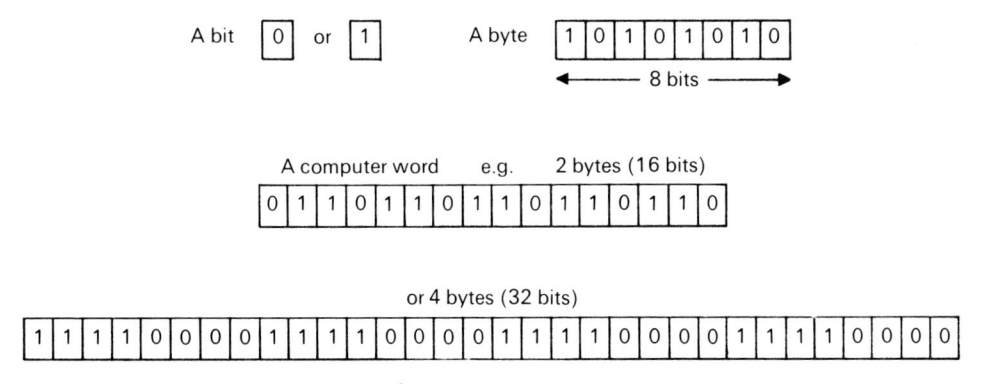

A bit | 0 | or | 1 |

A byte | 1 | 0 | 1 | 0 | 1 | 0 | 1 | 0 |
◄────── 8 bits ──────►

A computer word   e.g.   2 bytes (16 bits)
| 0 | 1 | 1 | 0 | 1 | 1 | 0 | 1 | 1 | 0 | 1 | 1 | 0 | 1 | 1 | 0 |

or 4 bytes (32 bits)
| 1 | 1 | 1 | 1 | 0 | 0 | 0 | 0 | 1 | 1 | 1 | 1 | 0 | 0 | 0 | 0 | 1 | 1 | 1 | 1 | 0 | 0 | 0 | 0 | 1 | 1 | 1 | 1 | 0 | 0 | 0 | 0 |

Fig. 5.1 *Bits, bytes and computer words*

CHARACTER	ASCII CODE	CHARACTER	ASCII CODE
@	100 0000	0	011 0000
A	100 0001	1	011 0001
B	100 0010	2	011 0010
C	100 0011	3	011 0011
D	100 0100	4	011 0100
E	100 0101	5	011 0101
F	100 0110	6	011 0110
G	100 0111	7	011 0111
H	100 1000	8	011 1000
I	100 1001	9	011 1001
J	100 1010	:	011 1010
K	100 1011	;	011 1011
L	100 1100	<	011 1100
M	100 1101	+	011 1101
N	100 1110	>	011 1110
O	100 1111	?	011 1111
P	101 0000	Space	010 0000
Q	101 0001	!	010 0001
R	101 0010	"	010 0010
S	101 0011	#	010 0011
T	101 0100	$	010 0100
U	101 0101	%	010 0101
V	101 0110	&	010 0110
W	101 0111	'	010 0111
X	101 1000	(	010 1000
Y	101 1001	)	010 1001
Z	101 1010	*	010 1010
[	101 1011	+	010 1011
\	101 1100	,	010 1100
]	101 1101	−	010 1101
↑	101 1110	.	010 1110
−	101 1111	/	010 1111

American Standard Code for Information Interchange (ASCII)

You could make up your own code for characters, but in practice it is convenient if everyone uses the same codes. One widely used character code was accepted internationally in 1968. It is called the **ASCII code** and uses seven bits.

Look at the codes for A, B and C. You can see that the code for B is a larger number than for A while C is larger than B, and so on. This is used when a computer sorts letters and words into alphabetical order.

Parity bits An eighth bit is added to the left-hand end of the ASCII code to make the total number of 1's even. For example:

PARITY BIT
↓
A 0 1 0 0 0 0 0 1 (a zero added)
C 1 1 0 0 0 0 1 1 (a one added)
M 0 1 0 0 1 1 0 1 (a zero added)
Z 0 1 0 1 1 0 1 0 (a zero added)

You can see that the code for each letter of the alphabet has an even number of 1's in it (e.g. A has two 1's, Z has four 1's). This extra bit added on is called a **parity check bit**. The 8 bits stay together all through the processing inside a computer. (However, when the code is stored in memory the parity bit is ignored.) When data is moved around, the number of 1's in each character code is checked by the system. If the number of 1's is even, processing continues. If the number is odd, an error message is sent out and processing stops.

This is called **even parity**—the total number of 1's in the pattern has to be even. Sometimes, **odd parity** is used—the number of 1's should then be an odd number.

Instructions and addresses

A computer is a data processor. So it's no use having data inside a computer if you can't tell the computer what to do with it. It needs **instructions**. Part 3 explains how a computer is given instructions in the form of a program. Most programs are written in a language that you can understand (e.g. BASIC) but they need to be converted or coded into a language the *machine* can understand: machine code.

Before a computer can process data it needs to know two things:
- where the data is stored, i.e. its address
- what it has to do with the data, i.e. an instruction.

Details of instructions and addresses are given in Unit 5.6.

KEY POINTS

1 All the data inside a computer has to be represented by patterns of 1's and 0's.

2 A group of 1's and 0's used to represent data or instructions is called a binary word.

3 Character codes are widely used binary patterns which represent the letters of the alphabet, numbers, punctuation marks and so on.

4 Binary codes are also used for the instructions used by a computer, and the addresses in memory where they are held.

Questions

1 Copy this passage and fill in the blanks:
'The term "bit" is short for _____ _____. A collection of bits is called a _____. With eight bits you could make _____ different binary patterns. Patterns of 1's and 0's are stored in _____ inside the computer. The collection of 1's and 0's in a _____ is called a binary _____.'

2 Using the ASCII code, shown on page 88, put:
a) your initials
b) your date of birth into binary code.

3 a) How many alphanumeric characters are there in PJX1982?
(i) 0 (ii) 3 (iii) 4 (iv) 7
b) How many bits would a binary store need to represent the numbers 0 to 9 and letters in lower case and in capitals?

89

D

c) What is a byte? What is a bit?
(NWREB 1982)

4 What is the maximum number of characters that can be represented in a computer which uses a 6-bit character code?
(SREB)

5 State the relationship between a bit and a byte.
(WJEC)

6 Characters within a certain computer are represented by 8 binary digits in which the first digit is used as a parity bit and the remaining 7 bits are the character code. For example, the number 1 is represented as:

Parity	Character code
1	0110001

a) What type of parity is being used?
b) In your own book:
(i) complete the representation for the number 2
(ii) show how the number 3 would be represented.

	Parity	Character code
(i)	2 ____	0110010
(ii)	3 ____	____

(YREB 1982)

7*A small microcomputer is said to have 4K bytes of read-only memory (ROM) and 8K bytes of random access memory (RAM). (A byte is 8 bits).

a) What does the term bit refer to?
b) What does the symbol 'K' stand for?
c) How many bits can be stored in the 8K RAM?
d) Explain the differences between ROM and RAM memory devices?
(OLE)

8 A group of bits may be used to hold a character in main store.
a) What name is given to this group of bits?
b) How does one character differ from another in main store?
c) What is the smallest number of bits that is needed to store the 26 letters of the alphabet and the digits 0 to 9?
(SEREB)

9 a) How many different characters can be represented in a 4-bit character code?
b) Design your own 3-bit codes to represent A, B, C, and D using the third bit for an even parity check.

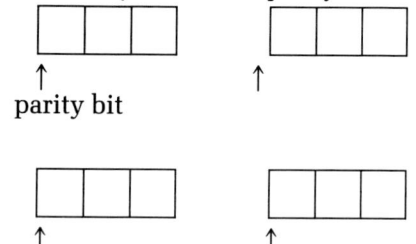

↑
parity bit

(ALSEB)
*'O'-Level question

5.2 Representing whole numbers

This unit tells you how whole, positive numbers are represented in a computer using the binary system. It also explains two other number systems, octal and hexadecimal, that can be used as shorthand for long patterns of 1's and 0's.

Binary to decimal and back again

Today most people use decimal or **denary** numbers. These are base-10 numbers. They use the digits 0, 1, 2, 3, 4, 5, 6, 7, 8 and 9. As you count past 9 you go on to 10, 11, 12 ... and so on. We use this number system partly because we have ten fingers. (Some ancient civilizations used other bases for their numbers. The Babylonians used base 60 for counting. Others have used base 20, perhaps using fingers *and* toes!)

Humans—ten digits are used:

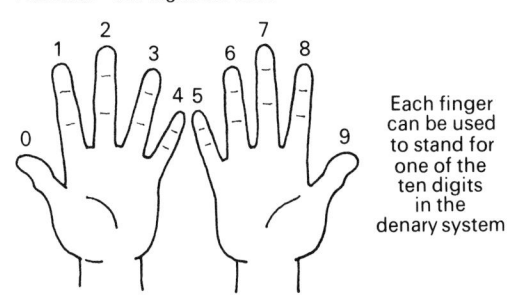

Each finger can be used to stand for one of the ten digits in the denary system

Computers—two digits are used:

Pulse — 1
No Pulse — 0

Fig. 5.2 *The two commonest counting systems*

Look at the decimal number 3267 and the binary number 1110. To show that one is a base-10 number and that the other is a base-2 number, we write them as:

$$3267_{10} \text{ and } 1110_2$$

Reading a decimal number from right to left, the first digit tells you the number of 'units', the second the number of 'tens', the third the 'hundreds', the fourth the 'thousands', and so on.

1000	100	10	1
3	2	6	7

The 'column headings' 1, 10, 100, 1000, ... are called **place values**.

With base-2, or binary, numbers the first digit on the right tells you the number of 'units', the next digit tells you the number of 'twos', the next the 'fours', the next the 'eights', and so on. We write this as:

8	4	2	1
1	1	1	0

Binary numbers have place values of 1, 2, 4, 8, 16, 32, ... and so on.

Only *two* different digits can be used in binary: 1 or 0, while *ten* digits are used in denary: 0, 1, 2 ... 9. The highest digit in a number system is always *one less* than the base (9 in denary, 1 in binary).

Information given to a computer is usually in decimal numbers, but data in the central processing unit can only be handled in binary form. So a computer system must be able to convert numbers from one base to another and back again.

Converting binary to decimal Any binary number can be converted to denary by multiplying each digit by its place value and then finding the sum of the products.

$$1110_2 \rightarrow (1 \times 8) + (1 \times 4) + (1 \times 2) + (0 \times 1)$$
$$= 8 + 4 + 2$$
$$= 14$$

i.e. $1110_2 \rightarrow 14_{10}$

Example
Convert 1101011_2 into denary.

Step 1: Work out the place values for each of the digits:

    64 32 16 8 4 2 1
    1 1 0 1 0 1 1

Step 2: Add up the numbers which have a '1' underneath them:
    $64 + 32 + 8 + 2 + 1 = 107$
    i.e. $1101011_2 \rightarrow 107_{10}$

Converting decimal to binary Converting this way round takes slightly longer, but there are two methods you can use.

Example
Convert 83_{10} to binary.

    Method 1
Step 1: Find the highest binary place value that can be subtracted from the decimal (83). In this case it is 64.
    $83 - 64 = 19$
Place a 1 in the 64's column as shown:

    64 32 16 8 4 2 1
    1

Step 2: Find the next highest value that can be subtracted from the remainder. In this case it is 16.
    $19 - 16 = 3$
Place a 1 in the 16's column.

Step 3: Find the next highest place value that can be subtracted from the remainder. In this case it is 2.
    $3 - 2 = 1$
Place a 1 in the 2's column.

Step 4: Keep going until the remainder is a 1 or 0 and place it in the units column. In our example a 1 goes in the units column.

Step 5: Fill the remaining empty columns with zeros.

    64 32 16 8 4 2 1
    1 0 1 0 0 1 1

and the binary representation of 83 can be read off:

$83_{10} \rightarrow 1010011_2$

This method can be quite lengthy and slow. Method 2 is quicker.

    Method 2
Step 1: Divide the decimal number over and over again by 2 until you reach zero. After each division the remainder is written down—it will be either 1 or 0.

    $83 \div 2 = 41$ remainder 1
    $41 \div 2 = 20$ remainder 1
    $20 \div 2 = 10$ remainder 0
    $10 \div 2 = 5$ remainder 0
    $5 \div 2 = 2$ remainder 1
    $2 \div 2 = 1$ remainder 0
    $1 \div 2 = 0$ remainder 1

Step 2: The *last* remainder is your first binary digit. Write down all the remainders, from the bottom upwards, to give your binary number. In this case it is 1010011.
    i.e. $83_{10} \rightarrow 1010011_2$
the same result as Method 1.

The next section shows you how whole positive numbers are represented in binary form in a computer. Unit 5.3 explains how negative numbers are dealt with, and fractions are covered in Unit 5.4.

Using 1's and 0's to stand for whole numbers

Pure binary representation A whole number is called an integer. One way of using 1's and 0's to stand for an integer inside the computer is by converting the integer *directly* into binary. For example:

    $6 \rightarrow 110$
    $9 \rightarrow 1001$

With larger numbers, more bits are needed. For example:

    $235 \rightarrow 11101011$

Here, 8 bits are needed. These bits could be stored in a location inside the computer. The location then *contains* the number 235.

This is called **pure binary representation**. One location in the computer is needed to hold one number. The problem is this: the size of the number that the computer can represent is limited by the number of bits in a location, e.g. with 8 bits in a location the highest number would be 255. Another way of storing numbers is by **Binary Coded Decimal** (BCD).

Binary coded decimal To change a decimal number to a binary coded decimal you take one decimal digit at a time, and convert it to binary. Each digit from 0 to 9 can be converted to binary using only 4 bits.

DECIMAL DIGIT	BINARY CODE
0	0000
1	0001
2	0010
3	0011
4	0100
5	0101
6	0110
7	0111
8	1000
9	1001

To convert the decimal number 23 to BCD you first convert the 3, then the 2:

2   3   denary number becomes
↓   ↓   ↓
0010 0011 binary coded decimal

This needs 8 bits. Using 8 bits, numbers as high as 99 can be represented:

9   9
↓   ↓
1001 1001

With 12 bits you can go up to 999:

9   9   9
↓   ↓   ↓
1001 1001 1001

Sixteen bits will represent numbers as high as 9999, and so on.

In some computer processing binary coded decimal is useful and efficient, for example, where numeric data is being processed but not used in calculations. This is because only 4 bits are needed for each character. However, pure binary representation is normally more efficient—16 bits in BCD can only represent numbers up to 9999, compared to 65535 in pure binary.

Shorthand for binary code

A long string of 1's and 0's can be very difficult for human beings to remember. Imagine remembering a binary code made up of 16 bits like 1011010110101110. A long binary code also takes a long time to write. For these reasons a shorthand version is often used to help people, for example, when a computer program is being checked.

Hexadecimal (hex) Many microprocessors have a word length of 8 bits. These words can be split into two groups of 4 bits, e.g. 0011 1101. Each of these 4-bit groups can be arranged in 16 different combinations. **Hexadecimal**, or **base-16 numbers**, can be used as shorthand to stand for these bits because the hexadecimal system uses 16 different digits. The hex system uses the letters A, B, C, D, E, and F to stand for the decimal numbers 10, 11, 12, 13, 14, and 15.

BINARY CODES (using 4 bits)	HEXADECIMAL SHORTHAND
0000	0
0001	1
0010	2
0011	3
0100	4
0101	5
0110	6
0111	7
1000	8
1001	9
1010	A
1011	B
1100	C
1101	D
1110	E
1111	F

Binary codes can easily be converted into hex (by first making groups of four bits) and hexadecimal numbers can easily be changed into binary.

BINARY TO HEX	HEX TO BINARY
0110 1101 ↓ ↓ 6 D	B 7 ↓ ↓ 1011 0111
1111 0010 ↓ ↓ F 2	F A ↓ ↓ 1111 1010
1010 0011 ↓ ↓ A 3	2 E ↓ ↓ 0010 1110

Octal A binary code of 12 bits breaks down easily into groups of three. Each group of 3 bits can be arranged in 8 different patterns. The octal, *base-8*, number system has a digit for each of these binary patterns (see table).

BINARY CODES (using 3 bits)	OCTAL SHORTHAND
000	0
001	1
010	2
011	3
100	4
101	5
110	6
111	7

You may have seen hexadecimal numbers on a VDU when a microcomputer is loading a program. These act as a counter showing the number of blocks of the program that have been loaded, for example, 'OC' on the screen tells you how many complete blocks have been loaded.

Hexadecimal codes are widely used with microcomputers as shorthand for 8-bit and 16-bit binary codes. One other type of shorthand is sometimes used with 12- and 24-bit word length computers (e.g. minicomputers). This is the **octal** system.

The octal number system uses only 8 digits: 0, 1, 2, 3, 4, 5, 6 and 7.

Binary numbers can easily be changed into octal by first putting them in groups of three bits, e.g. 110111 → 67 in octal i.e. $110111_2 = 67_8$

Here are two more examples.

BINARY TO OCTAL	OCTAL TO BINARY
011 101_2 ↓ ↓ 3 5_8	6 2_8 ↓ ↓ 110 010_2

KEY POINTS

1 Computers use binary numbers because the electronic devices inside them can be in only two states.

2 Decimal numbers can be converted to binary numbers by following certain rules. These rules can be followed by computers.

3 Whole numbers can be represented in a computer by pure binary representation or by binary coded decimal.

4 Octal and hexadecimal numbers can be used as shorthand for long binary numbers. Today 'hex' is most common.

Questions

1. What number base is used by:
   a) denary b) binary
   c) hexadecimal d) octal numbers
   How many different digits does each of the systems (a)–(d) use. What do you notice about the base-number and the number of digits?
2. Explain why the binary number system is used by computers. Why do you think most people use the denary system?
3. Convert each of these binary numbers into denary:
   a) 0111   b) 1110   c) 1001
   d) 1010   e) 011101   f) 111010
4. Convert each of these denary numbers into binary:
   a) 26   b) 53   c) 267   d) 512
   Show the method you use, and your working, in each case.
5. Represent 27_{10} and 6_{10} in 8-bit binary notation.
6. Convert each of these denary numbers into binary-coded decimal:
   a) 29   b) 998   c) 1984
7. A certain computer uses an 8-bit word to store numbers. Complete the table below. The first two examples have been completed for you:

BINARY CODE	DECIMAL
0 0 0 1 0 0 0 0	10
0 0 1 0	26
0 0 1 1	
	19

(SEREB)

8. Convert 1011011_2 to:
   a) octal b) hexadecimal
9. Convert the binary code 10110001 into either octal, decimal or hexadecimal stating which base you have used.
   (YREB 1982)
10. a) What is the binary number represented by the hexadecimal number 48?
    b) Convert the binary number 11100 to a hexadecimal number.
    (SWEB)
11.*Convert the positive decimal integer 536 to binary.
    (OLE)
12.*Explain the term two-state device in relation to the electronic components of computers, and discuss briefly why the binary number system is a convenient representation.
    (OLE)

*'O'-Level question

5.3 Representing negative numbers

Computers need to be able to represent negative numbers as well as positive ones. This unit explains two ways of representing negative numbers: sign-and-magnitude and two's-complement representation.

Sign-and-magnitude representation

A positive number like +9 can be written down in binary as +1001. On a piece of paper we can write −9 as −1001. But how can this be represented inside a computer? A computer has no way of storing a + sign or a − sign. So a binary digit must be used. This bit is used simply to show whether a number is positive or negative. It is called a **sign bit**. A sign bit of '$\underline{1}$' shows a negative number, '$\underline{0}$' indicates a positive number.

Using sign-and-magnitude coding the *left-hand bit* of the binary pattern stands for the *sign* of the number. This is called the **most significant bit**. The other bits stand for the size or *magnitude* of the number. For example:

```
     BINARY        DENARY
     0 1 0   =      +2
     1 1 0   =      −2
   1 1 0 0 0 =      −8
   0 1 0 0 0 =      +8
```

The sign bit in each case is underlined.

Using an 8-bit word you can represent numbers ranging from:

```
       0 1 1 1 1 1 1 1 = +127
to:    1 1 1 1 1 1 1 1 = −127
```

The main disadvantage with this way of coding is that there are two zeros! Half way between +127 and −127 there is:

$\underline{0}$ 0 0 0 0 0 0 0

and also

$\underline{1}$ 0 0 0 0 0 0 0.

Both stand for zero. This can cause problems, so another method is used in modern computers.

Two's-complement representation

Suppose you wanted to do this sum:
5 − 3
This sum is the same as:
5 + (− 3)
In other words, subtracting a number is the same as *adding the negative* of that number. For example:
7 − 2 = 7 + (− 2)
12 − 9 = 12 + (− 9)
11 − 8 = 11 + (− 8)
This is how most computers subtract numbers—by making the number negative then adding it. The number is made negative by the **two's-complement method**. Using this method, the bit on the far left of a binary number actually carries a *negative* value instead of a positive one.

The place values for a 3-bit, two's-complement number are, for example:

```
   −4  2  1
    1  1  0  = − 4 + 2 + 0 = − 2
```

The bit on the far left, the *most significant bit*, stands for a negative quantity.

Here is an example with 6 bits:

```
 −32  16  8  4  2  1
   1   0  1  1  1  0  = −32 + 8 + 4 + 2
                      = −18
```

Figure 5.3 shows you the two's complement of some simple numbers using only three bits. Follow the numbers on this diagram from +3 back round to −4. It is rather like turning the clock back.

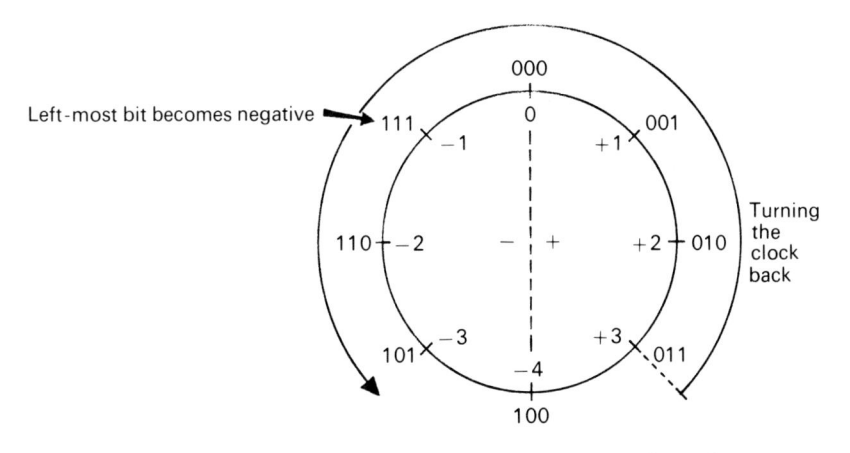

[Circular diagram showing 3-bit two's-complement representation with values 000=0, 001=+1, 010=+2, 011=+3, 100=−4, 101=−3, 110=−2, 111=−1. "Left-most bit becomes negative" points to 111. "Turning the clock back" labels the outer arrow.]

Using 3 bits you can represent −4 to +3
For example:
$$\begin{array}{ccc} -4 & +2 & +1 \\ 1 & 1 & 1 \end{array} = -1$$

Fig. 5.3 Two's-complement representation using 3 bits

Try adding +3 to −3. You can see that the result is zero:

```
  0 1 1   (+3)
  1 0 1   (−3)
─────────
(1) 0 0 0   Zero, using 3 bits only
```

The left-hand bit, which must be ignored, is called the **overflow bit**.

Figure 5.4 shows you two's-complement representation using 4 bits. Try adding +6 to −6:

```
  0 1 1 0   (+6)
  1 0 1 0   (−6)
──────────
(1) 0 0 0 0   Zero, using 4 bits only
```

Again, the result is zero. (Notice that there is only one representation of zero with this method.)

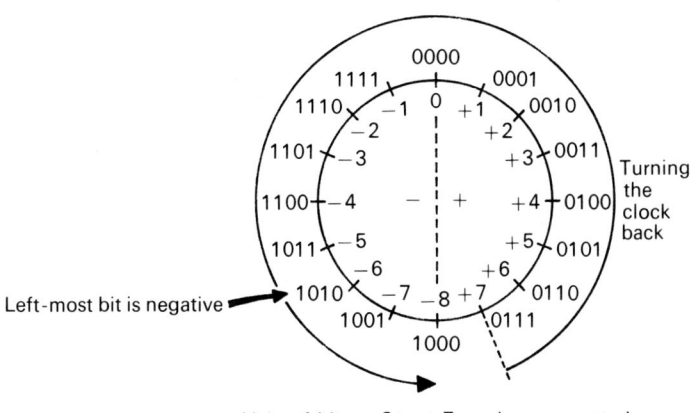

[Circular diagram showing 4-bit two's-complement representation: 0000=0, 0001=+1, 0010=+2, 0011=+3, 0100=+4, 0101=+5, 0110=+6, 0111=+7, 1000=−8, 1001=−7, 1010=−6, 1011=−5, 1100=−4, 1101=−3, 1110=−2, 1111=−1. "Left-most bit is negative" points to 1010. "Turning the clock back" labels the outer arrow.]

Using 4 bits, −8 to +7 can be represented
Example:
$$\begin{array}{cccc} -8 & +4 & +2 & +1 \\ 1 & 1 & 1 & 1 \end{array} = -1$$

Fig. 5.4 Two's-complement representation using 4 bits

The more bits used, the wider the range of numbers that can be represented. Eight bits can be used to represent numbers from −128 up to +127. Try adding +127 to −127. What result do you get?

EIGHT BITS		DENARY NUMBER
Positive numbers	01111111	+127
	....	.
	....	.
	....	.
	00001000	+8
	00000111	+7
	00000110	+6
	00000101	+5
	00000100	+4
	00000011	+3
	00000010	+2
	00000001	+1
	00000000	0
Negative numbers	11111111	−1
	11111110	−2
	11111101	−3
	11111100	−4
	11111011	−5
	11111010	−6
	11111001	−7
	11111000	−8
	....	.
	....	.
	10000000	−128

The table below shows you the ranges of numbers that can be represented with more and more bits.

NUMBER OF BITS	RANGE OF NUMBERS THAT CAN BE REPRESENTED
3	−4 to +3
4	−8 to +7
8	−128 to +127
16	−32 768 to +32 767
24	−8 388 608 to +8 388 607

Forming the two's complement of a number

There are two methods that you can follow for changing a positive binary number into its two's complement.

Example 1
Convert +11 into its two's complement using 6 bits.

> Method 1

Step 1: Convert +11 to pure binary.
> +11 → 0 0 1 0 1 1

Step 2: Change every 0 to a 1 and every 1 to a 0.
> 1 1 0 1 0 0

Step 3: Add 1.
> 1 1 0 1 0 1

Step 4: Check your answer.
> −32 + 16 + 4 + 1 = −11

Example 2
Change +22 into its two's complement using 6 bits.

> Method 2

Step 1: Convert +22 into pure binary.
> +22 → 0 1 0 1 1 0

Step 2: Copy down each digit from the right until you reach the first 1. Copy the first 1 but after that change every 1 to a 0 and every 0 to a 1.
> 1 0 1 0 1 0

Step 3: Check your answer.
> −32 + 8 + 2 = −22

Both methods give the same result. Try them out on some simple examples.

Checking There are three ways of checking that you have the right answer:
- All even numbers *end* in 0. All odd numbers end in 1.
- All positive numbers *start* with 0. All negative numbers start with 1.
- Try adding the negative number to its corresponding positive number, e.g. +22 + (−22). With a fixed number of bits the result should be zero.

Example
Show how the subtraction 125 − 8 is done using two's-complement binary representation.

Step 1: Convert +125 to pure binary.
+125 → 1 1 1 1 1 0 1

Step 2: Add a leading zero to indicate a positive number.
0 1 1 1 1 1 0 1   (+125)

Step 3: Convert +8 to pure binary.
+8 → 1 0 0 0

Step 4: Add leading zero or zeros to make the same number of bits.
0 0 0 0 1 0 0 0   (+8)

Step 5: Form the two's complement of +8.
1 1 1 1 1 0 0 0   (−8)

Step 6: Add the result of Step 5 to the result of Step 2.
```
    0 1 1 1 1 1 0 1   (+125)
    1 1 1 1 1 0 0 0   (−8)
 ─────────────────────
(1) 0 1 1 1 0 1 0 1
```

Step 7: Ignore the leading 1. The final answer is:
0 1 1 1 0 1 0 1   (+117)

Step 8: Check your answer!

Questions

1. Convert each of these denary numbers into a binary number, and then its corresponding negative number in two's-complement form:
   (i) 6   (ii) 12   (iii) 24
   (iv) 17   (v) 120
   How many bits are needed in each one?

2. Express −15 and 22 as 6-bit numbers, using two's complementation where appropriate. Use your answers to show the 6-bit result of the calculation 22 − 15.
   (NWREB)

3. Show the representation of −27 in a 16-bit word using two's-complement notation.
   (WJEC)

4.*Find the two's complement of the 10-bit positive binary number 0001010111.
   (OLE)

5. A computer uses an 8-bit complementary form word.
   a) What is the largest positive number that can be stored in one of these words?
   b) What is the smallest number?
   (SWEB)

6. A computer stores whole numbers in a 6-bit register. Negative numbers are held in two's-complement form with the left-most bit as the sign bit.
   a) What denary number would be held as:

1	1	1	1	1	1

   b) (i) What is the largest positive number that can be stored in this register? Give the answer in binary:

   (ii) What is the answer in denary (base ten)?

7.*In a particular computer, integers are stored in 6 bits where the first bit is used to indicate the sign (0 for a positive integer and 1 for a negative integer). Negative integers are stored in two's-complement form.
   a) What base-10 numbers are represented by:
   (i) 010011   (ii) 001010?
   b) What is the two's complement of 001010?

c) What is the largest positive number which can be stored?
d) What is the largest negative number which can be stored?
e) Explain how the answer to part b) can be used to do the binary subtraction sum corresponding to $19 - 10$ in base-10.
(SUJB)

8 a) Convert (i) 17 (ii) 26 from base-10 to base-2.

Parts b) to g) refer to a 6-bit integer register in which two's complements are used for negative numbers.

b) How would 17 be stored in this register?

c) What is the two's complement of 17 in this register?
d) How would a computer carry out $26 - 17$ in this register? Give the answer to its calculation in binary and in denary.
e) What would happen if $26 + 17$ was carried out in this register?
f) The register holds 111100; what denary number does this represent?
g) What are the largest (most positive) and smallest (most negative) numbers which this register can store? Give your answers in denary.
(SWEB)

*'O'-Level question

5.4 Representing fractions and real numbers

This unit tells you how fractions and real numbers can be stored inside a computer. The unit explains two types of binary representation called fixed-point and floating point representation.

Using 1's and 0's to represent fractions

A computer must be able to represent fractions as well as whole numbers. The table below shows the fractions that are easy to represent in binary.

FRAC-TION	POWER OF 2	BINARY FRAC-TION	DECIMAL
1	2^0	1	1
$\frac{1}{2}$	2^{-1}	0.1	0.5
$\frac{1}{4}$	2^{-2}	0.01	0.25
$\frac{1}{8}$	2^{-3}	0.001	0.125
$\frac{1}{16}$	2^{-4}	0.0001	0.0625
$\frac{1}{32}$	2^{-5}	0.00001	—
$\frac{1}{64}$	2^{-6}	0.000001	—

Fractions and whole numbers followed by a fraction, are easy to represent in binary if they are made up from fractions in this table. For example:

$\frac{3}{4} = 0.1 + 0.01 = 0.11$

$7\frac{1}{4} = 111.01$

$\frac{7}{8} = 0.11 + 0.001 = 0.111$

$4\frac{3}{16} = 4 + \frac{1}{8} + \frac{1}{16} = 100.0011$

Errors Some fractions are much harder to change into binary. One example is $\frac{4}{5}$. Using 6 bits you get:

$\frac{4}{5} \rightarrow$

	$\frac{1}{2}$	$\frac{1}{4}$	$\frac{1}{8}$	$\frac{1}{16}$	$\frac{1}{32}$	$\frac{1}{64}$
.1	1	0	0	1	1

But $\frac{1}{2} + \frac{1}{4} + \frac{1}{32} + \frac{1}{64} = \frac{32}{64} + \frac{16}{64} + \frac{2}{64} + \frac{1}{64}$
$= \frac{51}{64}$
$= 0.7969$

In fact, $\frac{4}{5} = 0.8000$

So this binary fraction is *not* exactly equal to $\frac{4}{5}$. More and more bits are needed to bring it closer and closer to the true value. There is a similar problem when you change some fractions to decimals. For example: $\frac{2}{3} = 0.6666666666\ldots$ and so on, for ever. The fraction has to be cut off or **truncated** after a certain number of decimal places, e.g. $\frac{2}{3} = 0.6666$. Because the two are not exactly equal this is called a **truncation error**. In binary: $\frac{2}{3} \rightarrow 0.101010$, if you can only use 6 bits. (= 0.65625 in decimal)

Rounding Fractions are often 'rounded off', for example, $\frac{2}{3}$ is rounded off to 0.6667 in decimal. The last 6 is changed to a 7. Binary fractions can be rounded too. For example, $\frac{2}{3} = 0.101011$, rounded to 6 binary places. The rule is: the last 0 is changed to a 1 if the next figure would have been a 1. The binary representation is still not exact, but the error, called a **rounding error**, is not as bad as a truncation error. These errors are present in all computer arithmetic (see Unit 5.5).

Fixed point representation

Numbers which are not whole numbers (integers) are called real numbers, e.g. $2\frac{1}{2}$, $6\frac{3}{4}$, $7\frac{1}{16}$. These can be stored inside an 8-bit location by changing them to binary and assuming that the decimal point (sometimes called the **bicimal point**) is fixed in a certain position. For example:

$7\frac{1}{16}$ → | 0 | 1 | 1 | 1 | 0 | 0 | 0 | 1 |

↑ Sign bit   ↑ Bicimal point

$2\frac{1}{2}$ → | 0 | 0 | 0 | 1 | 0 | 1 | 0 | 0 |

↑ Bicimal point

$6\frac{3}{4}$ → | 0 | 0 | 1 | 1 | 0 | 1 | 1 | 0 |

↑ Bicimal point

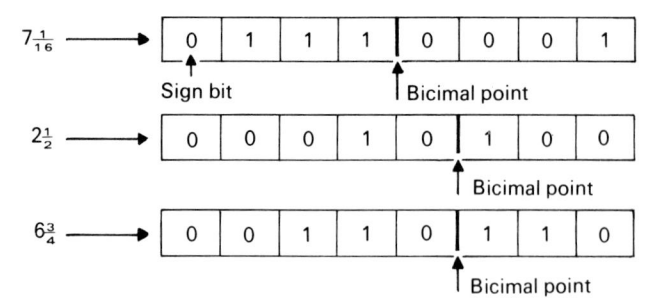

Fig. 5.5

There is no arrow inside the machine showing the bicimal point! The bicimal point is *assumed* to lie in a certain fixed position inside the word in a particular machine. This is called **fixed-point representation**. The three examples above are easy ones. They fit nicely into an 8-bit word, but what about a larger number like 105.125? Change this to binary and it becomes: 1101001.001. This needs 10 bits. If you try to put it into an 8-bit location it fills it up then 'overflows' (like a quart of milk in a pint jug!) This is one type of **overflow error** (see Unit 5.5). A way of avoiding this is to use a 'floating' bicimal point.

Floating-point representation

The speed of light is 300 000 000 metres per second. To save writing these 8 noughts all the time you can just write

$$3 \times 10^8.$$

The Earth is 150 million kilometres from the Sun. This number can be written as 1.5×10^8 km. To change back you must move the decimal point *eight* places to the right:

$$1.5 \times 10^8 = 150\,000\,000.0$$

A similar method is used to store binary numbers in a computer. The first part of the word tells you the number itself. The second part tells you how far the bicimal point must be moved to the right. For example:

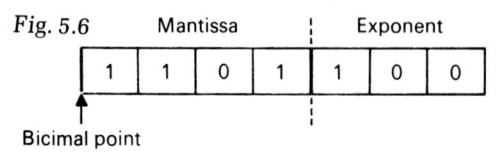

Fig. 5.6   Mantissa   Exponent

| 1 | 1 | 0 | 1 | 1 | 0 | 0 |

↑ Bicimal point

The first part (the number) is called the **mantissa**. The second part, telling you where to put the bicimal point, is called the **exponent**. The bicimal point always starts at the far left of the mantissa—the exponent then tells you where to move it. In this example the exponent is 100 (binary), or 4 (decimal). So you move the bicimal point four places to the right. The number, or mantissa, then becomes 1101, or 13. This way of coding numbers is called **floating-point representation** because the bicimal point starts off by 'floating' to the far left of the mantissa.

Two more bits are needed before you can represent every number with this method:

■ a sign bit is needed for the mantissa to show whether the number is negative or positive
■ a sign bit is needed for the exponent to show whether the bicimal point must be moved right (to represent numbers bigger than 1) or left (to represent numbers smaller than 1).

A complete representation using a floating bicimal point might then be:

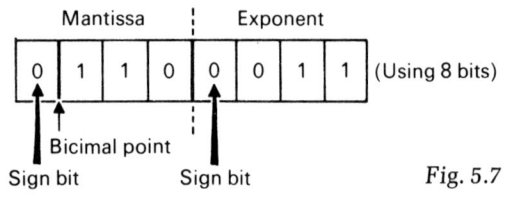

Mantissa   Exponent

| 0 | 1 | 1 | 0 | 0 | 0 | 1 | 1 | (Using 8 bits)

↑ Sign bit ↑ Bicimal point   ↑ Sign bit

Fig. 5.7

Looking at the exponent you see that the point needs to move 3 places to the *right*, because the sign bit is 0. So the binary number is 110, and it is positive. (Notice that the bicimal point starts off just to the right of the sign bit.)

Representing negative numbers A positive number has the same exponent as a negative number, but its mantissa will be different. For example:

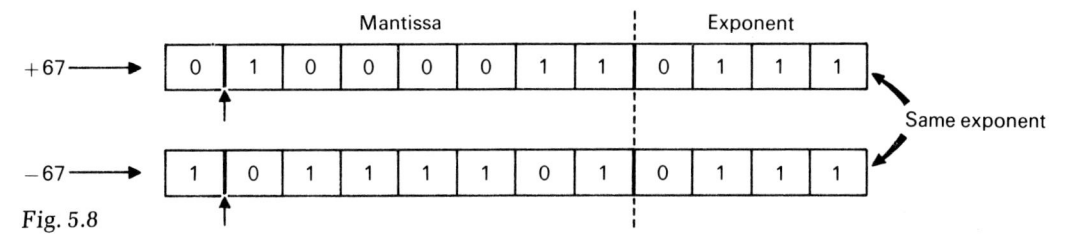

+67 → | 0 | 1 | 0 | 0 | 0 | 0 | 1 | 1 | 0 | 1 | 1 | 1 | (Mantissa | Exponent)

−67 → | 1 | 0 | 1 | 1 | 1 | 1 | 0 | 1 | 0 | 1 | 1 | 1 |

Same exponent

Fig. 5.8

As you can see, the exponents of +67 and −67 are the same. But the mantissa of −67 is the *two's complement* of +67.

Representing fractions With every fraction the exponent has to be *negative*. The negative exponent is usually represented in two's-complement form. For example:

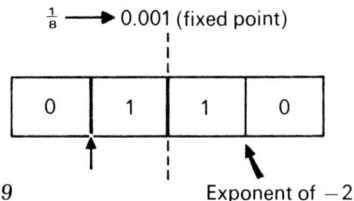

$\frac{1}{8}$ → 0.001 (fixed point)

| 0 | 1 | 1 | 0 |

Fig. 5.9   Exponent of −2

The exponent of −2 (10 in two's-complement form) shows that the bicimal point must be moved two places to the *left*.

This worked example gives you step-by-step instructions for changing decimal numbers into floating-point representation.

Storing real numbers

Computers may use one, two or even four words to store a floating-point number. Often, 23 bits will be used for the mantissa and 9 bits for the exponent:

This could be stored in a 32-bit word, or two 16-bit words. Obviously, the larger the exponent the larger the number that can be stored.

As you have seen, floating-point representation can be used to stand for a wide range of sizes and types of number inside the computer. It can be used for integers, real numbers, negative numbers and fractions.

Example 1
Convert the positive denary number +57 into binary using floating-point representation.

Step 1: Change +57 to binary.
+57 → 1 1 1 0 0 1.

Step 2: Add 0 for the sign bit.
0 1 1 1 0 0 1.

Step 3: Move the bicimal point just to the right of the sign bit.
0 . 1 1 1 0 0 1
         ↑
This is the mantissa.

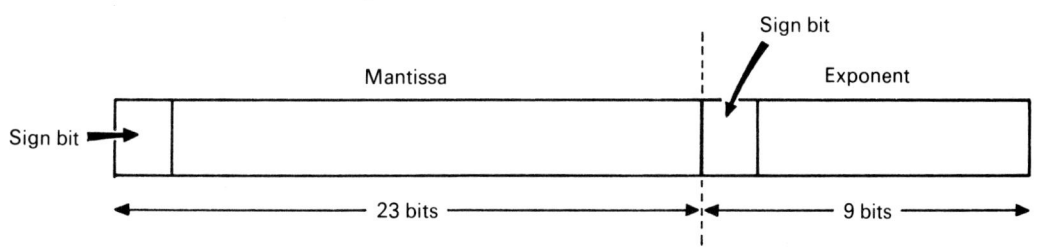

Sign bit → | Mantissa | Sign bit | Exponent |
← 23 bits → ← 9 bits →

Fig. 5.10

Step 4: How many places did you have to move the point? In this case 6 places to the left. Change +6 to binary:
$$+6 \rightarrow 0\ 1\ 1\ 0.$$
This is the exponent.

Step 5: Write down the mantissa then the exponent. The complete word is:

Mantissa							Exponent			
0	1	1	1	0	0	1	0	1	1	0

Fig. 5.11

Example 2

Convert the negative denary number −67 into binary using floating point representation.

Step 1: Change +67 to binary.
$$+67 \rightarrow 0\ 1\ 0\ 0\ 0\ 0\ 1\ 1.$$

Step 2: Change +67 to −67 using the two's-complement method.
$$-67 \rightarrow 1\ 0\ 1\ 1\ 1\ 1\ 0\ 1.$$

Step 3: Move the bicimal point just to the right of the sign bit.
$$1\ .\ 0\ 1\ 1\ 1\ 1\ 0\ 1$$
↑
This is the mantissa.

Step 4: How many places did you move the point? In this case 7 places left. Change +7 to binary.
$$+7 \rightarrow 0\ 1\ 1.$$
This is the exponent.

Step 5: Write down the mantissa then the exponent. The complete word is:

Mantissa								Exponent			
1	0	1	1	1	1	0	1	0	1	1	1

Fig. 5.12

Questions

1. Write down the binary fraction which corresponds to:
   (a) $\frac{1}{2}$ (b) $\frac{1}{16}$ (c) $\frac{3}{8}$ (d) $\frac{3}{16}$

2. Put each of these real numbers into an 8-bit location:

   (i) $7\frac{1}{16}$ (ii) $6\frac{7}{8}$ (iii) $2\frac{3}{4}$ (iv) $4\frac{1}{4}$

3. Why are some fractions, such as $\frac{4}{5}$, difficult to represent in binary? What are the errors associated with representing them called?

4. Explain the meaning of the terms: fixed-point representation and floating-point representation. Which type is most flexible? Why?

5.*Show how the fixed-point, base-10 number 12.25 would be represented:
   a) in base-10 floating-point form
   b) in base-2 fixed-point form
   c) in base-2 floating-point form using 8 bits for the mantissa and 4 bits for the index (or exponent).
   The leading bit of each part is a sign bit which is 0 for a positive number and 1 for a negative number.
   (SUJB 1981)

6.*Use the base 10 number $5\frac{3}{4}$ to illustrate the difference between fixed-point and floating-point numbers in base 2.
   (SUJB)

7.*a) Show how the integers 103 and −25 can be represented in:
   (i) two's-complement notation, using 8 bits;
   (ii) simple binary-coded decimal.
   Indicate the advantages and disadvantages of the two forms of representation.
   b) (i) Describe how numbers can be represented in floating-point form, using a 6-bit mantissa and a 4-bit exponent.
   (ii) Give a floating-point representation for the number 6.75, indicating how you have arrived at your answer.
   (Cambridge)

*'O'-Level question

5.5 Computer logic

It is often said: 'A computer is just a collection of switches.' This unit will examine how true this statement is by looking at the electronic switches or gates inside a computer.

Logic gates: what are they?

Binary bits are represented inside the computer by electrical pulses. These pulses are passed around the computer's electronic circuits through switches or **logic gates**. A gate may 'open' to pass on a pulse, or 'close' to stop it. (But note that logic gates have no moving parts.) Using these gates, pulses can be routed along different paths inside a computer.

Electrical pulses can also be *combined* according to certain logical rules. This is another job done by logic gates. A certain combination of binary pulses *into* a logic gate gives a certain combination of binary pulses *out*. This combining of inputs to provide certain outputs is called **computer logic**.

Three common logic gates

The NOT gate A very simple logic gate is called the 'NOT gate'. If it receives an input pulse (a '1'), its output is no pulse (a '0').

If it receives no pulse (a '0'), its output is a pulse (a '1').

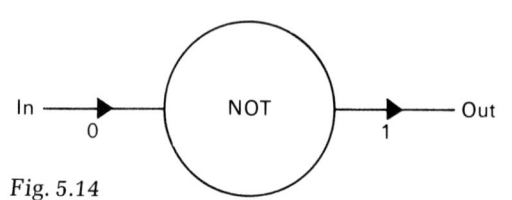

Fig. 5.14

The signal put in is always reversed. You can show this with a simple table.

INPUT	OUTPUT
1	0
0	1

This is called a **truth table** or an **operation table**.

The AND gate The next simplest gate has two inputs and one output. When both the inputs are 1 the output is 1.

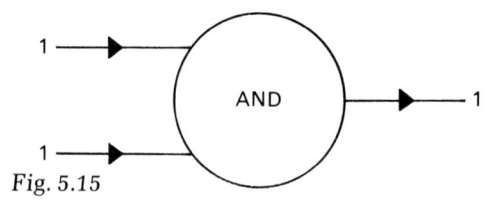

Fig. 5.15

This is called an 'AND gate'. If either of the inputs is 0, then the output is 0.

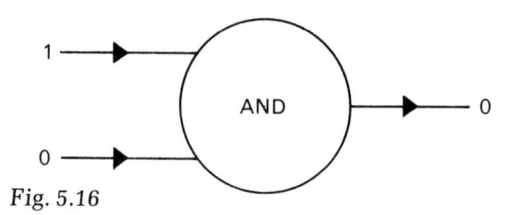

Fig. 5.16

The different combinations of 1's and 0's can be shown in a truth table. Call the two inputs A and B, and the output C.

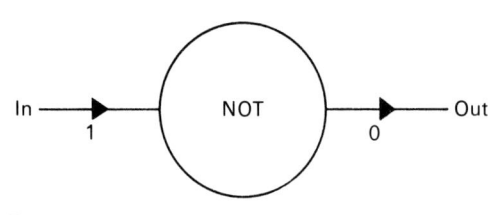

Fig. 5.13

106

INPUTS		OUTPUT
A	B	C = A and B
0	0	0
0	1	0
1	0	0
1	1	1

4 combinations

The output C is 1 *only if* A and B are both 1. For all the other combinations of A and B the output C is 0.

An AND gate can have more than two inputs. If three inputs were used the same rule would apply—the output is only 1 if *all* the inputs are 1.

The OR gate Like the AND gate, an OR gate can have two, or more, inputs and has one output.

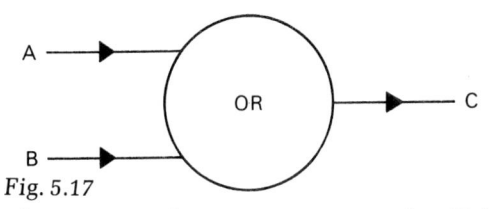

Fig. 5.17

This gate produces an output pulse C if *either* of the input pulses is 1 or both inputs are 1.

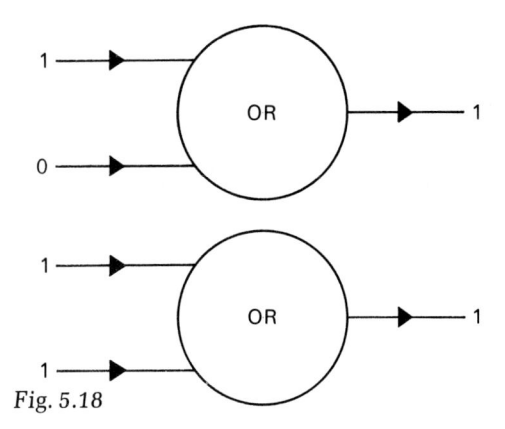

Fig. 5.18

The output is 0 *only if* both inputs are 0.
The different combinations for an OR gate can be shown by a truth table.

INPUTS		OUTPUT
A	B	C
0	0	0
0	1	1
1	0	1
1	1	1

The three logic gates described above (AND, OR and NOT) can be put together to make **logic circuits**.

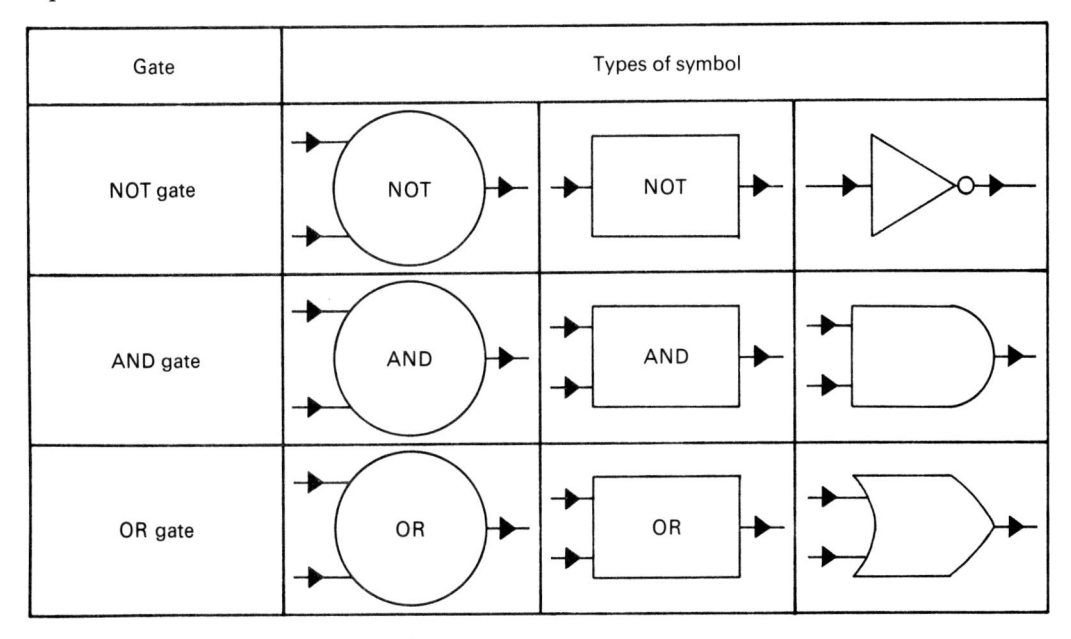

Gate	Types of symbol
NOT gate	NOT / NOT / (triangle symbol)
AND gate	AND / AND / (D-shape symbol)
OR gate	OR / OR / (shield-shape symbol)

Fig. 5.19 *Symbols for AND, OR and NOT gates*

AND gate

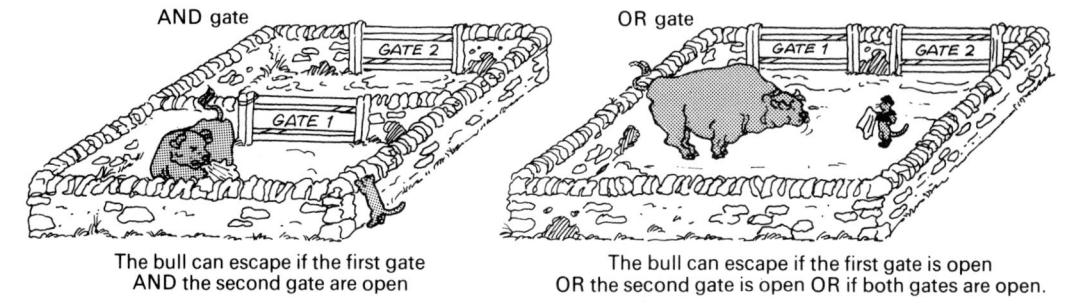

OR gate

The bull can escape if the first gate
AND the second gate are open

The bull can escape if the first gate is open
OR the second gate is open OR if both gates are open.

Fig. 5.20 These drawings should help you to understand the operation of AND gates and OR gates

Using logic gates to make logic circuits

A logic circuit or **logic network** is a combination of logic gates joined together. All computer logic circuits can be built up from the three basic gates already described: AND, OR and NOT. A simple example of a logic network using these three gates is shown below. The three inputs are A, B and C. The output from the AND gate is called X. This output will be 1 *only if* A and B are both 1. The NOT gate then reverses X—giving output Y. Finally, the two pulses Y and C meet at the OR gate. The output from this gate is called Z. This output, Z, will be 0 *only if* the input pulses Y and C are both 0. The complete truth table for this logic network is also shown.

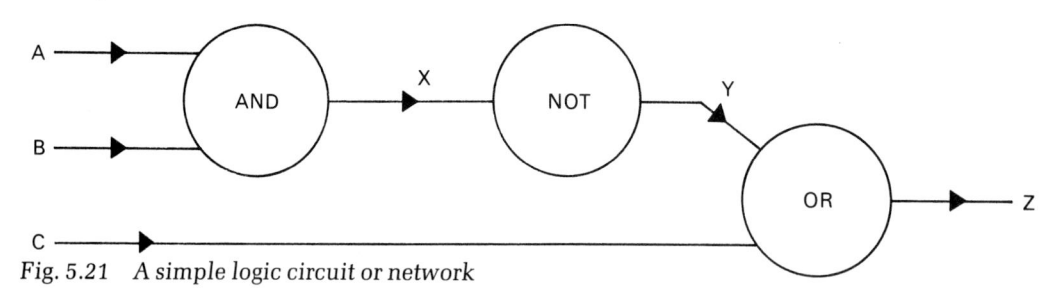

Fig. 5.21 A simple logic circuit or network

THREE INPUTS			A and B	NOT X	FINAL OUTPUT (Y or C)
A	B	C	X	Y	Z
0	0	0	0	1	1
0	0	1	0	1	1
0	1	0	0	1	1
0	1	1	0	1	1
1	0	0	0	1	1
1	0	1	0	1	1
1	1	0	1	0	0
1	1	1	1	0	1

Truth table for the simple logic network in Fig. 5.21

More complicated logic circuits can be built up from the three basic AND, OR and NOT gates. In fact, *all* computer logic circuits can be built up using only these gates.

Jobs done by logic circuits

What kind of jobs do these logic circuits do inside a computer? Here is a general idea of some of their uses:
- for *comparing* binary words
- for *transferring* data, and *controlling* the flow of data from one place to another
- for *decoding* instructions, e.g. recognizing certain binary patterns
- for *calculating*, e.g. adding two binary numbers
- for *storing data*, e.g. by the use of 'flip-flops' (two-state memory devices).

The next section describes two logic circuits for adding numbers. These circuits are called the **half-adder**, and the **full-adder**.

Adding with logic circuits

Adding two binary digits Look back at the unit on binary numbers. There are four rules for adding two binary digits. They are:

	DIGIT	CARRY	SUM
0 + 0 =		0	0
0 + 1 =		0	1
1 + 0 =		0	1
1 + 1 =		1	0

A logic network is needed to do these simple additions inside a computer. It must have a truth table exactly corresponding to these four rules of addition.

TWO INPUTS		OUTPUTS	
A	B	CARRY	SUM
0	0	0	0
0	1	0	1
1	0	0	1
1	1	1	0

Compare this table with the four rules of addition above. There is no simple logic gate which has this truth table so a logic network has to be made up with two outputs called a **sum** and a **carry**. The network is shown below. It is called a **half-adder**.

Check this half-adder for yourself. Trace the different inputs (starting with A = 0 and B = 0) through the network to see that it produces the right sum and carry for each combination.

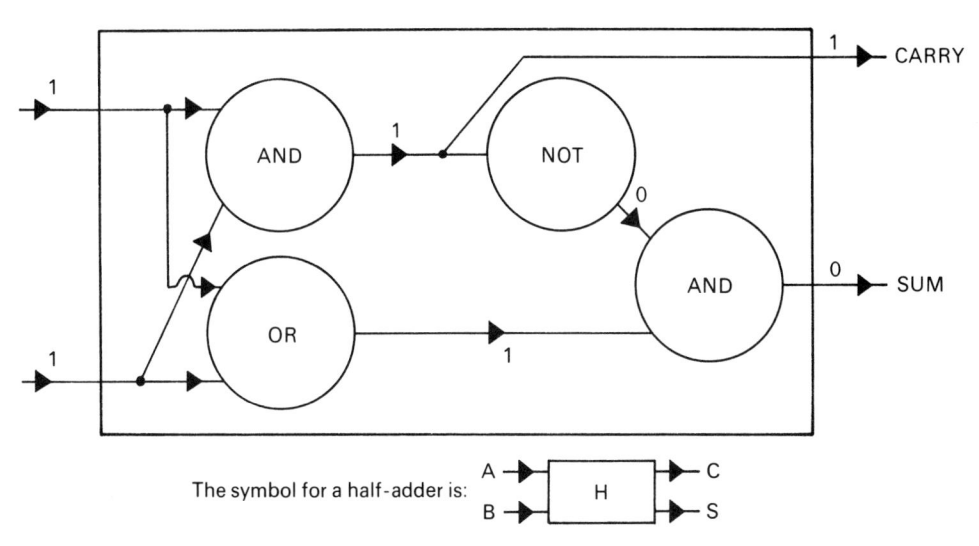

Fig. 5.22 A half-adder logic circuit (with one example shown)

Adding three binary digits The half-adder works perfectly for two digits. But it is often necessary to add 3 bits—1 bit from each of the numbers to be added and the carry bit from the previous addition. A more complex circuit is needed for adding three binary digits. This is the **full-adder**.

For three digits there are eight different rules.

DIGIT	CARRY	SUM
0 + 0 + 0 =	0	0
0 + 0 + 1 =	0	1
0 + 1 + 0 =	0	1
1 + 0 + 0 =	0	1
0 + 1 + 1 =	1	0
1 + 0 + 1 =	1	0
1 + 1 + 0 =	1	0
1 + 1 + 1 =	1	1

The logic network for adding three digits must have a truth table exactly corresponding to these eight rules of addition.

THREE INPUTS			OUTPUTS	
A	B	C	CARRY	SUM
0	0	0	0	0
0	0	1	0	1
0	1	0	0	1
1	0	0	0	1
0	1	1	1	0
1	0	1	1	0
1	1	0	1	0
1	1	1	1	1

Compare this table carefully with the eight rules of addition above.

The logic network for adding three digits, i.e. a full-adder, is made by joining two half-adders. A full adder which produces the correct sum and carry is shown below. Check this for yourself. Trace the different inputs through the network for each of the eight combinations.

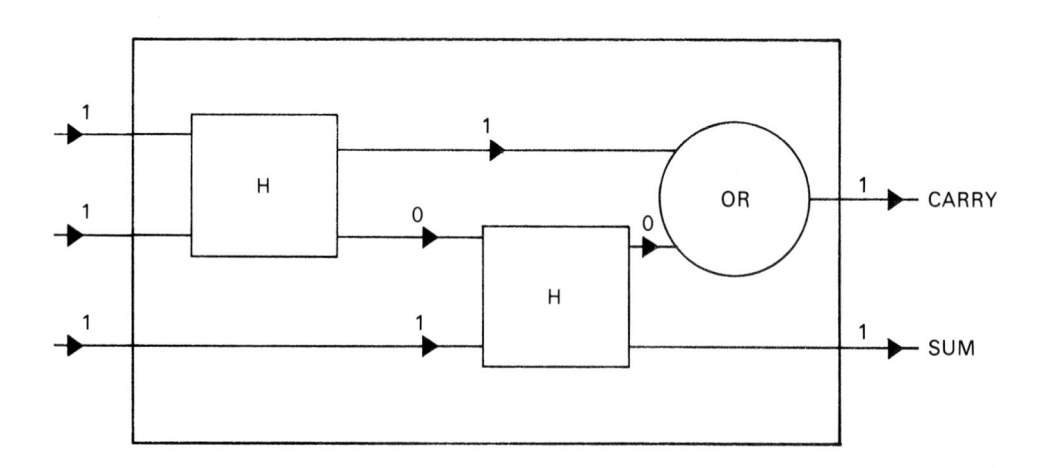

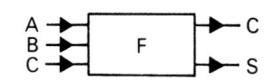

Fig. 5.23 A full-adder logic circuit (with one example shown)

The symbol for a full adder is:

Adding longer binary numbers Binary numbers of any length can be added by joining 'adding' circuits together. For example: a 3-bit binary number can be added with three full-adders; an 8-bit binary number can be added with eight full adders. Figure 5.24 shows a circuit for adding two 4-bit numbers. Within one clock pulse (i.e. in less than one millionth of a second) the result is produced on the output wires.

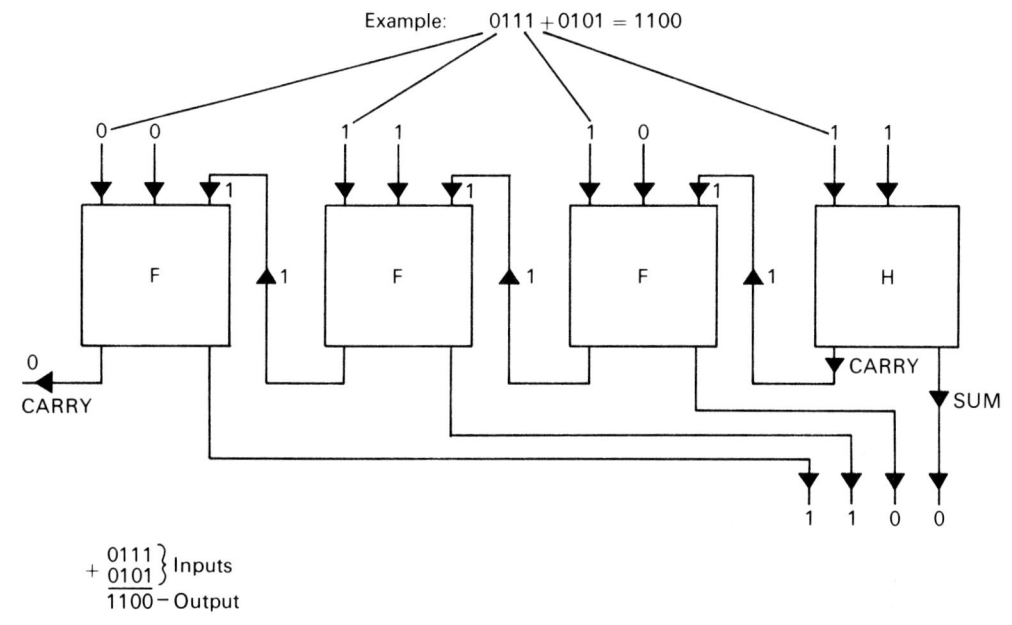

Fig. 5.24 Adding two 4-bit numbers with a parallel adder

Inputs:
$$+\begin{array}{r}0111\\0101\end{array}$$
Output: 1100

Notice that a half-adder is shown in Figure 5.24 in the units column. But in practice a full adder is placed there so that the same circuit can be employed for subtraction using the two's-complement method. The complete circuit is called a **parallel adder**. A special register in the CPU is used to signal whether overflow has occurred at the final full-adder, i.e. if the last carry is a 1. This is called a **flag register**.

How computers do their sums

Computers can do all kinds of arithmetic: adding, subtracting, multiplying and dividing. Computer calculations are complicated, but, in fact, the *basic* operation is addition. For example, one number can be subtracted from another by making it negative then adding it:

$$6 - 3 = 6 + (-3) = 3$$

Many computers subtract numbers in this way. The negative number is found by the two's-complement method already explained. It is then added.

Multiplication can be done by adding numbers over and over again, for example:

$$6 \times 2 = 2 + 2 + 2 + 2 + 2 + 2$$

Division can be done by repeated subtraction.

The logic circuits rarely go wrong but they can sometimes give unexpected results when they do a calculation. One reason is that certain fractions cannot be represented exactly in binary form, or decimal form (e.g. $\frac{1}{3} = 0.333333...$). The number has to be truncated to fit it into a binary word.

Another problem is overflow. The result of a calculation may contain too many bits to fit into a storage location.

Errors in computer arithmetic

Errors in computer arithmetic are unavoidable. An **error** is the difference between the *true value* and the *value stored* in the computer. Errors result from trying to store numbers in a binary word of fixed, *finite* length. Normally, the shorter the word length the greater the probability of error. The table gives a summary of errors in computer arithmetic.

Computers which carry out huge, complex calculations have been designed to reduce these errors to a minimum. Their calculations are certainly accurate enough to send astronauts to the moon and back!

TYPE OF ERROR	MEANING	EXAMPLE
Overflow	The result of a calculation is too large to fit into the storage location intended for it (the computer word)	The answer to a multiplication is outside the range of numbers a computer can represent—an error message is output
Truncation	A fraction is cut off (truncated) after a certain number of binary or decimal places	$\frac{2}{3} = 0.101010_2$ $\frac{2}{3} = 0.6666_{10}$ to four places
Rounding	Binary fractions are rounded by raising the last figure to 1 if the next figure would have been a 1. Decimal fractions are rounded by raising the last figure by 1 if the next figure would have been above 5	$\frac{2}{3} = 0.101011_2$ $\frac{2}{3} = 0.6667_{10}$
Underflow	The result of a calculation is too small to be held in the computer word	A result of 0.000000001 becomes 0.00000000 in 8 bits

Errors in computer arithmetic

Other logic gates

AND, OR and NOT are not the only logic gates. This section explains three others: **NAND, NOR** and **EXCLUSIVE-OR**.

The NAND gate A NAND gate is made by putting a NOT gate after an AND gate.

NAND is short for NOT-AND. Its truth table is the exact reverse of the AND gate.

A	B	NAND
0	0	1
0	1	1
1	0	1
1	1	0

The NOR gate This is made by putting a NOT gate after an OR gate.

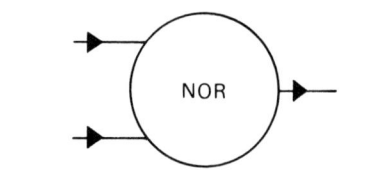

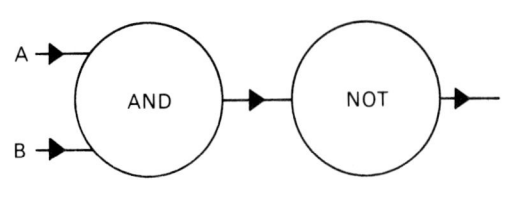

Fig. 5.25

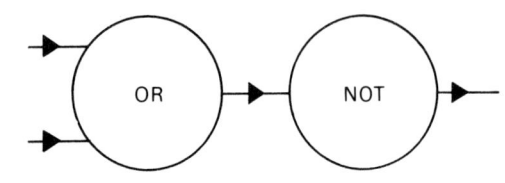

Fig. 5.26

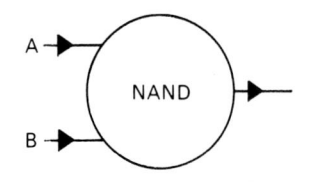

NOR is short for NOT-OR. Its truth table is the exact reverse of the OR gate.

A	B	NOR
0	0	1
0	1	0
1	0	0
1	1	0

Every computer logic circuit can be built only from NAND gates or only from NOR gates. In fact, all the other logic gates can be built by combining NAND gates in the right patterns.

The EXCLUSIVE-OR gate This final gate gives an output of 0 when both the inputs are the *same*, i.e. when both inputs are equivalent. It is sometimes called the **NOT-EQUIVALENT gate**.

A	B	XOR
0	0	0
0	1	1
1	0	1
1	1	0

More than one symbol is used to show an EXCLUSIVE-OR (XOR) gate.

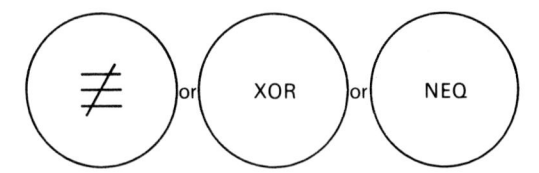

Fig. 5.27 Symbols for the EXCLUSIVE-OR/ NOT-EQUIVALENT gate

This gate actually means: 'Either A or B but not both'. You can see from the truth table that this gate gives the *sum* of two binary digits, e.g. $1 + 0 = 1$. So it can be used as part of the logic circuit for a half-adder, as Figure 5.28 shows. Check this circuit with different patterns of 1's and 0's to see that it works.

This unit has explained the job that different logic gates do. You do not need to know how these logic gates are made, or what goes on inside them. This is the concern of the electronic engineer. As far as computer studies goes, the logic gate is the lowest level you need to go down to.

Half-adder

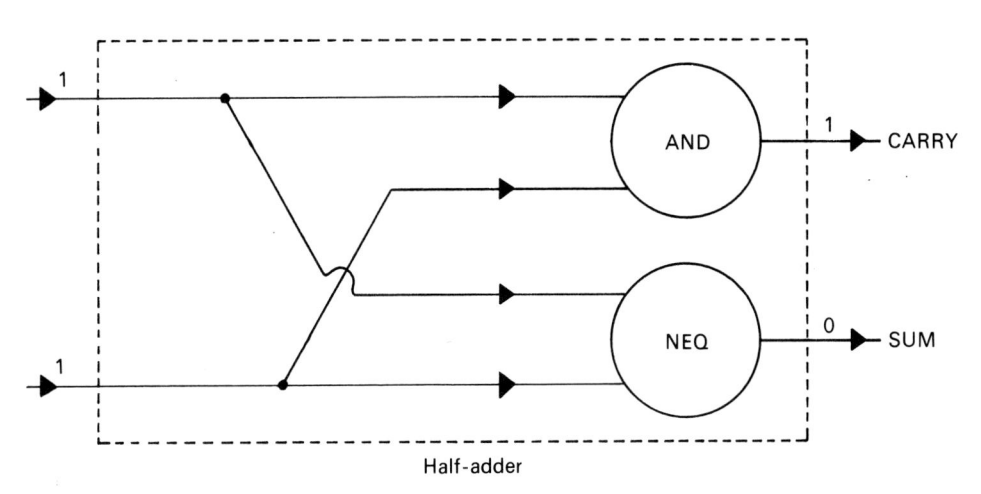

Fig. 5.28 A half-adder made from an AND gate and a NOT-EQUIVALENT gate

KEY POINTS

1 Electrical pulses travel around the circuits of a computer through logic gates.

2 Three basic gates are the AND, OR and NOT gates. Their operation is shown by using a truth table.

3 These gates can be combined to form logic circuits or logic networks.

4 Logic circuits can be used for comparing, transferring, calculating and decoding data.

5 A logic circuit for adding two binary digits is a half-adder. A circuit for adding three bits is a full-adder.

6 Three other important logic gates are the NAND, NOR and EXCLUSIVE-OR gates. All logic circuits can be constructed using only NAND gates.

Questions

1 Complete each of these truth tables:

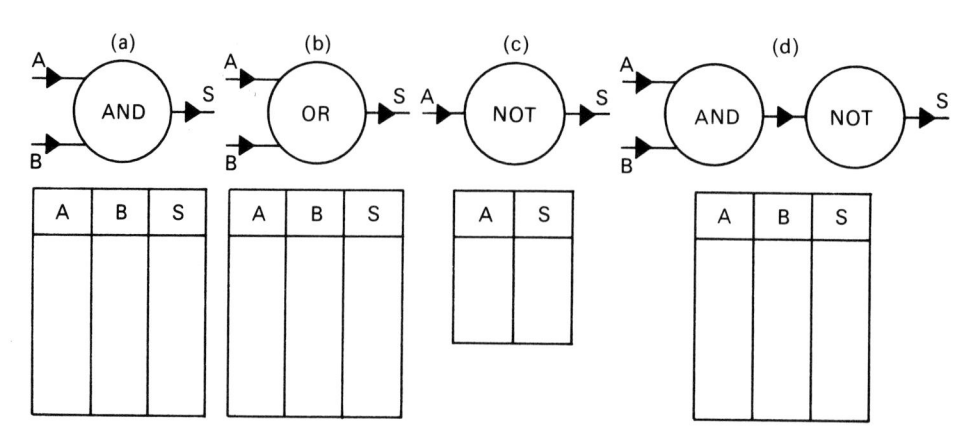

(a) A, B → AND → S

(b) A, B → OR → S

(c) A → NOT → S

(d) A, B → AND → NOT → S

A	B	S

A	B	S

A	S

A	B	S

Fig. 5.29

2 Copy these statements into your book and fill in the blanks:
 a) 'The output is 1 only when both inputs are 1' describes the _____ gate.
 b) 'The output is 0 only when both inputs are 0' describes the _____ gate.
 c) 'The output is 1 when one of the inputs is 0 and the other input is 1' describes the _____ gate.
 d) 'The output is always 1 when the input is 0 and always 0 when the input is 1' describes the _____ gate.
 (YREB 1982)

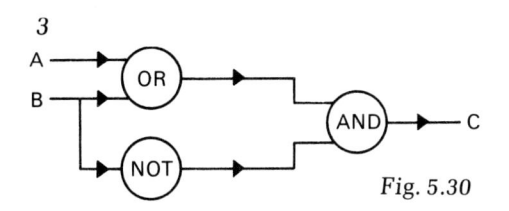

3

Fig. 5.30

State what the value of C is in this logic circuit if:
 a) A is 1 and B is 0
 b) A is 0 and B is 1
 c) A is 1 and B is 1

4 Copy out and complete the truth table for the following logic circuit:

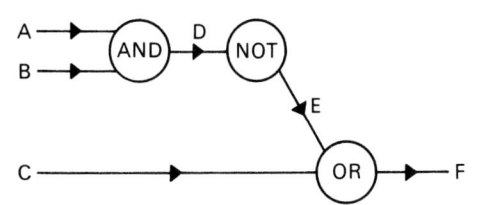

Fig. 5.31

A	B	C	D	E	F
0	1	1			
1	0	0			
1	1	0			
1	1	1			

(SREB)

5 a) Copy out and complete the following truth table so that it represents the output from an AND gate:

A	B	A AND B
0	0	
0	1	
1	0	
1	1	

b) Study the truth table for this logic circuit. Three of the values in the D column are incorrect. Draw the table in your note book with a ring around each of the three incorrect values:

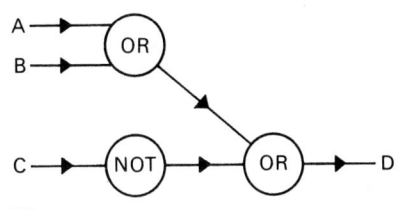

Fig. 5.32

A	B	C	D
0	0	0	0
0	0	1	1
0	1	0	1
1	0	1	1
1	1	0	1
1	1	1	0

(SEREB)

6 Draw logic circuits to represent the expressions:
 a) A OR NOT (B AND C)
 b) A AND (B OR NOT C)
 (WMEB)

7 Construct a truth table for the outputs at C and D for the following circuit.

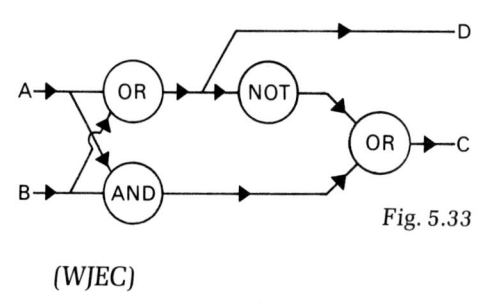

Fig. 5.33

(WJEC)

8 Construct the truth table for the output, Z, of this logic circuit:

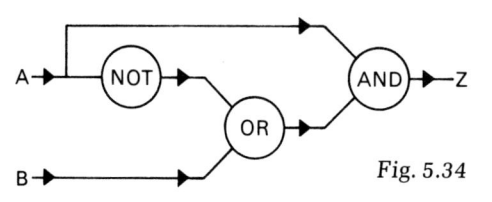

Fig. 5.34

9*a) Construct the truth table for the following logic network.

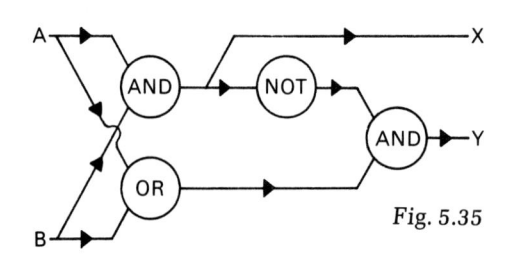

Fig. 5.35

b) Suggest a use of this logic network within the CPU of a computer.
(JMB)

10 The diagram below shows a simple piece of decoding logic. Draw and complete the truth table for the inputs given.

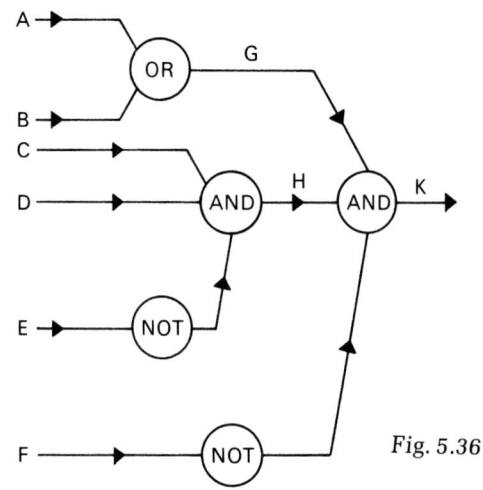

Fig. 5.36

A	B	C	D	E	F	G	H	K
1	0	1	1	0	0			
0	1	1	1	1	1			
0	1	1	1	0	1			

11*Copy and complete the truth table for this logic circuit.

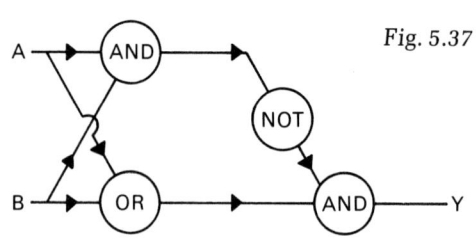

Fig. 5.37

116

A	B	Y
0	0	
0	1	
1	0	
1	1	

By considering the addition of binary digits, explain how this circuit can be modified to form a half adder.
Explain what is meant by a full adder and show how one can be made from half adders.
(SUJB)

12*a) Construct a truth table for each of the following logic gates.
   AND   OR   NOT   NAND   NOR
b) Show that the two circuits in Fig. 5.38 are equivalent.
(OLE)

Fig. 5.38

*'O'-Level question

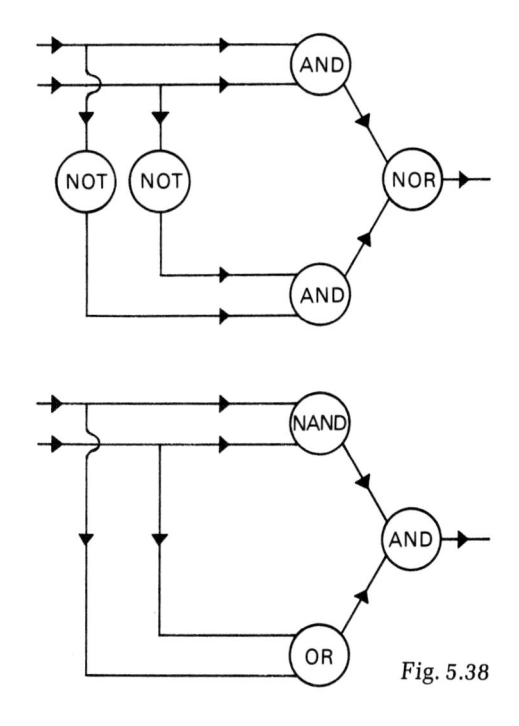

5.6 The heart of the computer: the central processing unit

At the heart of any computer is the device which carries out the program instructions—the central processing unit. Every computer has a CPU. This unit explains how it operates.

The parts of the CPU

The CPU has inside it:
- a control unit
- an arithmetic and logic unit
- some special registers.

The main memory is attached to the CPU. The CPU takes instructions from the main memory and *executes* them, i.e. it carries out the instructions. The instructions use data—this is also stored in memory.

Data and programs occupy *locations* in memory. Each location has an *address*. A location might be 8 bits (1 byte) long.

Addresses Some instructions take data from or store data in memory. To do this they must be given the address of the location containing the data. The number of bits needed to specify an address depends on how many locations there are altogether in the memory. The lowest address is always zero.

If the memory has 4 kilobytes (i.e. 4096 bytes) then the number of bits needed for an address is 12 bits. This is because the addresses range from 0 to 4095. The binary value for 4095 is 111111111111, i.e. 12 bits set to 1. The table below shows the number of bits needed to address all the locations in different sizes of memory.

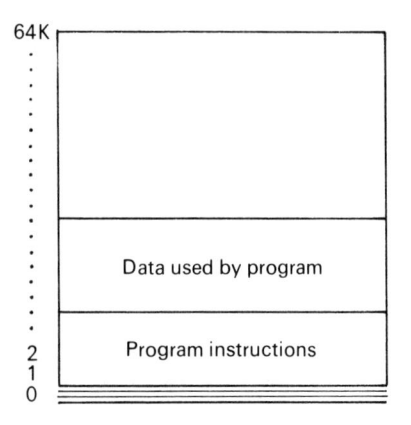

Fig. 5.40 *Program and data stored in the memory*

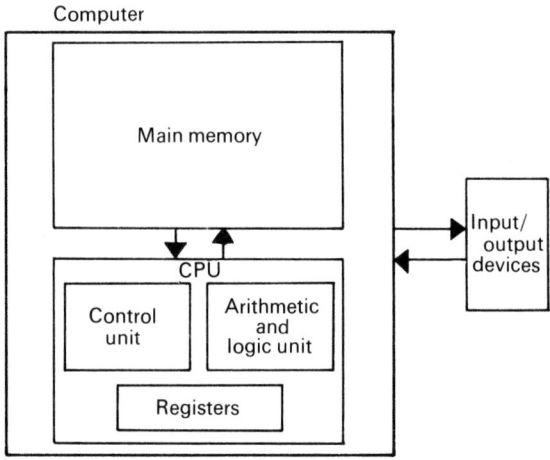

Fig. 5.39 *General layout of the CPU and memory*

SIZE OF MEMORY (BYTES)	ADDRESSES	NUMBER OF BITS REQUIRED
2^{11} = 2K = 2048	0–2047	11
2^{12} = 4K = 4096	0–4095	12
2^{13} = 8K = 8192	0–8191	13
2^{14} = 16K = 16384	0–16383	14
2^{15} = 32K = 32768	0–32767	15
2^{16} = 64K = 65536	0–65535	16
2^{17} = 128K = 131072	0–131071	17
2^{18} = 256K = 262144	0–262143	18

Number of bits needed to address various sizes of memory

The control unit The control unit is the part of the CPU which is responsible for executing instructions. It retrieves the next instruction in the program from main memory. It decodes this instruction and sets the circuits of the computer ready to carry out the instruction. For instructions which use data it also obtains the data from the correct memory address.

Arithmetic unit A lot of program instructions carry out arithmetic on data, e.g. adding two numbers, multiplying, etc. These operations are carried out by the arithmetic unit under control of the control unit.

Special registers These are storage locations similar to those in main memory. But they can be accessed more quickly than main memory locations because they are physically closer to the control unit and arithmetic unit. Also, each register has a name and does not have to be accessed by an address.

Some registers are used for temporarily holding data during calculations. These are often called **general registers** or **accumulators**. Other registers have a special purpose. Some examples are listed below:
- **Instruction Register** (IR)
- **Memory Address Register** (MAR)
- **Program Counter** (PC) or **Sequence Control Register** (SCR).

These registers are used in the execution of an instruction.

Instructions

The instructions executed by the CPU are in *machine code*. Remember, these are held as strings of binary digits. A computer is designed to execute a given **instruction set**. This means that the circuits within the CPU are capable of executing a particular set of instructions. Instruction sets vary from computer to computer. For instance the instruction set for an ICL 2900 is very different to an IBM 370's. A Zilog Z80 CPU chip has a different instruction set to a MOS technology 6502 chip, and so on.

An instruction is identified by an **operation code**. A computer may have a hundred or more operation codes in its instruction set. Each of these is represented as a different binary pattern.

There are 4 main types of instructions. These are:
- data transfer
- arithmetic and logic
- test and branch
- input and output.

If the instruction is one which operates on data in main store, it will also include an address as a binary number.

Operation code	Address
← 8 bits →	← 16 bits →

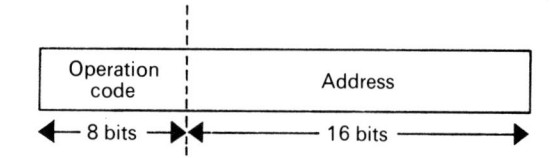

Fig. 5.41 A typical instruction

The diagram above shows the layout of an instruction which contains an address. The operation code uses 8 bits, the address uses 16 bits. This means that the maximum number of different instructions is 255 and the highest possible address is 65 535 with this layout.

The program in the example below loads two values from memory, adds them and puts the answer back in memory. The machine code shown is for a Z80 CPU. The comments explain what the code is doing. The code is also shown in assembly code. Notice how the LD B,A and ADD A,B instructions use one byte but that the others use 3. This is because a Z80 can address up to 64K bytes. An instruction needs 16 bits (or two bytes) for an address. Some CPU's (e.g. Z80) can use 2 bytes for op-codes, thereby increasing the number of available instructions.

Example A machine code program to add 2 numbers.

COMMENTS	MEMORY LOCATION (hex)	MNEMONIC	MACHINE CODE
Load contents of address 2000H into A	100	LD A,(2000H)	3A0020
Load A into B	103	LD B,A	47
Load contents of address 2001H into A	104	LD A,(2001H)	3A0120
Add B to A	107	ADD A,B	80
Load A into address 2002H	108	LD (2002H),A	320220
Halt the program	10B	HALT	76
First number	2000	DEFB 4	04
Second number	2001	DEFB 8	08
Space for number	2002	DEFB 0	00

The memory locations contain (after execution):

LOCATION	CONTENTS (binary)	CONTENTS (hex)
100	00111010	3A
101	00000000	00
102	00100000	20
103	01000111	47
104	00111010	3A
105	00000001	01
106	00100000	20
107	10000000	80
108	00110010	32
109	00000010	02
10A	00100000	20
10B	01110110	76
2000	00000100	04
2001	00001000	08
2002	00001100	0C

The fetch and execute cycle

A computer operates in a continuous rhythm of *fetching* an instruction from memory and *executing* the instruction.

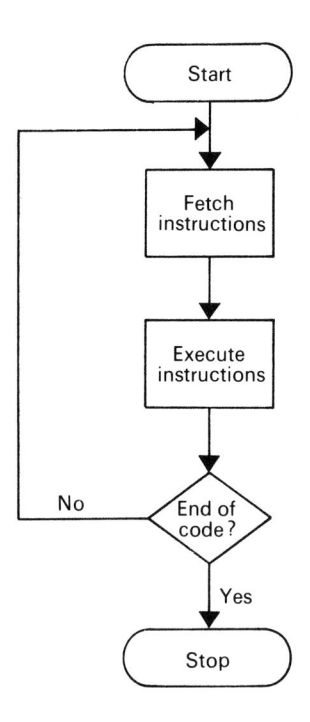

Fig. 5.42

Fetch cycle The flow diagram for the fetch cycle is shown below. The program counter (PC) register contains the address of the next instruction in memory. This is used to address the right location in memory for the next operation code. It is intially set for the first instruction in the program. The operation is loaded into the instruction register (IR). The control unit decodes the op-code and sends control signals to the other circuits in the computer. If the op-code is one which has an address associated with it, then the next 2 bytes of memory must be obtained. These are put in the memory address register. The program counter is used for this. After the instruction has been fetched, the program counter is set correctly for the next instruction. Before that though, the current instruction must be executed. This is done in the execute cycle.

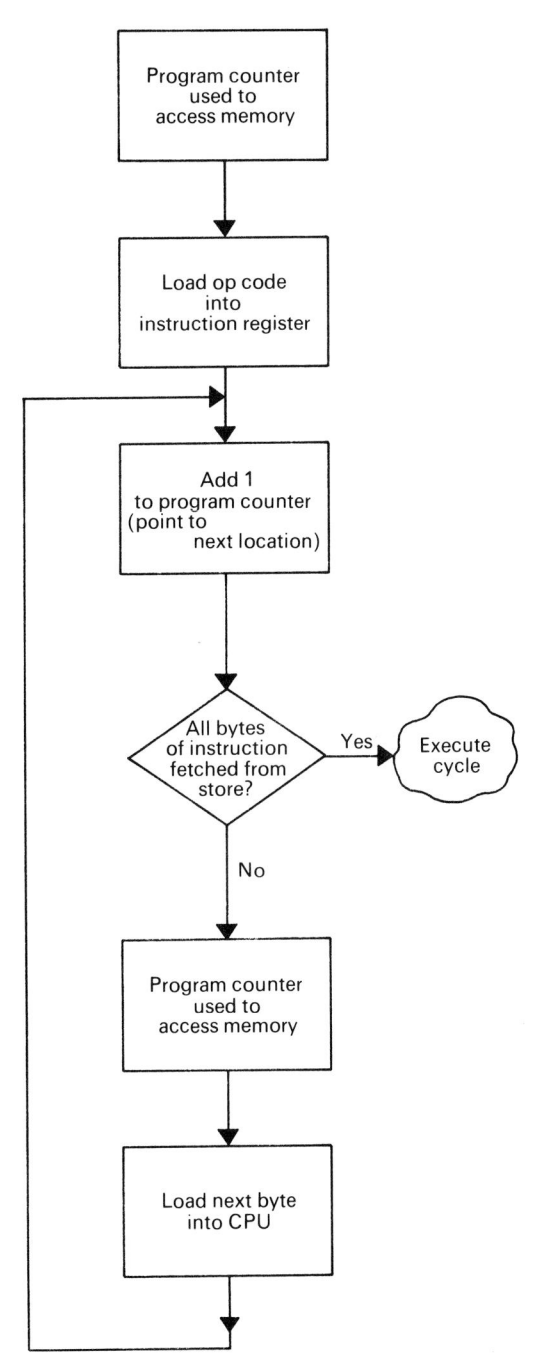

Fig. 5.43 *The fetch cycle*

Execute cycle What happens in the execute cycle depends on the op-code and the contents of registers. To understand the execute cycle generally, you need a more detailed picture of the CPU.

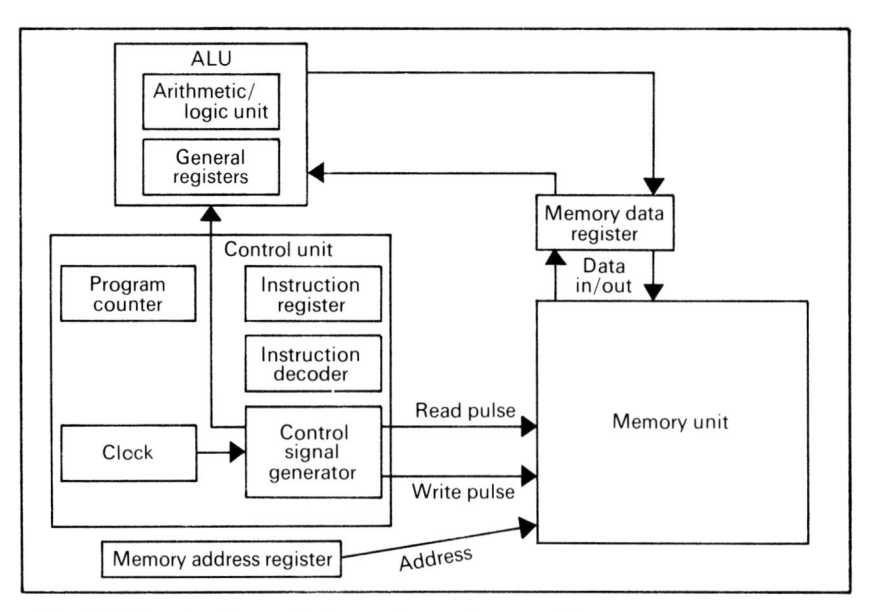

Fig. 5.44 *The CPU showing flow of information and control lines*

The execute cycle is as follows.
1. The instruction is in the instruction register (IR). The instruction decoder (ID) sets the control signal generator to send out the correct control signals.
2. If the instruction requires data from memory (e.g. LD A, (ADDR)) a *read pulse* is generated. This takes the contents of the location whose address is in the memory address register (MAR). Remember this was set in the fetch cycle. The contents of the location are put in the memory data register (MDR).
3. The data can now be taken from the MDR and put into the arithmetic and logic unit (ALU). The control unit generates the signal for this and the signals for the operation to be performed (e.g. ADD).
4. If the instruction is one which places data in memory (e.g. LD (ADDR), A) then the control unit generates signals to transfer data from the ALU into the MDR.
5. Once in the MDR the data may then be transferred to memory. This is done by the control unit generating a WRITE pulse. The address of the location to be used is again, in the MAR.

Notice that the steps required are different for loading data into the CPU from memory and storing data into memory from the CPU.

In the example shown earlier the instructions LD A, (ADDR) follow steps 1, 2, 3. The instruction LD (ADDR), A follows steps 1, 4, 5. The LD A,B and ADD A,B instructions do not access memory. The control signals for these would be to the ALU only.

Branch instructions Some instructions branch to an instruction other than the one immediately following. This is equivalent to a GOTO instruction in BASIC. A branch instruction contains the address of the instruction to branch to.

INSTRUCTION
Branch to address 256

ASSEMBLER CODE
JP   ADDR

MACHINE CODE
1100 0011 | 0000 0000 0001 0000
Op. Code | Address

In this case the address in the instruction is placed in the program counter. The next instruction executed will be the one at the address specified and not the next instruction.

Controlling the operations

Clock pulses All the steps in the fetch and execute cycle take time. To keep the computer running properly each operation must be done in a strict time sequence. To do this the control unit contains a **clock circuit**. This generates periodic clock signals to the control circuit. Each step must begin on a **clock pulse**. A step may take several clock pulses to execute.

This diagram shows the timing sequence for a typical computer. One instruction cycle takes eight clock pulses.

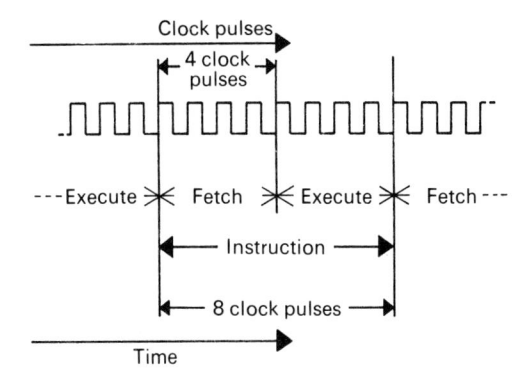

Fig. 5.45 A typical timing sequence

- **KEY POINTS**

  1. At the heart of any computer is the central processing unit.
  2. The CPU has 3 main parts: the control unit, the arithmetic and logic unit, some special registers.
  3. The CPU is connected to the main memory.
  4. The CPU takes instructions from the memory and executes them. This is known as the fetch-execute cycle.
  5. Some instructions take data from or put data in the memory. They need the address of the memory location containing the data.
  6. The control unit contains a clock circuit. This generates clock pulses which keep the computer running in a proper time sequence.

Questions

1. Copy out this sentence and fill in the blanks.
   A CPU has inside it _____, _____ and _____.

2. Complete this sentence.
   Data and programs are stored in _____.

3. How many bits are required to address a memory of 64K bytes?

4. a) Name the three parts of a computer which make up the central processing unit.
   b) Which one of these three parts ensures that the parts of the computer work in the correct order?

5. Complete this sentence.
   The main store of a computer is divided up into storage locations

and each is identified by its own _____.
(SREB 1982)

6* A certain computer uses 12-bit words, each of which can contain one machine code instruction. In each machine code instruction, the operation code occupies 4 bits. A single accumulator is used.
a) The machine code instruction 1 0 0 0 1 1 0 1 0 1 1 1 indicates that data should be loaded into the accumulator from the location in main store having the binary address 1 1 0 1 0 1 1 1. Draw a simple diagram showing the principal elements of the central processing unit. On this diagram, show the data paths and control signals which would be needed to decode and execute the instruction shown above, after it has been fetched from store. Write notes to describe this process of decoding and execution.
b) Why is it likely that, in practice, a computer would use:
(i) operation codes occupying more than 4 bits
(ii) machine code instructions occupying more than 12 bits?
(Cambridge 1982)

7*a) (i) Complete this sentence. The initials CPU stand for _____.
(ii) The accumulator, program counter and instruction register are three registers which are in the arithmetic unit (AU) or control unit. State in which unit each is found.
The accumulator is in the _____ unit.
The program counter is in the _____ unit.
The instruction register is in the _____ unit.
(iii) State two differences between a register in the CPU and a location in main memory.
b) (i) The instruction ADD A,B means: 'Add the number in B onto the number in the accumulator. The result is kept in the accumulator.'
Complete the following sentence. To execute the instruction ADD A,B it is fetched from _____ and copied to _____.
How do the contents of the program counter change when this instruction is fetched and executed?
(ii) The instruction JP AGAIN means: 'Jump to the program instruction labelled AGAIN'. What are the contents of the program counter when this instruction has been executed?
(Cambridge 1983)

8* A simplified system of machine instructions uses the first 3 bits of an 8 bit instruction for the operation code and the other 5 bits are used for the binary number representing the memory address. The following table gives the interpretation of a selection of the operation codes.

OPERATION CODE	INTERPRETATION
010	Copy number from accumulator to memory
100	Copy number from memory to accumulator
110	Add number in memory to accumulator.

a) Explain the instruction 10000101, specifying the memory address in base 10.
b) Write two further instructions to follow that in part (a) which would add the number in memory 6 to the accumulator and store the result in memory 15.
(SUJB)

*'O'-Level question

5.7 Linking the inside of the computer to the outside world

To be useful the computer must be able to communicate—it must accept input and produce output. Computers communicate via input and output peripherals. This unit describes how the computer does this.

Handling input and output

The CPU executes program instructions which transfer, calculate and compare data. The program may also input data from, or output data to, peripherals. A peripheral could be:
- a keyboard
- a printer
- a disk drive
- a magnetic tape drive.

These are peripherals to a general-purpose computer. If the CPU is part of a microprocessor-controlled system the peripheral could be:
- a temperature sensor
- a traffic light controller
- a pressure gauge
- a light meter
- a pressure valve.

The list is almost endless.

Input/output instructions Instructions were described in the previous section. An instruction set contains instructions for processing data and for the input and output of data. Input and output to and from a computer takes place through one or more **ports**. (Data passes through a computer port as cargo passes through a shipping port.) Often the data is sent from, or received into, a general-purpose register in the CPU.

Here are the input and output instructions for a Z80 CPU.

IN A, (port); input character to register A
OUT (port), A; output character from register A

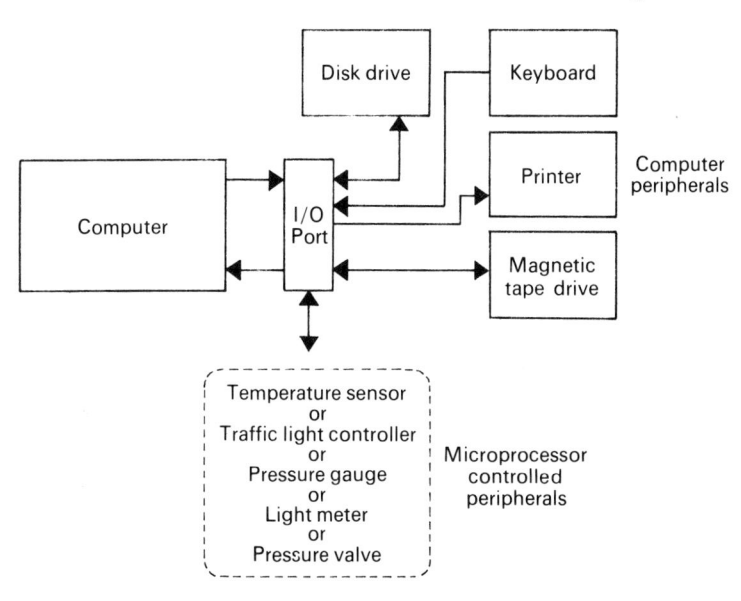

Fig. 5.46 Data passes through input/output ports

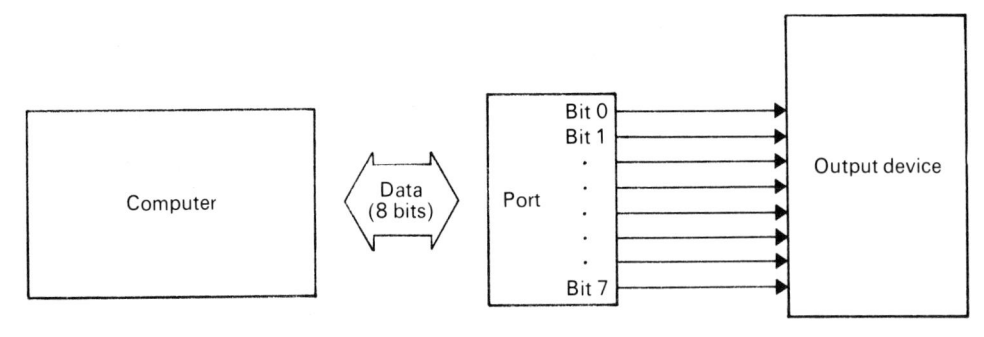

Fig. 5.47 *Parallel data transfer*

Parallel input/output Each byte of data transferred is a fixed number of bits (e.g. 8 bits). If the data is transferred in *parallel* then this means that each of the 8 bits is transferred at the same time. The connections between the peripheral and the computer must be capable of carrying the 8 bits. This method is often used with control peripherals (e.g. a temperature sensor).

Serial input/output Most communication devices, for example a VDU or telephone lines, are designed to transmit data in strings of 0's and 1's. These strings are *serial*. A pattern of bits represents a character. For example, a computer may wish to transmit the letter 'A' to a VDU. If the computer and VDU are designed to use the ASCII code the bit pattern is 11000001.

In this case the port takes the character from the computer and passes it 1 bit at a time along the communication line. The data is transmitted as a series of electrical pulses and no electrical pulses. A '1' is represented as a pulse, a '0' by no pulse. The letter 'A' transmits as:

Extra bits are added to the string to indicate the beginning and the end of a string. These are called **start bits** and **stop bits**. The start bits allow the computer or peripheral to 'get ready' to accept the character. The stop bits indicate that the character has finished. A parity bit may also be added so that the receiving device can detect if errors in transmission have occurred. Different computers use different numbers of bits for start and stop bits. Here is a typical character transmission.

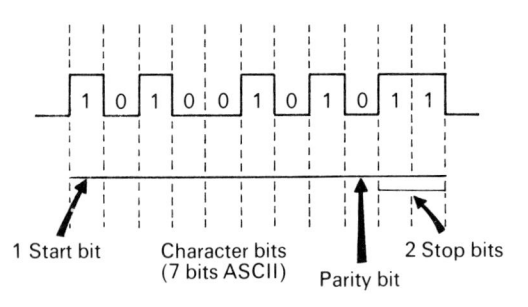

Fig. 5.49 *Character transmission showing stop, start and parity bits*

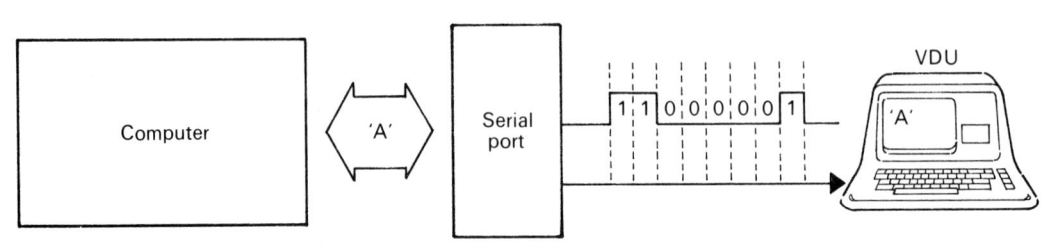

Fig. 5.48 *Serial data transfer*

Analogue-to-digital conversion Most computers are digital computers, so they deal with data in binary digits. But some input devices are analogue devices (e.g. a thermometer or a pressure gauge). Input from these devices must be converted into digital data. This is done by including an **Analogue-to-Digital Converter** (ADC) in the transmission line.

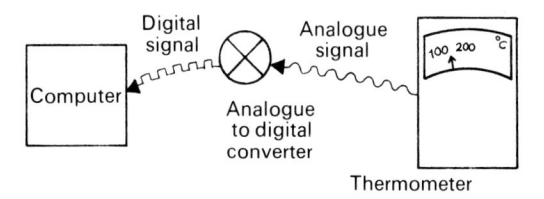

Fig. 5.50

Digital-to-analogue conversion This is the reverse of analogue-to-digital conversion. If the output device is an analogue device, then a **Digital-to-Analogue Converter** (DAC) must be included in the transmission line.

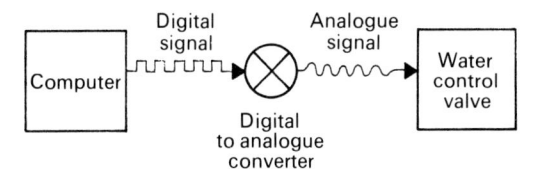

Fig. 5.51

Digital/analogue and analogue/digital converters allow computers to communicate with a wide variety of control instruments. Another example of analogue input is the 'joystick' in a Space Invaders game.

Interrupts

The CPU executes instructions at very high speed. Peripherals operate much more slowly. While data is being transferred to or from a peripheral, the CPU could be doing a lot of other processing. To make full use of the CPU a computer often runs more than one program at once. This means that when one program starts to input or output data another program runs on the CPU. When the peripheral has finished transferring data it signals to the CPU that it is ready. The signal is sent on a wire connected to the control unit. This wire is called the **interrupt line**. At this point the CPU stops executing the main program and runs another small program which deals with the peripheral device.

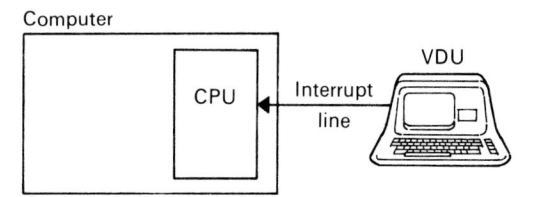

Fig. 5.52 The interrupt line

After servicing the device, the CPU continues with the main program where it left off. This is called an **interrupt**. The peripheral device 'interrupts' the main program. The CPU then runs an **interrupt service routine**. Here are the steps involved.
1 The main program receives an interrupt signal.
2 Execution of the main program stops.
3 Contents of the program counter and general registers are stored away in memory.
4 The program then jumps to the start of the interrupt service routine.
5 The interrupt service routine runs.
6 At the end of the interrupt service routine the contents of the program counter and general registers are reset.
7 The main program continues.

Interrupt priorities If the computer is connected to several peripherals, it could receive another interrupt while it was still servicing one. Should the computer ignore the second interrupt or stop servicing the first interrupt? To help answer this question interrupts may be given **priorities**. Those interrupts which must be serviced straight away are given a higher priority. Lower priority interrupts may be interrupted by higher priority interrupts.

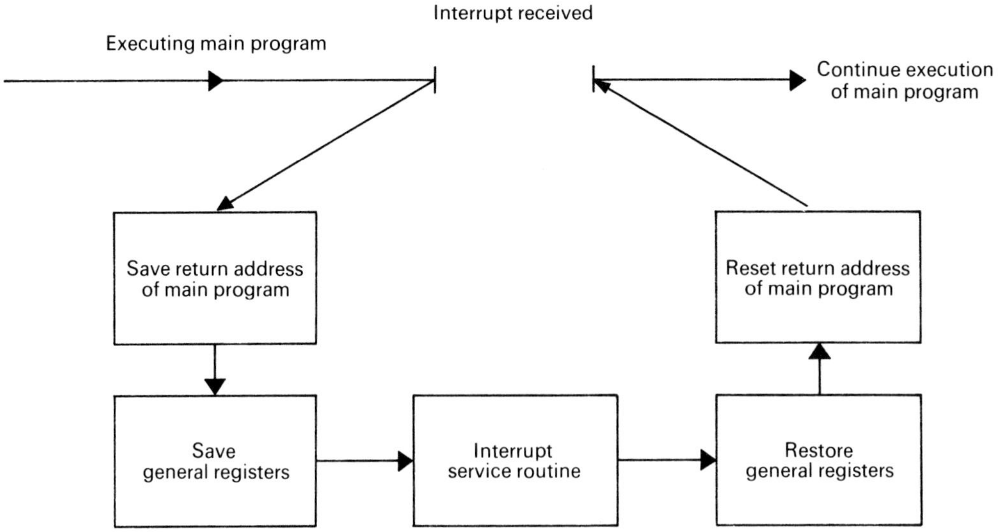

Fig. 5.53 The interrupt sequence

Input/output buffers

As mentioned previously the CPU operates at a much higher speed than peripherals. To reduce the operating speed difference a **buffer** is often used. A buffer is an area of main memory which is used to hold data temporarily. It may hold the data:
- before it is transferred to the peripheral from the computer
- after it is transferred from the peripheral to the computer.

With this arrangement the computer can put data into, and take data from, the buffer more quickly. The program reads and writes data items into and out of the buffer. This is especially useful when inputting and outputting data from, and to, magnetic disk and tape.

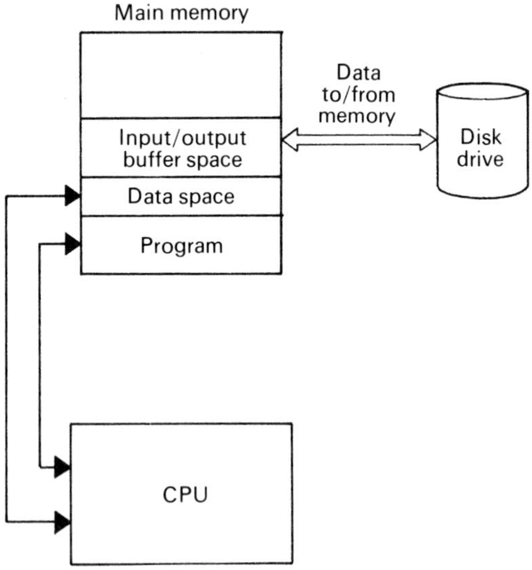

Fig. 5.54 An input/output buffer holds data temporarily

Computers in control

Common applications of computers are in the control of:
- industrial machinery and processes
- domestic appliances, e.g. washing machines
- robots
- experiments in industry, schools and colleges.

The computer controls activities according to the program stored in its memory. The control is exercised by outputting signals to start and stop motors, open and close valves, etc. The timing of the output signals may be dependent upon input signals received. For example, the movements of a robot are achieved by the computer switching motors on and off for set time periods or until a particular event occurs.

The case study on the automatic washing machine deals with control in more detail.

This unit has talked about making the computer communicate with peripherals. Computers also communicate over longer distances, sometimes to peripherals and sometimes to other computers. The next unit describes how computers do this.

KEY POINTS

1 Computers have to communicate with the outside world. They may be connected to input/output peripherals or to instruments in a microprocessor-controlled system.

2 Input and output may be parallel or serial.

3 The data is always transferred via an input/output port.

4 If the input is from an analogue device, an analogue-to-digital converter is needed.

5 If the output is to an analogue device a digital-to-analogue converter is needed.

6 Peripherals may have an interrupt line connected to the CPU.

7 Input/output buffers are used to speed the input and output of data between the computer and peripherals.

8 Computers may be used to control machinery, industrial processes, etc.

Questions

1 Copy out this sentence and fill in the blank.
  Data passes between the computer and peripherals via _____.
2 Data may be transferred in two ways. These are: a) _____ and b) _____.
3 Is the following statement true or false?
  'Serial data transfer is faster than parallel transfer.'
4*Explain why it is necessary to have interrupts of different priorities, and describe how these interrupts are handled by a computer.
  (Cambridge 1983)
5 A buffer allows:
  a) peripherals to work at different speeds from the CPU
  b) programs to crash gently without damage to the computer
  c) a computer to operate when the power is switched off
  d) one program to run into another.
  (NWREB 1983)

*'O'-Level question

5.8 Computer networks: linking computers together

Computers may be connected to other computers or to input/output devices. These may be in the same room as the computer, but they could be in different rooms, different buildings, or different countries. This unit describes how computers may be connected over a distance using computer networks.

Wide area networks

Many large organizations have several offices in different parts of the country and maybe in different parts of the world. If they use computers it is often necessary for each office to have access to the same data. For example, a company may have a head office in London and offices in Sheffield and Glasgow. The company could connect the computer in London to the ones in Sheffield and Glasgow using telephone lines. This is called a **communications network**. Data can be sent between computers and processed in London, Sheffield or Glasgow. If the company also had an office in New York it could connect its New York computer to the London computer. Data could be transmitted via a telecommunications satellite.

This type of communications network is called a **wide area network** (WAN) or **remote communications network**. This is because the computers are a long way from each other, maybe thousands of miles. Many large organizations connect their computers in this way. It has the following advantages:

- if one computer breaks down another one could do its processing
- if one computer has too much work to do, another one in the network can take some of the load
- data updated at one site is immediately available to all the other sites.

Local area networks

A **local area network** (LAN) is a group of computers connected together in a *small* area. It has the same advantages as a wide area network. The main difference between the two types of networks is that a local area network does not need telephone lines for communication. A local area network often involves a group of microcomputers connected in the same room or the same building (e.g. office block, hospital, school).

The various ways in which local area networks may be organized are shown

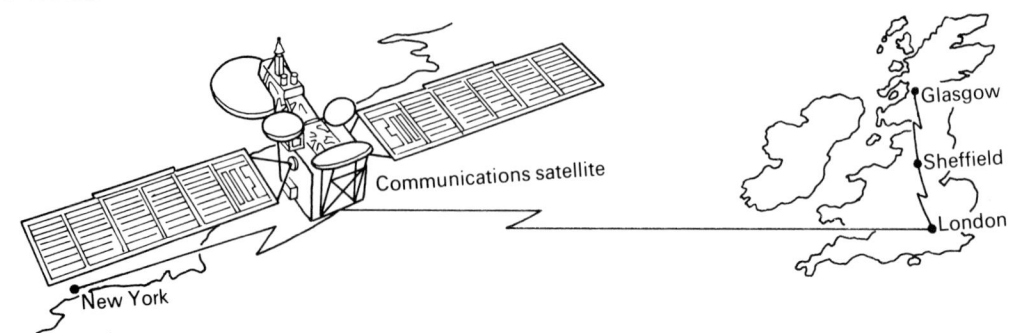

Fig. 5.55 *A remote communications network*

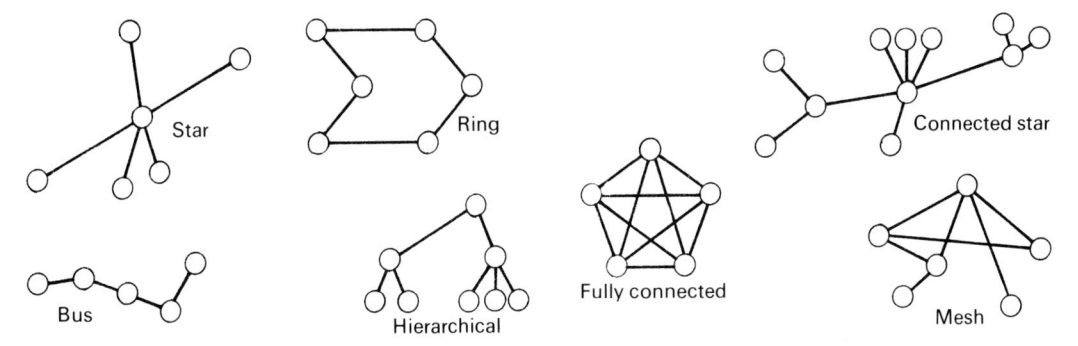

Fig. 5.56 Some common LAN organizations

above. One micro in the network may have a large disk drive or a printer connected to it. The other micros in the network can send output to the micro with the printer or store data on the disk.

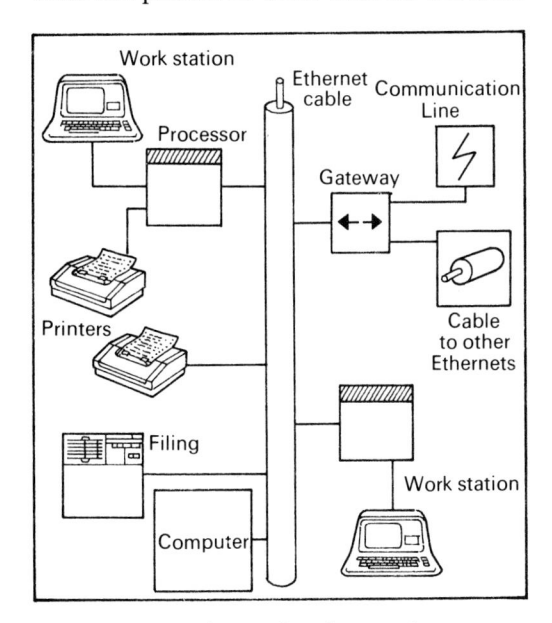

Fig. 5.57 An Ethernet local network

Local area networks are extremely useful because they can make expensive peripherals such as printers and disk drives available to many micros.

Local area networks are often sold under different names (e.g. ETHERNET, ECONET, DECNET, Cambridge Ring). Each of these have different methods for transmitting data.

LAN's may be connected to large computers and to wide area networks.

Communicating data

Data may be passed between computers using telephone lines. The lines may be private lines, i.e. belonging to an organization, or public lines. The public telephone system is the one you use to make any telephone call. The telephone lines may be used to transmit data as well as conversations. The telephone system operates on *analogue* signals. For computers the signals must be *digital*. To allow data to be transmitted over telephone lines it must be converted into analogue signals and back again into digital signals.

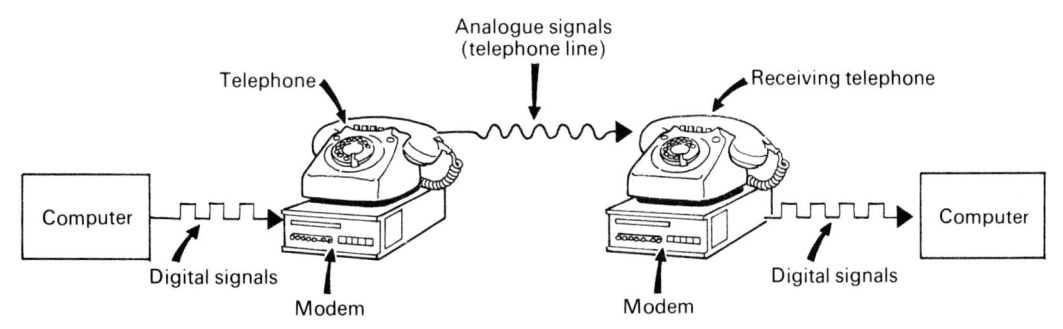

Fig. 5.58 Computers connected using modems

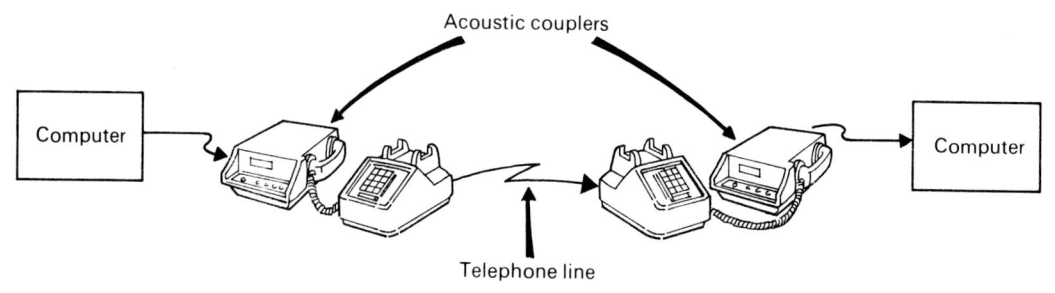

Fig. 5.59 Computers connected using acoustic couplers

The **modem** (modulator/demodulator) is used to carry out the conversion of signals. Another device used to convert the signals is called an **acoustic coupler**. This uses the telephone handset to transmit data as sound, like a conversation. Modems can transmit data much more quickly than acoustic couplers. The public telephone system is capable of transmitting data at approximately 9600 bits/second.

New telephone systems Existing telephone systems operate on analogue signals. This is not convenient for data communications because digital data has to be converted. However, modern telephone systems are being developed to operate on digital signals. These will make data communication easier and faster because no conversion will be necessary. In this country Plessey are developing a new telephone system called **System X**. This will provide digital conversation and data communication facilities. We will all be talking in bits!

Security in networks Because data passes over communication lines there is a problem of **data security**. Data can be obtained illegally from the communication lines. A lot of data is confidential (e.g. personal details, bank balances). Data must be protected from illegal access. Often the data is 'scrambled' by the sending computer, i.e. the data is made unreadable on the communication line. The receiving computer has to 'unscramble' the data before it can be processed.

Developments in data communication and the spread of computers as described here are very important occurrences. They form the basis for the 'electronic office'. One example of this is 'electronic mail'. Word processors may be used to 'send' letters via the network. Part 7 on information technology deals with this in more detail.

KEY POINTS

1 Computers may be connected via wide area networks or local area networks.

2 The major difference between the two types of network is that wide area networks use telephone lines for communication.

3 Networks provide many advantages.
   - If one computer breaks down another in the network can do its work.
   - Work may be shared by the computers in the network.
   - The same data is made available at many sites.

4 Existing telephone systems operate on analogue data. Digital data must be converted before it is communicated. Modern telephone systems are being developed which operate on digital data.

5 Data is often 'scrambled' before being communicated and 'unscrambled' by the receiving computer. This provides data security.

6 Networks provide the basis for 'electronic office' systems.

Questions

1 What do the letters WAN stand for?
2 List three advantages of computer networks.
3 The major difference between wide area and local area networks is _____. Complete the sentence.
4 Draw a diagram of a LAN connected in a 'Star' organization.
5 Why are MODEMS or acoustic couplers needed in a wide area network?
6 In what way will new telephone systems differ from existing systems?

Comprehension Extract

THE GUARDIAN Thursday September 10 1981

Mr Kenneth Baker, the Minister for Information Technology, has called that area of little companies working with microcomputers, assembling the machinery to provide a particular service, Britain's fastest growing industry.

One good example of that work is a board, 18 inches by 16, studded with nearly 200 silicon chips. It looks like a town planner's model of a housing-cum-light industry estate, though produced by a modular-minded planner who detests curves.

It is, of course, a powerful computer, the current equivalent of the elephantine computers of the 1960s—except that it works faster. But the new town analogy is real. Each section of that board has a community function, though for electrons instead of people.

The section of monopoly-board houses, four streets of semi-detacheds south of the main highway, is the memory—the collection of chips that hold the information. You could house a short novel in there.

The five bigger building blocks across the way look like factories and are factories. That is the central processing unit, the cluster of logic chips that do the actual work.

The bit that looks like a power station is a power station—its ugly lumps control the power supply. The long strips at the edge that look like railway stations are railway stations—the input and output channels though which the microscopic world communicates with the clumsier reality outside. And, of course, there is a town clock that is a clock.

The analogy only breaks down beneath the pavements. Such a single-board computer is solid state—no wires required beneath it to carry the messages around. It's all done by road.

That particular board, made by Dicoll Electronics at Basingstoke, adds value to imported microchips by being, in toto, a machine to control factories, in this case any plant producing materials in sheet form. Its prototype has just completed six weeks of round-the-clock work monitoring a paper mill at Basingstoke.

It takes information from transducers spread around the production machinery and translates that data into words, figures, and colour graphics on a display terminal. Thus the foreman can check at a glance that the tension, moisture, and so forth of the paper flowing along the production line is within the allowable tolerances. If it's not, the computer rings the alarm bell.

That board costs £2,600—less if you want several. Its equivalent would have cost at least 100 times as much two decades ago—and you couldn't have found room for it on the factory floor, and it wouldn't have worked there anyway: it would have demanded an air-conditioned room.

Yet that board is only a shade away from the contents of the personal computer you can buy off the shelf.

Questions

1. Explain the meaning of each of these terms used in the article: 'silicon chips', 'the memory', 'central processing unit', 'logic chip', 'input and output channels'.
2. What does the writer mean by: 'the elephantine computers of the 1960's'? Why did they 'demand an air-conditioned room'?
3. The writer makes a comparison (or analogy) between a computer on a board and a new town. Explain each part of this analogy. Where does the analogy break down?
4. Describe in detail how one particular board is used in the paper mill at Basingstoke. What is a transducer?
5. This article was written in 1981. How do you think computers and chips have changed since then?

Wordsearch

Copy this grid into your workbook. In the grid you will find 8 words which are to do with the 'heart of the computer'. The clues will help you.

1. Only two digits are allowed in this number system.
2. Sixteen digits are allowed in this number system.
3. Bytes pass into and out from the computer via this.
4. This stops the computer doing one thing and starts it doing another.
5. This type of storage location is very close to the CPU and is used to store data temporarily.
6. An _____ 'tells' the computer what to do next.
7 & 8 The temperature reading from a thermometer may well have to pass through an _____ to _____ converter before being input to a computer.

HARDWARE WORDSEARCH

```
A R G M H B C Q H K Q O H R L
O I N T E R R U P T X W E A E
F C M G X B C M K Z J T T E C
E A A P A T I U L W S I U C Z
F Z U Q D Q E V I I G G L A X
G R V T E I J O G I O G Y R T
L H Y N C K A E D L R R L O J
Q Y U S I L R J A K P T K P X
V T E T M R I N R H S D F W E
H L X W A C A T A E X D W C T
F D G J L R B E G A S R Q R E
P Y C I N S T R U C T I O N C
T H U Y Z E M A P F P P Q P A
B I N A R Y E H O L X S S L B
O X C N U Q P X I Z G H K S M
```

Case Study
– A washing machine controller

Microprocessors are widely used to control industrial processes and machines. This case study shows how a microprocessor may be used to control the operation of an automatic washing machine. The techniques used in this example apply to many situations in industry.

Using a microprocessor-controlled washing machine

Inputs and outputs

The microprocessor is connected to (or **interfaced** with) various devices within the washing machine.
These are the:
- hot water control valve
- cold water control valve
- water heater
- tub motor
- pump motor

These devices may be controlled by the microprocessor by switching them on or off. They are treated as *output devices* because the microprocessor sends signals *to* them. Two other devices send signals to the microprocessor. These are the:
- 'tub full' indicator
- water thermostat

These are treated as input devices. All the signals pass through input/output ports.

The program in the microprocessor

A program must be written which takes the washing machine through a sequence of steps. This program is stored on the microprocessor and starts to run when the machine is switched on.
The program carries out the following basic actions:
- switches a device on
- waits for a fixed time period by running in a *delay loop* or keeps testing for a condition change
- when the time expires, or the condition changes, the program switches the device off

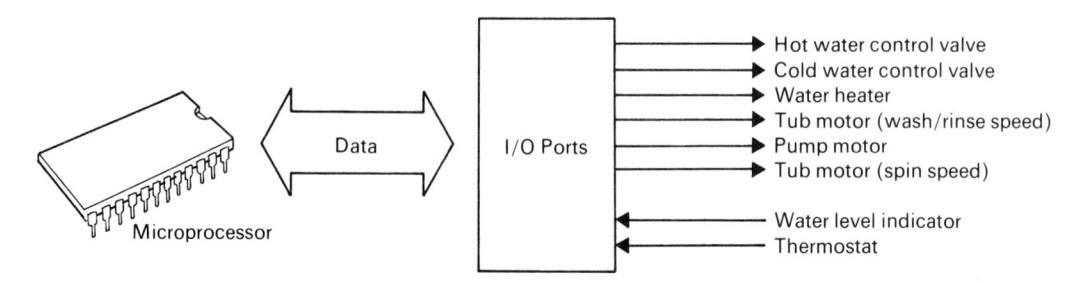

Fig. 5.60 Signals pass through the input/output ports

1. Fill tub with hot water until full.

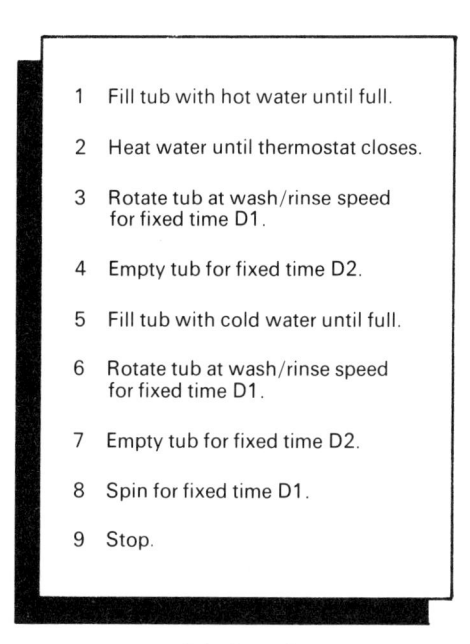

2. Heat water until thermostat closes.

3. Rotate tub at wash/rinse speed for fixed time D1.

4. Empty tub for fixed time D2.

5. Fill tub with cold water until full.

6. Rotate tub at wash/rinse speed for fixed time D1.

7. Empty tub for fixed time D2.

8. Spin for fixed time D1.

9. Stop.

Fig. 5.61 *Simplified wash/rinse sequence for a washing machine*

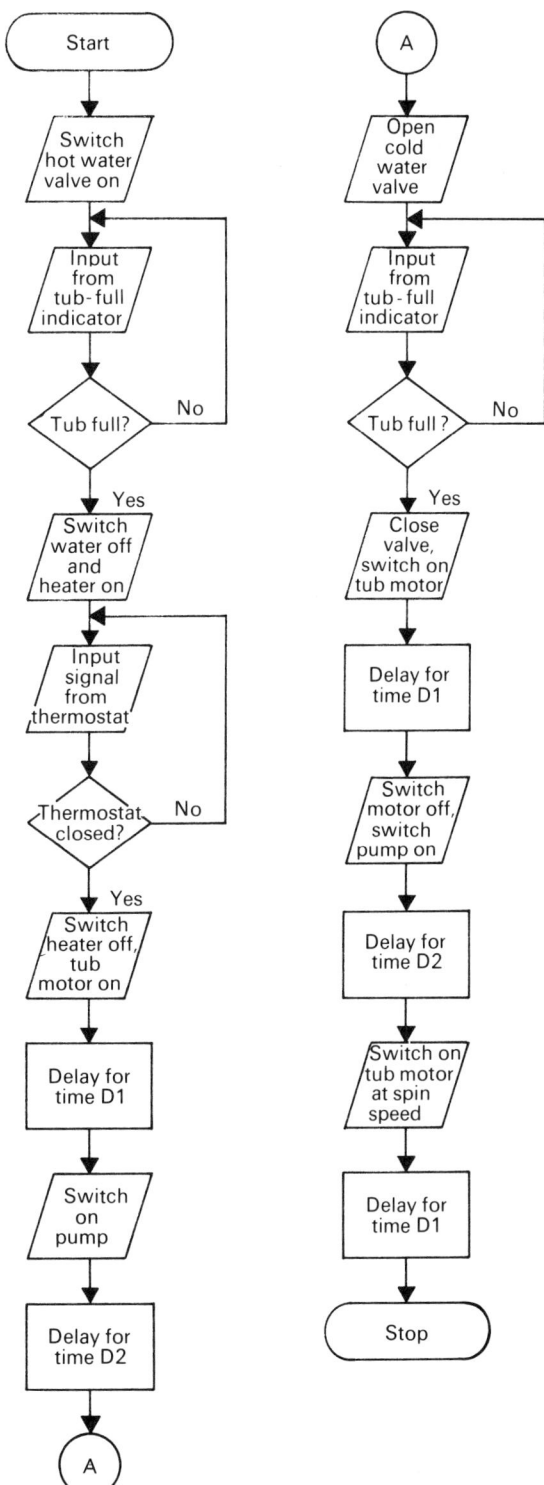

Fig. 5.62 *Flowchart of the wash/rinse sequence*

Delay loops

The delay loops are created by having a set of instructions in the program which are repeatedly executed a fixed number of times. Each instruction in a program takes an exact, known amount of time, e.g. 1000th of a second. Executing an instruction which takes 1000th of a second a thousand times gives a 1 second delay. To do this a loop may be coded into the program to give exact time delays.

This code will take 1 minute to execute, i.e. 60 × 1000 × 1000th of a second. Executing all these instructions 60 times gives a delay of 1 hour, and so on.

Condition testing

To detect a change of condition, e.g. the 'tub not-full' signal changing to 'tub full' signal, the program must keep reading the value of the signal from the input port. This is done by making the program loop, testing the condition each time through the loop. When the condition changes, the program exits from the loop.

Washing machines may be controlled by electro-mechanical methods, but using a microprocessor reduces the number of moving parts and is therefore more reliable.

This case study has taken a simplified wash/rinse and spin cycle as an example. In reality the sequences may be more complicated. Also, a washing machine usually has a choice of several different washing cycles. These can be provided simply by putting different programs onto the microprocessor.

A program may be developed and tested on a computer. When the program is working properly the code may be 'burned' (i.e. permanently stored) onto a PROM chip—this is the microprocessor.

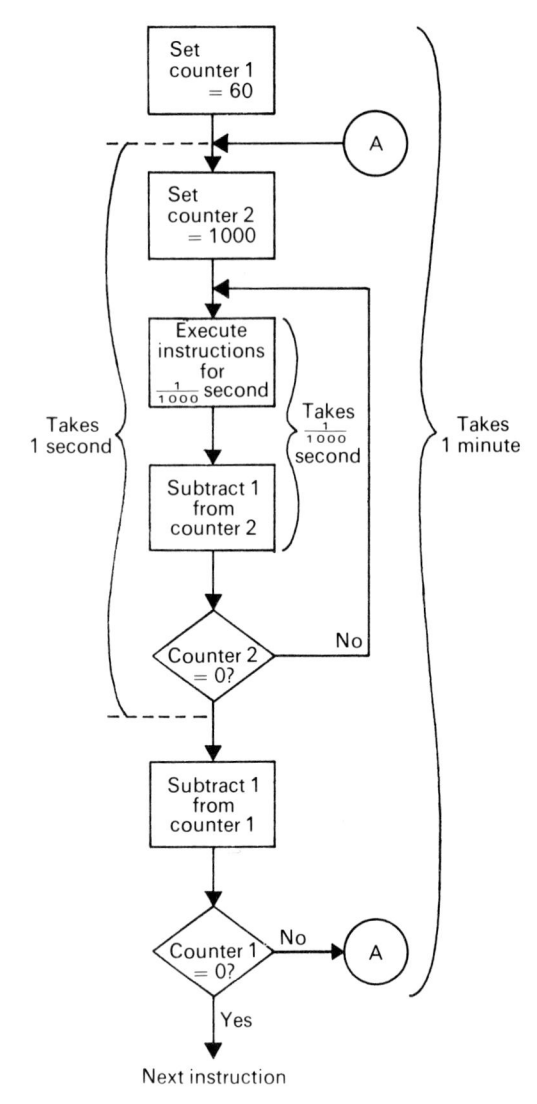

Fig. 5.63 Delay loop for 1 minute duration

Part 6

Putting Computers to Work

6.1 Computer-based systems

Computers are electronic machines which can process vast amounts of data to produce information. To make use of these machines they have to be put into a system. The system may be in a business, an industry or a hospital. This unit describes how computers are used in the real world. It describes computer-based systems.

What computers are good at

Computers are used in industry, business, hospitals, local government, etc. This is because they are very good at doing certain tasks. A lot of these tasks could also be done by people, but a computer can be programmed to do them more quickly or reliably. Computers are good at:
- calculating at very high speed
- inputting and outputting at high speed
- storing and retrieving large amounts of data.

This table shows examples of where those abilities are useful.

What is a system?

The word 'system' is used in all sorts of ways. Just think of some systems you know, for example: the solar system, the central heating system, the cooling system in a car. The list is probably endless.

A computer-based system has three basic parts:

    input ⟶ process ⟶ output

Often, systems have another main part. This is **control**. To 'control' is to keep a check on the process and alter the input or change the process if things aren't right. For example, in a central heating system, the thermostat controls the amount of heat

COMPUTER FACILITY	WHERE USEFUL
Calculate at very high speed	Arithmetic Calculate costs, wages, profits and losses Statistical trends Weather forecasting Space-flight trajectory calculations
Input and output at high speed	Produce wage slips Warehouse contents list Census data—large numbers of questionnaires Item/price tickets Gas, electricity, 'phone bills Personalized mail
Store large amounts of data	Business records Medical records Production plans Weather pictures Maps of the earth, space and sea

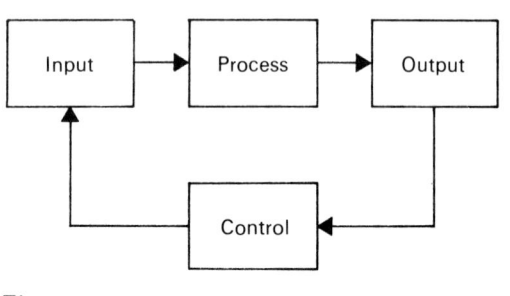

Fig. 6.1

input. If the temperature is too high it causes the boiler to switch off. If the temperature is too low it causes the boiler to switch on.

Data processing

The input to a computer-based system is *data*. It is *processed* to produce *information* as output. This is called **data processing**.

Example 1 A warehouse system.
- inputs: number of items leaving
  and number of items coming in (data)
- process: add items in to stock level
  and subtract items out from stock level
- output: new stock level (information).

Control information may be a message: 'Stock level too low—order more stock.' The warehouse manager could inform the buyer who may act upon this information and buy more stock.

Example 2 Warehouse movements rates.
- input: the date the item was last taken out of stock
- process: compare this date with 'slow movements date'
- output: 'Stock item movement too slow'.

The sales manager may then start a sales campaign to increase sales of this item.

These examples show how data is used as input to a system. This data is processed to produce output information. This information may then be used to make decisions.

The process part of a computer-based system can be made up from computer programs, but part of the processing may also be carried out by people. The next unit describes some of the jobs involved in creating and running computer-based systems.

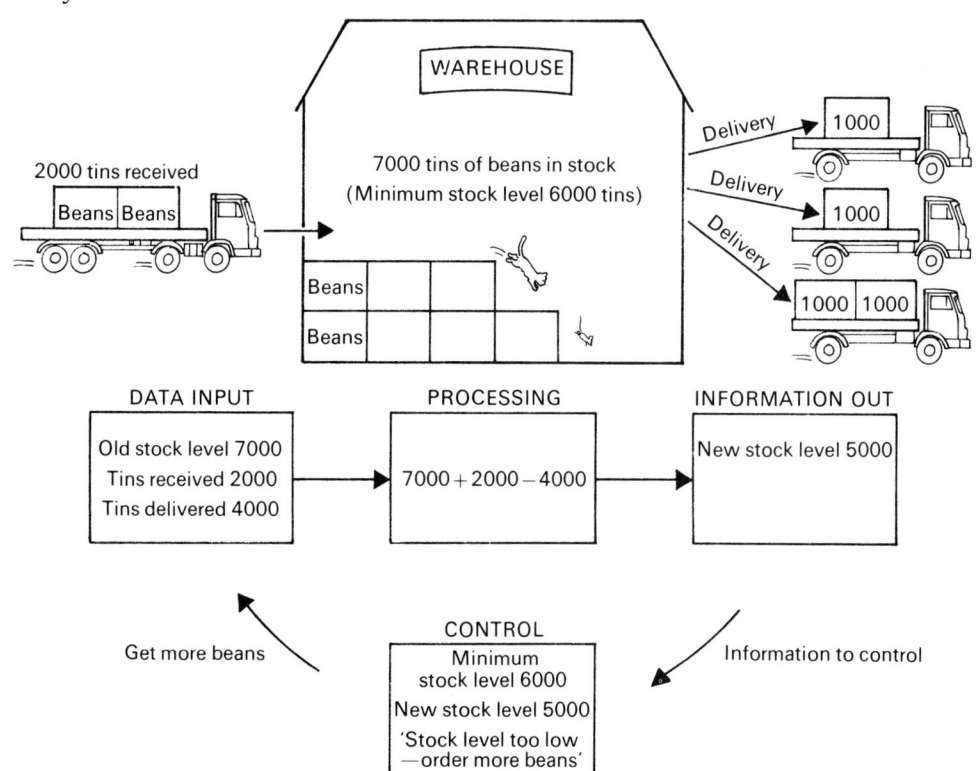

Fig. 6.2 *Stock control in a warehouse*

> **KEY POINTS**
>
> 1 Computers are used in many situations because they are good at:
>   - calculating at high speed
>   - inputting/outputting at high speed
>   - storing large amounts of data.
>
> 2 The word 'system' is used in lots of ways. Generally, a system is a 'complex whole made up of connected parts arranged to work together'.
>
> 3 Computer-based systems have: input, process, output and control as their main elements.
>
> 4 Data is input and processed to produce output, the output is called information.
>
> 5 Computer programs and people are involved in computer-based systems.

Questions

1 Complete the following sentences.
   a) A computer-based system has 3 basic parts, these are _____, _____, and _____.
   b) _____ is used to check a process and alter the inputs or process.

2 What does 'data processing' mean?

3 Write a few sentences describing what computers are good at and why they are used in organizations.

6.2 People who work with computers

People are involved with computers in lots of ways. Many people use computers in their work to help them. Other people are employed in producing computer-based systems. This unit identifies some of the jobs in producing computer-based systems.

CREATING THE SYSTEM	RUNNING THE SYSTEM
Systems analyst Systems designer Programmer	Computer operator Data controller Data preparation clerk

Jobs in creating and running computer-based systems

The jobs in the computer department are of two types:
- those involved in creating computer-based systems
- those involved in running the systems.

People are also needed to design, build and maintain the computer hardware. They are usually employed by the computer equipment manufacturers.

Systems analysts, designers and programmers create the computer systems

Engineers build and maintain the hardware

Users use the hardware and systems to help at their jobs

A large computer system has computer operators, a data controller and data preparation clerks to run the user's programs

Fig. 6.3 Jobs involved in creating and running computer-based systems

Systems analyst A systems analyst studies the way an organization operates. The organization may be a commercial or industrial company, national or local government department, hospital board, etc. The work of the systems analyst is in setting up and maintaining computer-based systems in an organization.

Systems designer A systems designer takes the results of the systems analysis and:
- designs the inputs to the new system
- designs the processes to be carried out on the data
- designs the outputs and control procedures for the system.

The designer considers both the computer *and* the person using the computer in the design. He/she draws up **systems flowcharts** (see unit 6.4) to describe the new system to managers, users, etc. The designer will also specify the functions of computer programs in the new system.

Computer programmer The computer programmer takes the **specification** for a computer program then writes and tests the program.

The project team The analyst, designer and programmer often work as a **project team** on the development of a new system. It is important that each member of the team understands what is required of them. Each member writes down the details of what they are doing. This is called **documentation**. A project team will use a standard way of documenting their work, so that each member understands what the other is doing.

Computer operator If the computer being used is a large mainframe computer it needs one or more people to operate it. The operators have responsibility for the computer's operation. They have to:
- load/unload magnetic tapes and disks and printers
- ensure the computer is running properly.

(When a minicomputer or microcomputer is being used it is often not necessary to have a computer operator.)

Data controllers With mainframe computers running a batch input/output system (see Unit 4.2) data control staff might be needed. Their job is to organize all the inputs and outputs for the computer. With these systems the input and output is often in large 'batches'. The right input data and running instructions must be provided for each job. When completed, all the output has to be sent to the right user. The output is usually on continuous stationery. This needs to be split and identified before sending to the user.

Data preparation Often a large amount of data is required for input to a batch run. Users may enter this data on coding forms by hand. The input to the computer may be required on punched card, paper tape or magnetic tape. Usually, magnetic tape is used.

Data preparation is the process of transferring data from handwritten forms onto magnetic tape. The data preparation operator sits at a keyboard, reads the handwritten data and types this on the keyboard. The data is then stored on magnetic disk or tape for input to the computer. (Unit 2.1 gives a detailed description of this process.) The data controller usually arranges the input to the computer.

Data preparation and data control clerks are not needed with **direct data entry systems**. Users enter their data and receive output at a terminal. With these systems the amount of input and output is small.

How the jobs fit together

Those who created the system will also often need to maintain it. They should correct any problems which arise when the system is running. This table shows how the jobs arise in the 'lifetime' of a system.

ANALYSE THE SYSTEM	DESIGN THE SYSTEM	WRITE THE PROGRAMS	TEST THE SYSTEM	RUN THE SYSTEM	MAINTAIN THE SYSTEM
Analyst	Designer	Programmer	Programmer Analyst Designer	Operators Data prep Control	Programmer Analyst Designer

Lifetime of the system ⟶

The next two units will look in more detail at the work of the systems analyst and systems designer.

● **KEY POINTS**

1 Computer-based systems are created and run by people.

2 People who use computers are often called users.

3 The main jobs in creating and running computer-based systems are:
- systems analyst
- systems designer
- computer programmer
- computer operator
- data controller
- data preparation clerk.

4 The systems analysts, systems designers and computer programmers create the system. They may also be involved in maintaining the system once it is running.

Questions

1 Name the three jobs involved in creating a computer-based system.

2 Copy out these sentences and fill in the blanks.
a) The person responsible for the analysis of a business system to assess its suitability for computer application is the _____.
(ALSEB 1983)
b) Data preparation staff are not needed for direct data entry systems because _____.

3 Why is documentation needed when developing a computer-based system?

4*a) Name three types of computer personnel in a typical data-processing installation.
b) For one of these types, describe the essential duties.
(OLE)

*'O'-Level question

145

6.3 Defining the system: systems analysis

Using a computer in an organization does not automatically mean improvements. A lot of thought should be given to what the changes brought about might mean. Systems analysis is the process of investigating current systems and suggesting improvements.

What the systems analyst does: a summary

The job of the systems analyst is to set up and maintain computer-based systems in an organization. The duties of a systems analyst are to:
- investigate how existing information is used in the existing systems in the organization
- report on the failings of the existing system
  (These may be high costs, delays and high clerical effort.)
- analyse the findings so that they may be used to improve the system
- suggest how the system may be improved and examine the feasibility of suggested improvements.

(The suggestions for improvements may or may not include using a computer.)

Systems investigation

Fact finding Before making any suggestions for changes the analyst must have a good understanding of the organization. He must establish the *facts* about the way the organization runs. This may be done in several ways. These are:
- reading reports about the structure of the organization
- interviewing personnel involved in the current system
- observing the processes in the current system
- examining documents used in the current system.

The aim of these investigations is to gain an understanding of the system and the people involved.

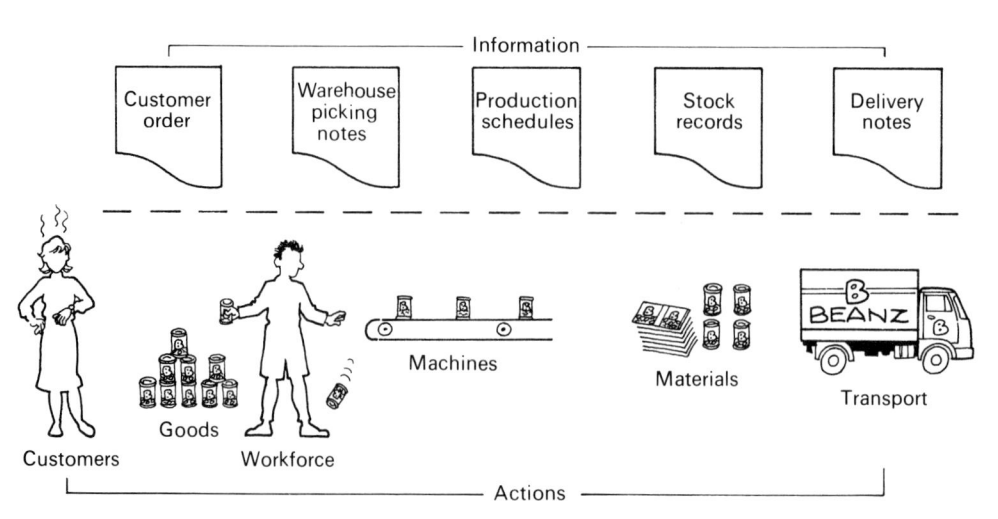

Fig. 6.4 Factors which the systems analyst must take into account

Interviewing Talking to people involved in the current system is very important—these people will know best about what they do. They will also feel that they should be involved in any changes being made—they will be the users of the new system. However, the analyst should be able to understand the whole system. An individual involved in the system may only understand their personal involvement.

People often feel threatened by change and suspicious of new ways of working. It is important that the analyst works *with* the users rather than against them. Often a written report of the interviews is made and a copy kept by the interviewer and interviewee.

Reporting on the current system

Having established all the facts about the current system, the analyst should report on these. The report should consist of:
- a description of current procedures
- a description of information flows in the system and documents used
- a report on where time delays occur or where a piece of information is difficult to obtain from the system
- suggestions about where procedures may be improved.

This report will then be passed to the managers in the organization. If the managers think it is worth improving procedures then they will ask the analyst to carry out a more detailed study. This study should include suggestions about what the new system should provide.

Feasibility

The proposed system might involve:
- buying new computer hardware
- writing or buying new computer software
- changing people's jobs.

Computer hardware and software are expensive. Software can take a long time to write. People can object to having their jobs changed.

The analyst should examine the feasibility of the proposed system. This means that costs, time and people should be considered. A new system will not be feasible if:
- the costs of creating or running it are too high
- it will take too much time to set up or run it
- the existing staff refuse or are not able to operate it.

Software packages Not all organizations have their own programmers, or their programmers cannot produce the programs in time or cheaply enough. Software development time and costs may be reduced by buying an applications or **software package**. A software package is a set of programs which are written by a **software house**. The package is designed to do a particular job, for example, to calculate the payroll for a business. Buying a software package is like buying a ready-made suit. The package is written for general use. It may be 'tailored' to suit a particular organization. This is usually cheaper than writing new software just for one application. The disadvantage is that the package might not do the exact job required.

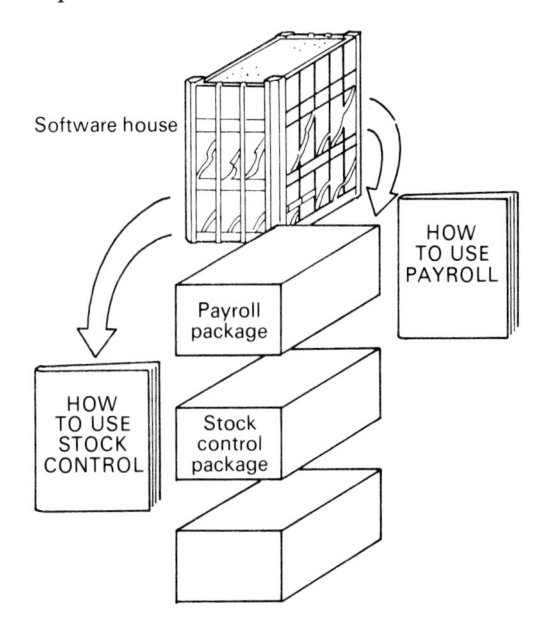

Fig. 6.5 *A software package is a set of programs written by programmers who work for a software house*

Computer bureaux An organization may want to buy its own computer equipment but not all organizations would find it feasible to buy their own computer. They may use a **computer bureau** to run their programs. Computer bureaux have computers and hire out computer time. Data is sent from an organization to the computer bureau. The bureau processes the data on its computer and sends back the output.

The input and output data can be transferred manually. This means taking the input data to the bureau on magnetic tape or punched cards. Computer print-outs are then taken back. Another method is to send input and output data over telephone lines.

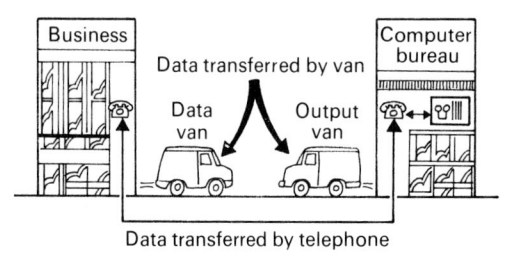

Fig. 6.6 Computer bureaux hire out time on their computer to businesses

The bureau charges according to the amount of processing time used. It may also carry out the data preparation.

The advantages and disadvantages of using a computer bureau are shown in the table.

ADVANTAGES	DISADVANTAGES
Organization does not have to buy and maintain computing equipment	Charges for time may be high
	Time lost in data transfer
	Difficulties sorting out errors

Invitation to tender If new computer hardware *is* to be purchased then the likely costs have to be discovered. An *invitation to tender* is sent to hardware suppliers. This asks the supplier to suggest equipment and costs for a system. The analyst can then discover who the best supplier might be. Sometimes particular software might only run on certain hardware. This means that the choice of suppliers might be limited.

Making the final decision

The report produced by the systems analyst may or may not be accepted by management. If the report is accepted, the go-ahead will be given to design the new system. The report could contain one or several proposals. The design of the new system should be based upon the specification in the report. Systems design is described in the next unit.

Fig. 6.7 The systems analyst reports to management

> **KEY POINTS**
>
> 1 Systems analysis involves examining existing information usage and flows in an organization.
> 2 The aim is to discover any problem areas such as time delays, high costs, etc. Any findings are analysed so that an improved system may be created.
> 3 The existing system is examined by interview, observation and reading information about the organization.
> 4 A report on the improvements is made, including a feasibility study.
> 5 A feasibility study should consider costs, time and people.
> 6 Software costs may be reduced by using a software package.
> 7 Computer bureaux may be considered to avoid buying a computer.
> 8 If new hardware is to be purchased costs are established by inviting hardware suppliers to tender their prices.

Questions

1*Describe briefly three duties of a systems analyst.
(OLE)

2 The systems analyst can 'find the facts' about a system by doing what?

3 A set of specialized programs and associated documentation to carry out a task, e.g. stock control, is _____. Complete the sentence.
(ALSEB 1983)

4 A company decides to use a computer to keep its accounts.
a) The accounts data can be processed by a standard package or by programs written by programmers working in the company. State one advantage for each method of processing.
b) The company could use a bureau to process the data, or could use its own computer. Give one advantage for each method.
(LREB 1983)

5*A shoe manufacturing company, which does not use a computer, has requested the advice of a systems analyst. By considering the following activities within the company, describe what the systems analyst might do:
a) the buying, storage and use of raw materials
b) the control of the distribution of the finished products from the warehouse.
(SUJB 1982)

*'O'-Level question

6.4 Designing the system: systems design

Systems analysis produces the starting point for designing the new system. This provides an outline of what is expected from it. The designer has the job of turning this idea into reality.

What is systems design?

Systems design is the process of defining all the activities and information flows in the new system. It involves:
- defining computer procedures
- defining clerical (human) procedures
- designing new documents and files for transferring and storing information.

Systems flowcharts

Systems flowcharts may be used to help in the design of a system. As in programming, standard symbols are used to stand for particular elements of the flowchart. Flowlines are used to show the next element in the flowchart. The symbols suggested by the National Computing Centre (NCC) are shown below.

Systems flowcharts may be used to show:
- a general sequence of events and data flows in a system
- a computer run chart
- a clerical procedure.

	Symbol	Type of chart: System	Clerical procedure	Computer procedure	Computer run
1	 ▭	All operations			
2	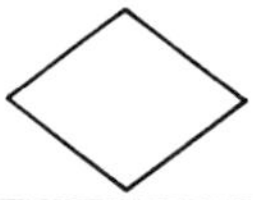 ◇	All decisions			
3	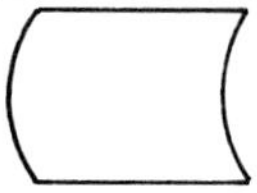 ⟅⟆	All storage media, both permanent and temporary		Not used	Computer backing storage
4	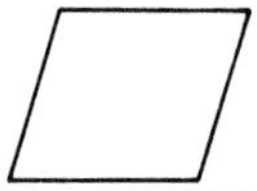 ▱		Individual document or set of documents	Not used	Data passing between the computer and the non-computer parts of the system
5	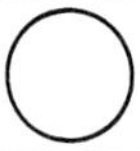 ○	Connector, to show continuity between symbols, where it is not possible to join them by a flowline			
6	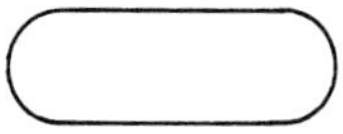 ▢	Terminal, to show entry to or exit from a procedure			
7	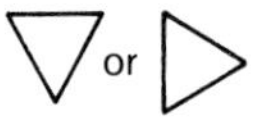 ▽ or ▷	Data moving from one location to another		Not used	Transmission by communications link

Fig. 6.8 Systems flowchart symbols

Figure 6.9 is a chart showing the daily routine of a system for processing sales orders. It shows all the general things that happen when an order is received. Notice how the chart is split into columns—SALES, COMPUTER, WAREHOUSE, DESPATCH, POSTROOM. These are the departments involved. Starting at 1) and working through the chart, you should be able to tell how information flows through the system. Some of the boxes show where information is filed. Some show where information is processed. Others show information passing to another department, process or file. (Don't worry if you can't understand some of the words used in the chart, e.g. sales ledger, invoice, etc.) Drawing up this chart helps the systems designer understand what happens in the system.

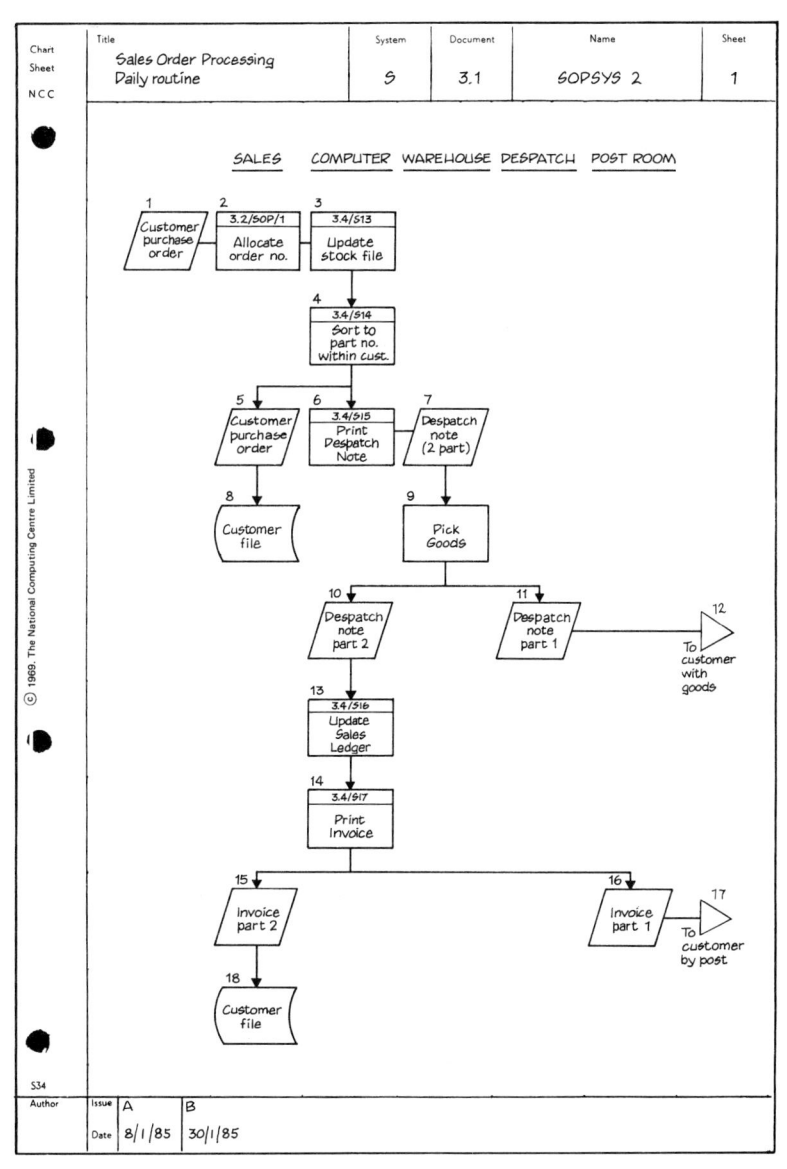

Fig. 6.9 *Flowchart of one system for processing sales orders*

The systems flowchart of a clerical procedure (Figure 6.10) shows the information flows and processes in a **manual system**. A manual system is one where all the processing is done without using a computer. This chart helps the designer understand the human involvement and where this might change.

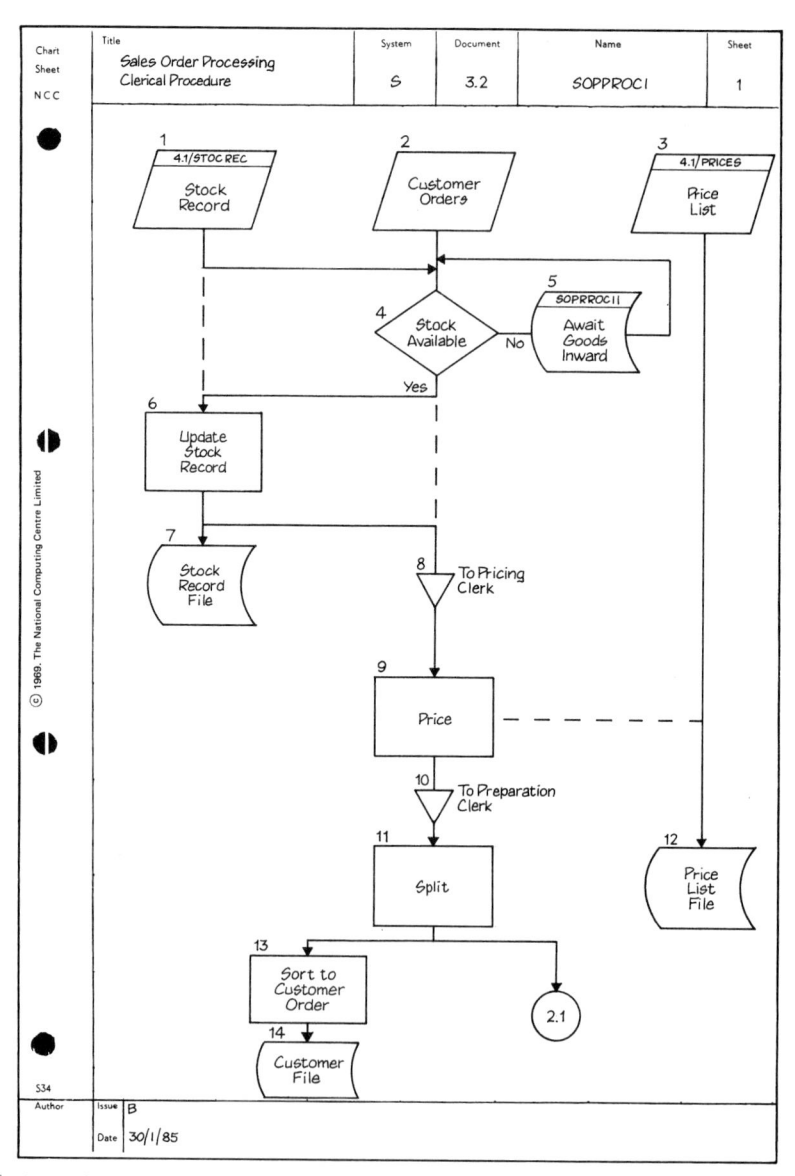

Fig. 6.10 A clerical procedure (manual system)

Figure 6.11 is a **computer run chart**. This shows the computer processes in a system.

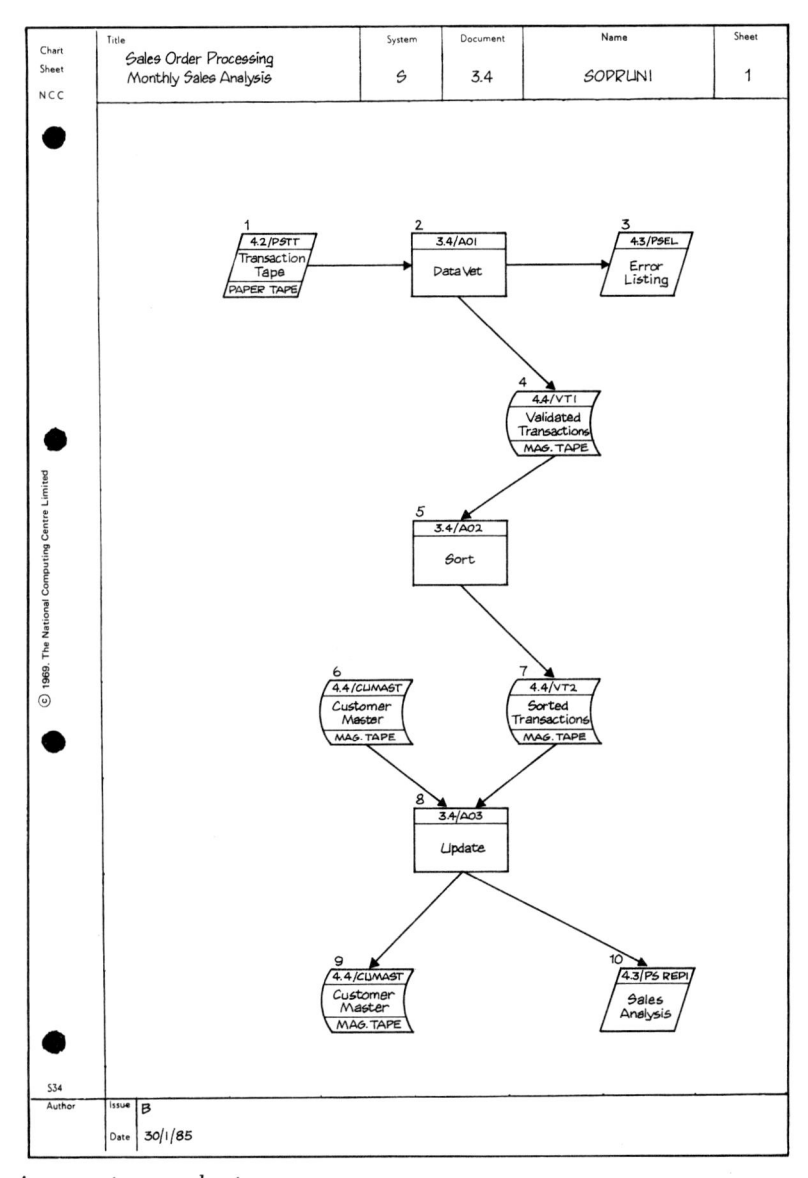

Fig. 6.11 A computer run chart

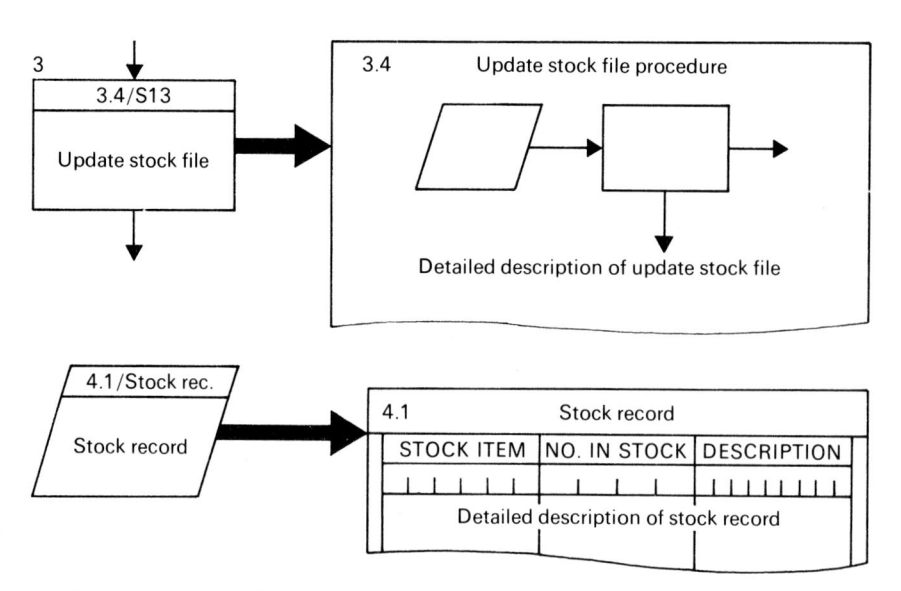

Fig. 6.12 References to more detailed descriptions

How the charts are used

Each of these charts may show how the existing system operates. By studying these the designer can gain a good understanding of the system. The new system is then described using a revised chart.

Note that the clerical procedure and computer run charts are detailed descriptions of processes. The general description shows where these processes fit in to the system.

In some of the boxes there are numbers and letters. The number and letters are references to the more detailed description of a process, document or file.

By using these charts the designer can describe the whole system on paper. This is called the **documentation** of the system. It is used to help the systems designer understand the system. It also describes the system to other people.

Collecting the data: choosing the data acquisition method

The designer has to decide on the best way to obtain the data. There are scores of input methods. Unit 2.1 describes some of the input devices available. Some systems require the input *on-line*, others *off-line*.

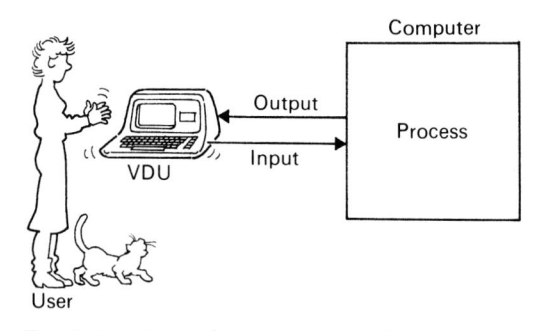

Fig. 6.13 Data which is input and used immediately is said to be on-line

Input on-line If data is input and used immediately in the system it is said to be processed on-line. This is useful when results of processing the data are required quickly.

Input off-line With off-line working, data is input and then processed at a later time. This is useful if lots of separate data items are required before the computer processes them. All the separate lots of data can be batched together before processing.

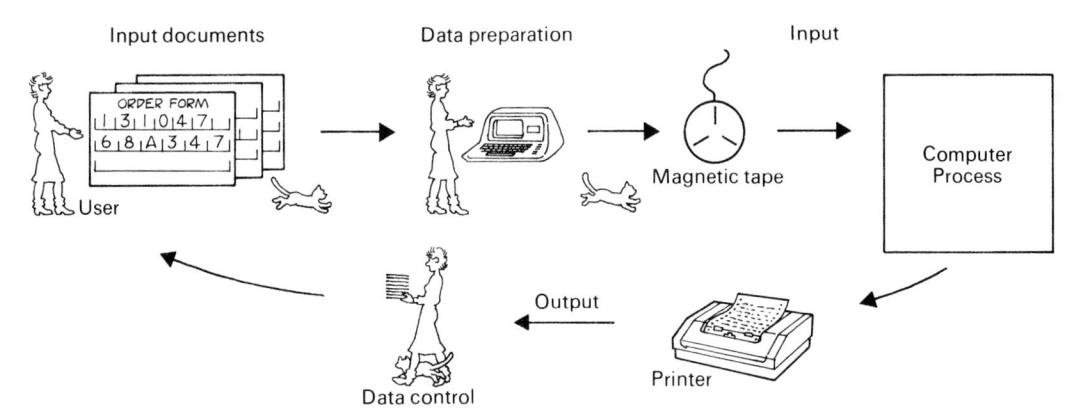

Fig. 6.14 Off-line processing

The diagram below lists some of the devices which are used for on-line data collection. They are examples of direct data entry devices.

- Visual display unit
- Hand-held data logger
- Light pen
- Laser reader
- Magnetic strip cards
- Data logging devices
- Pre-punched card readers

→ Computer

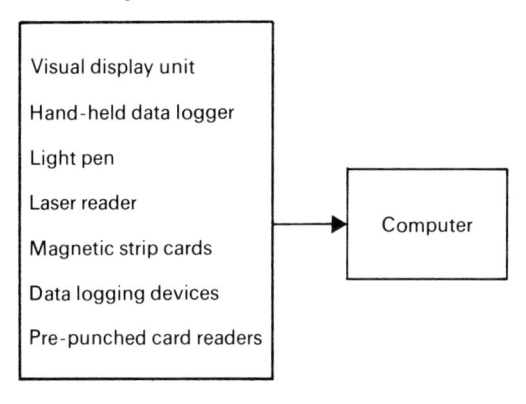

Fig. 6.15 Some direct data entry devices

Off-line data entry is done by writing the data down on **coding documents**. The written data is then keyed-in to the computer later. For example, every ten years when a National Census survey is held, the coding documents (census documents) are sent to each household. When completed they are sent to the Census Surveys Office. The data is then keyed on to magnetic tape or disk and processed by the computer.

In the above example on-line data collection would not be possible. However, cheaper on-line data collection devices have meant that more and more data is collected on-line. For example, electricity meter readings can now be collected on-line. (The traditional way of doing this is off-line.)

The portable billing machine receives data from the computer in preparation for the meter reader's day's work

Keying-in the meter reading

Handing over the bill

On-line meter reading

Design of input and output

The input and output to a computer system involves communication with *people*. So, a lot of thought should go into designing input and output layouts.

Off-line input: punch documents If data is collected off-line it is usually first entered on a 'punch document'. This should be designed so that it is easy to use for:
- the person filling in the document
- the data preparation clerk.

Each item of information should be clearly defined to reduce incorrect entry and keying of data.

As there may be several different types of documents used in a system, each type should be identified. This may be done by giving each one a different name or colour.

On-line input For on-line processing the VDU is usually the input and output device. One approach to designing the input is to display an input 'form'. Each entry item name is displayed with blanks for the value to be entered. The form is accepted when completed. Another approach is for the computer to ask for the next data item. For example:

ENTER NAME   ← (displayed by the computer)

JOE BLOGGS   ← (entered by operator)

As for off-line documents, the design should be easy to use.

Off-line output: print layout Off-line output is usually to a printer. The printer uses continuous stationery, i.e. a continuous sheet of paper perforated at every 'page'. The paper may be plain or **pre-printed**. If plain paper is used, the print program should print headings. The detail should be easy to read.

'Pre-printed stationery' is paper with headings and other information already printed onto it. The computer 'fills in the blanks' on the paper. An example of printing on pre-printed stationery is your telephone, gas or electricity bill. Try looking at your gas bill to see if you can identify the pre-printed and computer-printed parts.

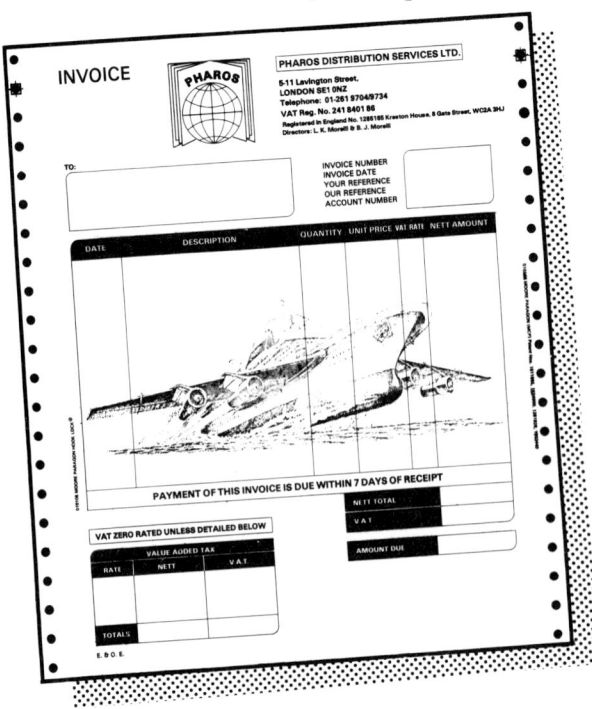

Fig. 6.16 This invoice is an example of pre-printed computer stationery

On-line output On-line output is usually to a VDU. This is useful if an instant response is required. For instance, in a ticket booking system the ticket agent can tell the customer straight away if tickets are available. However, if the information needs to be recorded it is better to print the output.

The system designer must design input and output very carefully. Badly-designed input and output can make the system difficult to use. The chance of making errors is increased, which reduces the effectiveness of the system.

Checking the input data: verification and validation

Computer-based systems have the ability to process data very quickly and to produce accurate and useful information. However, if there are errors in the data the computer can produce a lot of inaccurate and useless information. To avoid this, the input data should be checked as much as possible for errors. The checking for errors should be done at the *input* stage of a system.

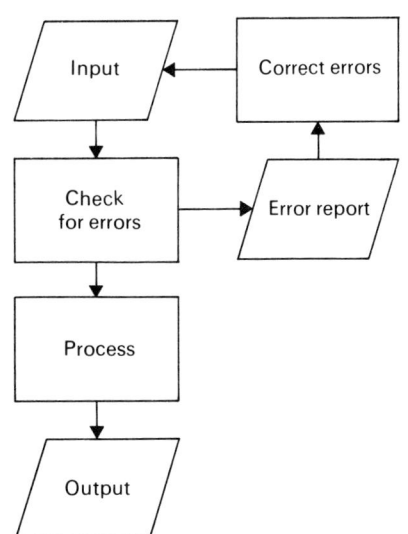

Fig. 6.17 Checking input for errors

Verifying data Off-line data entry involves a data preparation clerk keying data from an input document. There is a chance that the clerk will mis-key the data, so a second clerk keys the data a second time. The two results are compared and if they are different, a keying error has occurred. This type of input data checking is called **verification**.

A common error is that two digits in a number are keyed in the wrong order. For example:

```
Input_____2 1 2 4 3 1 5
Keyed_____2 1 4 2 3 1 5
```
These two digits have been swapped

Validating data Data **validation** is the process of checking that data is reasonable and accurate. There are several ways of checking that data is valid.

1 **Range checks**: check that a data item is within a range of values. For example, a pupil's age will be within the range—older than 4, younger than 18.

2 **Probability checks**: check that a value is reasonable. For example, a value for a person's weight is probably wrong if it is more than 112 kg.

3 **Consistency checks**: check that one data item is consistent with another. For example, if a person's age is less than 16 they are probably not married. Other examples are checks on car registration numbers, postal codes, etc. These are codes which have a particular **format**. A letter is allowed in part of the code, a number in other parts. Checks can be made for the correct format.

4 **Check digits**: are used to check code which has been entered wrongly, but which still appears valid and passes the checks mentioned above. The check digit is a digit which is put on the end of a code. It has a value which is the correct result of a calculation carried out on the rest of the code. The calculation is performed on the code. If the answer is equal to the check digit, the code is valid. If the answer is not equal, the code is not valid. Check digits are a very effective way of detecting when two digits have been keyed in the wrong order.

Every book has a check digit in its International Standard Book Number (ISBN). Can you find the ISBN for this book? (It is on the cover and at the front of the book—ISBN 0 216 91648 8.) The check digit is the last of the 10 numbers. It is known as a 'modulo 11' check digit because of the way it is calculated.

The original code number is written down and multiplied as shown.

$$\begin{aligned} 0 \times 10 &= 0 \\ 2 \times 9 &= 18 \\ 1 \times 8 &= 8 \\ 6 \times 7 &= 42 \\ 9 \times 6 &= 54 \\ 1 \times 5 &= 5 \\ 6 \times 4 &= 24 \\ 4 \times 3 &= 12 \\ 8 \times 2 &= 16 \\ \hline & 179 \end{aligned}$$

The results are added together to give the total: 179. This is next divided by 11.

$$\frac{179}{11} = 16 \text{ remainder } 3$$

The remainder is subtracted from 11.
$$11 - 3 = 8$$
This is the check digit.

How validation is done The input data is first processed by a **validation program**. This program contains the code which carries out all the validation checks on the data. If a data item passes the checks it is accepted. If it fails a check it is rejected. Usually the program will output a message. This message will say whether the data is valid or not valid.

The systems designer tells the programmer what checks to put into the validation program. The user corrects the data errors and re-enters the data.

This unit has described the system design process, and the design of inputs and outputs. Data is also stored in systems and this involves using computer files. The next unit describes computer files and how they are used.

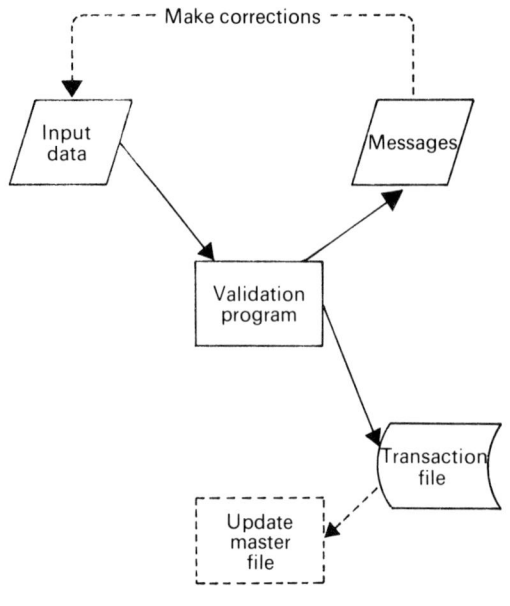

Fig. 6.19 *The validation program in a batch system*

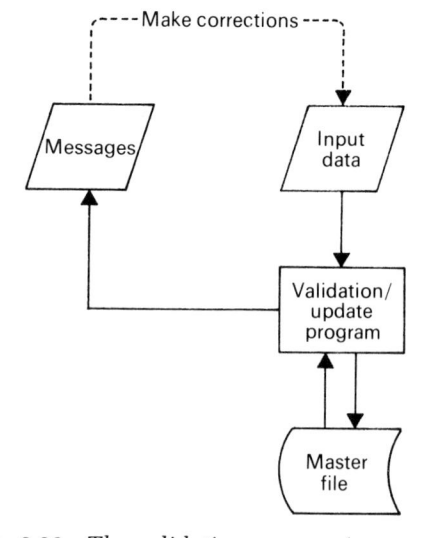

Fig. 6.20 *The validation program in an on-line system*

> **KEY POINTS**
>
> 1 Systems design is the job of defining a new system or changes to an existing one.
>
> 2 Systems flowcharts are used to document the system. They are used to show events, data flows, computer runs and clerical procedures in a system.
>
> 3 The designer chooses the method of data acquisition, getting data into the system. The inputs must be carefully considered. Poorly-designed input/output can reduce the effectiveness of a system.
>
> 4 Data verification and validation should be done as data is input to a system. This reduces the errors that might occur in the data.

Questions

1 Complete the following sentence. Systems design is the process of _____.

2 _____ are used to document the system. Complete the sentence.

3 Explain the difference between a program flowchart and a systems flowchart.
(London 1982)

4*For each of the applications given below state whether the method of data processing would be off-line/on-line, real time/batch. In each case give one reason for your choice.
a) A bank cash dispenser which can also give a report of the current balance in a customer's account.
b) An examination board system for collecting marks from examiners using mark sense forms.
c) An automatic device in a car which can set and maintain a given speed on a motorway.
(AEB 1983)

5*Explain the difference between verifying and validating data and briefly describe two different methods used in validation.
(SUJB 1983)

6*Describe clearly one named scientific or engineering application for a computer (for example, weather forecasting, computer-aided design, simulation of processes, process control). Include in your description:
a) the data needed, where it comes from, how it is checked, and how it is organized
b) the output produced
c) the nature of the calculations which take place
d) the advantages and the disadvantages of using a computer for this work.
(OLE)

7*a) Describe the analysis and design work which must precede the computerization of a task which was previously done manually.
b) What problems are likely to arise during the changeover?
c) What are the likely effects on employment?
(SUJB 1983)

*'O'-Level question

6.5 Files in a system

A computer can store data for long periods of time. If data is stored it has to be easy to get at—the computer has to 'know' where the right data is. This unit describes how data is stored and accessed using files.

Files, records and fields

Go into most offices and you will see a filing cabinet. The filing cabinet has drawers. In the drawers will usually be **files**. The files might be envelopes, folders or boxes. In the files will be information about a particular subject. The subject in the example is school reports. A particular school report is a **record**.

To get to the school report required you would:
Go to the correct filing cabinet
Open the correct drawer
Pull out the file required
Take the report wanted from the file
Hopefully, the report file contains a record of all the information required. Each of the items of information is called a **field**, e.g. date of birth, name, sex, etc.

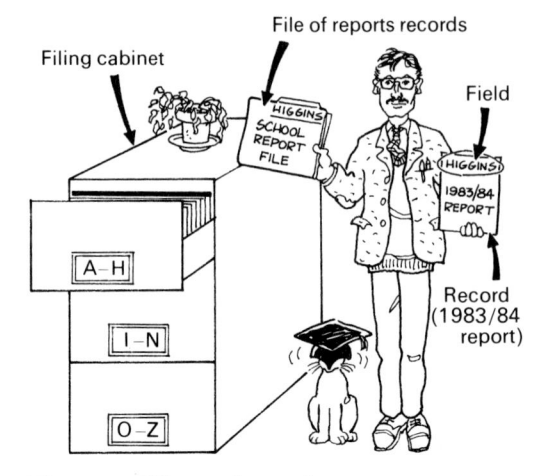

Fig. 6.21 Files and records

Computer files are basically organized in the same way. The difference is that the files and records are stored not in filing cabinets, but on magnetic tape or magnetic disk.

A file contains several records and each record contains many fields. For example, in the file of school reports, each record contains the date of birth as a field. The *value* of the data items may be different in each record. HIGGINS' date of birth is different to HILL's date of birth.

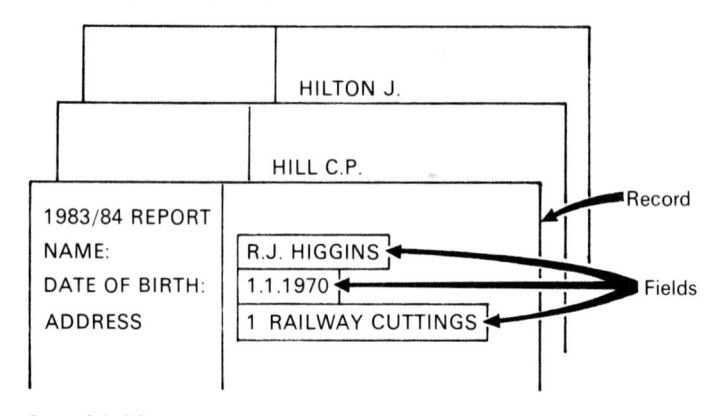

Fig. 6.22 Records and fields

160

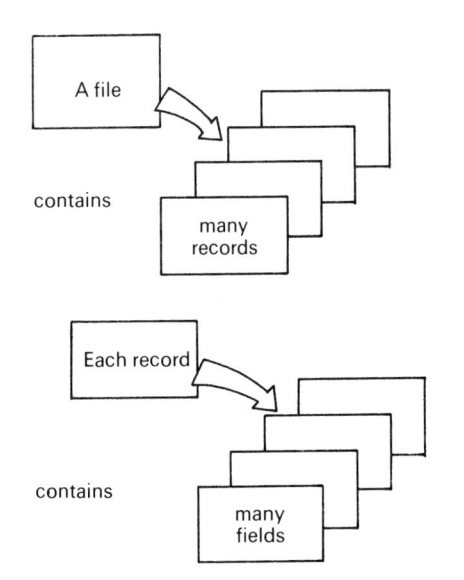

Fig. 6.23

Computer files To get at (or access) computer files and records you need a computer program. When a program writes the data onto the tape or disk it must be possible to read the data again. The program must 'know' where the data is. This is done by writing data to a file. By reading the correct file, the data can be extracted again.

Finding the right file Magnetic tapes and disks can store a large amount of data. Several files can be stored on one disk or tape. So, each file must have a name, e.g. SCHOOL REPORT FILE.

Before reading from or writing to a file, the correct file must be accessed. The file to be processed by a program is 'opened' by an instruction in the program. The OPEN instruction will give the name of the file to be accessed.

Finding the right record: record keys To get the right record from a file you need to know the name of the record. The name of a record is known as the **key**. The key to a record could be any field or several fields on the record. For example, in the school reports file a report is found by looking for the name of the pupil. To be able to do this, the name must appear in the same place in each record in the file. The key must also have a unique value for each record. Imagine that there are two R J HIGGINS in the school. One has an excellent report, one has a bad report. How does the headmaster know which parent should be sent which report? To be useful a key must:
- appear in the same position in each record
- have a unique value in the file.

Since two people may have the same name a person's name is not a useful key. Often a **code** is used to identify a record. Each pupil might be given a pupil number—this is a code number. Each pupil number will be *unique*.

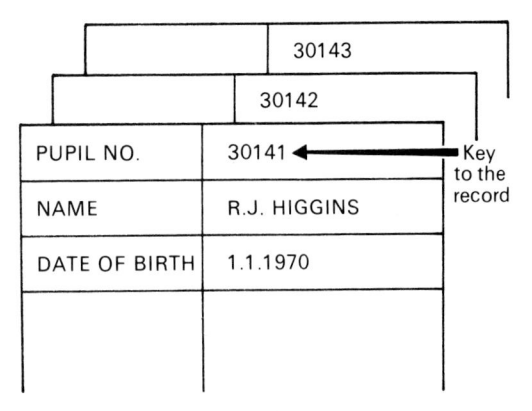

Fig. 6.24 *Keys to records*

How files are organized

Files may be organized in several ways. Some methods of organization allow records to be accessed *directly*. Other methods require starting at the beginning of the file and going through the file, one record at a time. These two forms of accessing are called **direct access** and **serial** or **sequential access**.

Serial or sequential access To read the file the computer has to start at the first record in the file. Each record is read in turn until the correct one is found. The program checks each key by comparing it with a known value.

Fig. 6.25 Sequential file in pupil number order

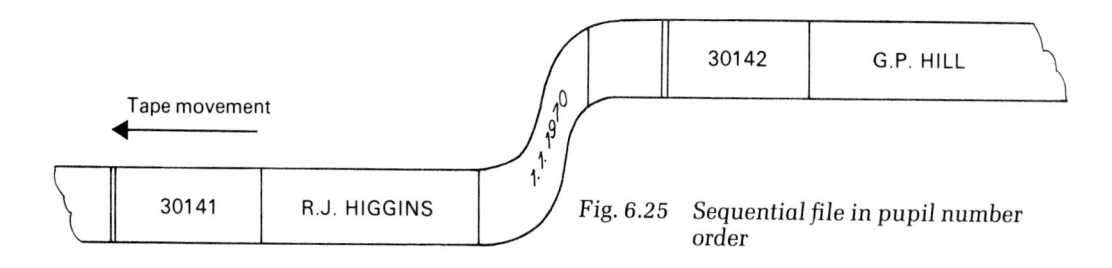

To find HIGGINS' report; for example, the computer would proceed as follows:

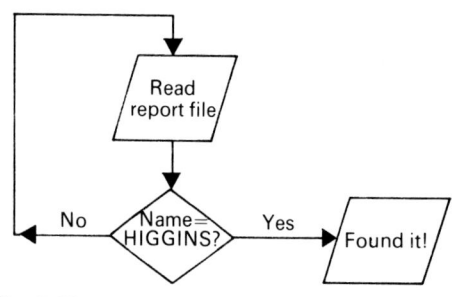

Fig. 6.26

New records are written at the end of the file (serial), or at a position dependant upon the value of the key (sequential). Writing new records often involves creating a new version of the file. A file is organized *serially* if there is *no* sequence to the record keys. It is organized *sequentially* if there *is* a sequence to the record keys.

For example, the SCHOOL REPORT FILE records might be accessed by name. The records could be organized alphabetically in name order. This means names beginning with 'A' first, 'B' second and so on. The file would be organized sequentially in name order. If there were no alphabetic order to the records it would be organized serially, i.e. no particular order.

Direct access With direct access methods the key item is used to access the record directly. In this case the program goes straight to the record required. No other records have to be read. This method accesses the record required far more quickly than the sequential method.

The table below shows which file organization can be used with which storage medium.

SEQUENTIAL/ SERIAL	DIRECT ACCESS
Magnetic tape Disk Floppy disk Winchester disk	Disk Floppy disk Winchester disk

File organization and storage media

Files on magnetic tape You will see from the table that magnetic tape allows only *sequential* or *serial access*. The read/write can be done in one direction only. To get to any point in the file, the tape must be read from the beginning.

Files on magnetic disks Data is stored on disks in sections or tracks (see Unit 2.1). The read/write head moves quickly across the surface of the disk and can access any part of the disk very quickly. This means that a record may be accessed *directly*, without reading any other records. Serial, sequential and direct-access file organization methods may be used on disks.

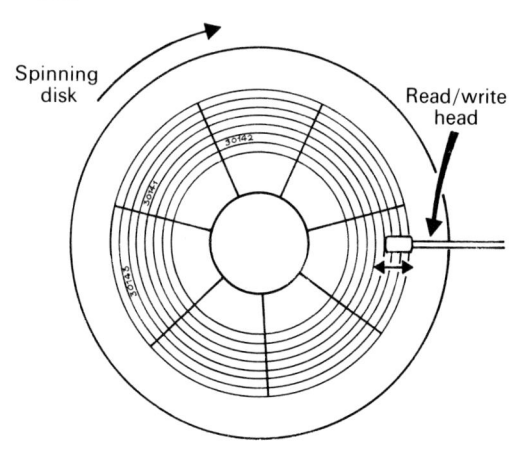

Fig. 6.27 Disks allow direct access

Processing sequential files

The records in a sequential file must be kept in a meaningful *sequence* of keys. Processing sequential files involves maintaining records in key sequence. There are two main ways of processing sequential files: **sorting** and **merging**.

Sorting Sorting is rearranging records into a new sequence of keys. For example:

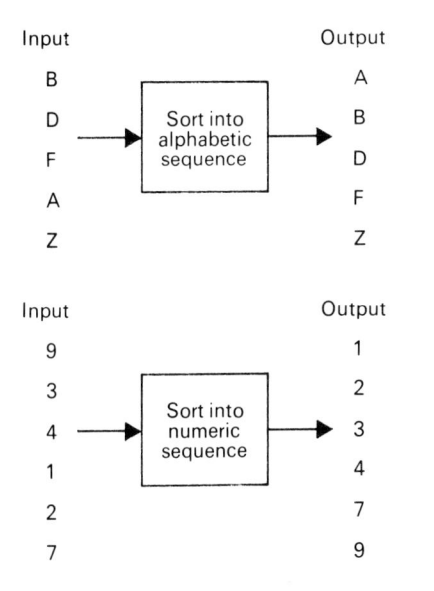

```
Input                               Output
B                                   A
D     ┌─────────────┐              B
F  ──▶│ Sort into   │──▶           D
A     │ alphabetic  │              F
Z     │ sequence    │              Z
      └─────────────┘

Input                               Output
9                                   1
3     ┌─────────────┐              2
4  ──▶│ Sort into   │──▶           3
1     │ numeric     │              4
2     │ sequence    │              7
7     └─────────────┘              9
```

Fig. 6.28 Sorting record keys

The sorting is done by a program called a **sort program**. Sort programs are used by a lot of computer installations and are often provided with the computer. It is an example of **utility software**. A sort program is usually designed to work for any file and any key. The program requires the file name and the key length and position in each record when it runs. The key sequence may be defined for numeric keys as *ascending*, for example:

```
          1045
          1056
          1310
          1400
```

or *descending*, for example:

```
          1400
          1310
          1056
          1045
```

The sequence may also be alphabetic.

Below is an algorithm for a 'bubble sort', i.e. the highest values 'float' to the top of the list. LIST is a list of numbers. I points to the items in LIST. SIZE is the number of items in LIST. NOEXCHANGES indicates when no more exchanges are needed, i.e. when the list is sorted. Try the algorithm with your own numbers or letters.

```
PROCEDURE BUBBLESORT;
VAR
    I, TEMPORARY: INTEGER;
    NOEXCHANGES: BOOLEAN;
BEGIN
    REPEAT
        NOEXCHANGES := TRUE;
        FOR I := 1 TO SIZE - 1 DO
            IF LIST[I] > LIST[I + 1] THEN
            BEGIN
                TEMPORARY := LIST[I]
                LIST[I] := LIST[I + 1];
                LIST[I + 1] := TEMPORARY;
                NOEXCHANGES := FALSE
            END
    UNTIL NOEXCHANGES
END;
```

Fig. 6.29 A 'bubblesort' algorithm

Merging Merging is similar to sorting. The difference is that two or more files may be input and *merged* to create a new file. For this to work properly the input files must all have their keys in the same position on their records.

Sorting is done for two reasons:
- The file is not in any key sequence
- The file is required in a new key sequence

(If the SCHOOL REPORT FILE is in pupil number sequence and the system is required to produce a print in name order, the file would first have to be *sorted* into name sequence.)

Merging is done when several smaller files are brought together to produce a larger file.

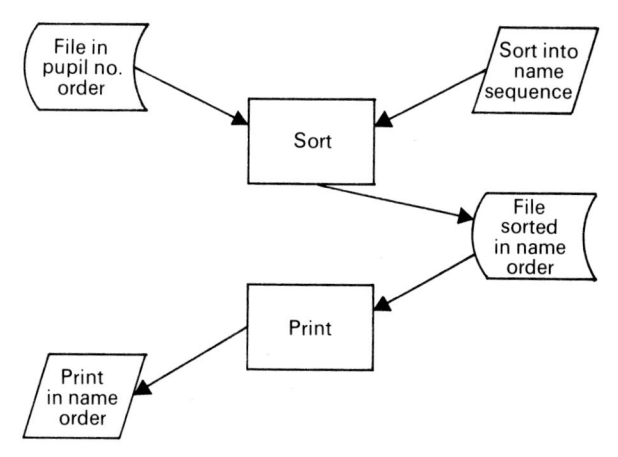

Fig. 6.30 Sorting a file

Types of files in a system

Master files A master file is a file containing the up-to-date information of each record in the file.

Transaction files Transaction files contain data which is used to **update** a master file. 'Update' means to keep the information held in the master file up to date. Types of transactions are:
- change
- delete
- add.

Master files exist for the lifetime of a system although they are usually regularly updated and rewritten. Transaction files might only exist for one computer run.

Updating a sequential master file The transaction file records and master file records must be *sorted* into the same sequence. The two files are read together by the update program. The keys from the two files are compared. If there is no transaction record for a master record, the original master record is written to the new master file without changing. If the keys are equal, the transaction record is tested for being a *delete* or a *change*. If it is a 'delete', the old master record is *not* written to the new master file. If it is a 'change', the transaction data will be used to change the old master record. The changed master record is then written to the new master file. If the transaction is an *add*, the transaction record is written to the new master file in the correct key sequence.

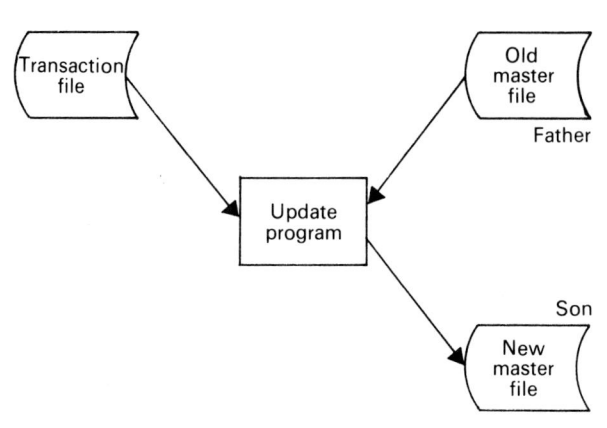

Fig. 6.31 Updating a master file

Updating a direct access master file
With a direct access master file additions, changes and deletions may be done in any key order. The amendments may be carried out directly onto the old master file. With this method the old version of the file is lost. The update program matches keys as for sequential files but updates the existing file.

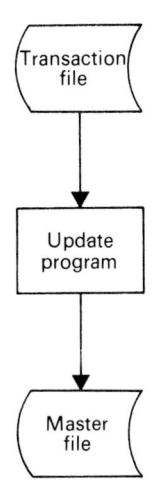

Fig. 6.32 Updating a direct access master file

Sequential files are more convenient where large numbers of records are processed. Sequential files are usually processed in batch systems.

Direct access files are required if updating is being done on-line. This is because transactions may arrive in any sequence.

Security of master files

Master files contain an organization's data over long periods of time. If this data were lost or damaged the organization would suffer. Imagine a bank with all its customers' accounts on a computer. The customer accounts are held in a master file. Customers would not be very happy if the bank 'lost' its records of customer accounts. Chaos would result.

Master files can be destroyed in two ways:
- by physical damage to disks or tapes (e.g. in a fire)
- by input of the wrong data when the file is updated.

To guard against this, **security copies** of master files are taken.

Security of sequential master files With sequential files a new copy is made every update run. Each new copy of the master file is called a **generation**, as for generations in families. The old master is the **father**, the new master the **son**. A security copy of each of these may also be taken. This method provides physical security and allows for an update run to be repeated if anything goes wrong.

Security of direct access files Regular copies must be taken of a direct access file. This is because there is only one up-to-date master file in existence at a given time. To guard against incorrect updates, a note must be kept of all transactions between each security copy run. If any errors have occurred, the security copy can be used with the transactions. This will re-create the master file.

Security copies are often made onto magnetic tape. The tape is then stored in a fireproof safe. Tape is useful because it is cheap, can store a lot of data and takes up little room. In large installations several copies of each master file may be kept.

If you have a microcomputer with floppy disks or cassette tape you will find it useful to keep copies of your files.

Many microcomputers and minicomputers have Winchester disk drives. Often a cheap, fast tape drive called a **streamer** is available. This allows the whole of the contents of the Winchester disk to be copied onto magnetic tape. The moral of the story is that for large computer installations or for a micro in the home: Security is vital!

The systems designer chooses the file access method and storage media. The choice will depend on many factors such as:
- volumes of data
- speed of access required
- storage devices available
  and many more.

The two case studies which follow this unit look at the design of files.

KEY POINTS

1. Storing data on magnetic media involves files, records and fields. A file contains many records, each record many fields.
2. A file is identified by a name so that it may be located by a computer program.
3. Each record is identified by a key, which is a field or group of fields in each record.
4. Magnetic tape may only be used to store serial or sequential files. Magnetic disk may be used to store serial, sequential or direct access files.
5. Common operations on sequential files are: sorting and merging.
6. Transaction files and master files are the two main types of file in a computer system. Transaction files are used to keep master files up to date.
7. Tapes and disks can be physically damaged, files can have wrong data put on them. Security measures must guard against both kinds of corruption.

Questions

1. A group of records treated as a complete unit of data during transfer to and from a backing store is known as a:
   a) byte
   b) fixed length record
   c) block
   d) program
   e) word.
   (ALSEB 1983)

2. Complete the following sentence. A predetermined section of a record is a _____.
   (ALSEB 1982)

3*. Explain the connections between the terms record, field and file, using for an example information about the subjects taken by children in a particular class.
   (SUJB 1982)

4*a) Explain what you understand by the terms serial access and direct access, and describe briefly a suitable application for each.
   b) Name two types of magnetic storage devices, and for each state whether it allows serial or direct access.
   c) Describe for the application involving serial access how data are organized on the magnetic storage medium.   (OLE)

5* Explain the following terms used in file maintenance:
a) merge
b) transaction file.
(AEB 1983)

6 If a son file was destroyed, how could it be replaced?
(WMEB 1982)

7* Read the following passage:
'In a shop, a microprocessor is incorporated into a cash till which is used as a point-of-sale terminal and is connected on-line to a central mainframe computer. Details of each sale are validated by the terminal before transmission to the mainframe where the data are used immediately to update the master stock file and calculate statistical information. The central computer is connected in this way to approximately 100 shops. After the shops close for the day, the central computer processes the updated stock file to produce new stock reports and other management information.'
Answer the following questions.
a) State, giving a reason, the type of file access which would be suitable for the master stock file.
b) Name and describe two possible reports produced by the central computer which would be of use to management.
c) Describe two file security methods that could be used, one for each of the following cases:
(i) in case of corruption of the master stock file
(ii) in case of a breakdown in the telecommunications network
d) In the context of this application, why is it necessary to validate the sales data?
(JMB 1982)

8* The Headteacher of a school wishes to use the school's own microcomputer to help in the running of the school. In particular, the Headteacher is considering storing some current information about pupils on the computer.
a) What details about each pupil would probably be held on the computer?
b) What benefits would the Headteacher expect to gain from this use of the computer?
c) What possible dangers could there be in storing pupil records on a computer, rather than keeping them in a filing cabinet?
d) What precautions and rules would be needed to reduce these dangers?
(JMB 1983)

9* Each record in a stock master file consists of three fields: a key field, MK; a current stock level field, CSL; and a minimum stock level field, MSL.
All the key values are positive whole numbers and all records have distinct keys. The records are stored in ascending key order. The file is terminated by a dummy record with key -1.
The master file is updated at the end of each week so that the current stock level becomes the new stock level, NSL, using a transaction file which records the week's sales.
Each record in the transaction file consists of two fields: a key field, TK; and a sales this week field, STW, which may be zero. There should be one transaction record for each commodity held in stock. The transaction records are arranged in ascending key order and the file is terminated by a dummy record with key -1.
Draw a flowchart for the updating of the master file and for the output of the key and the new stock level for any record where the new stock level is less than the minimum stock level.
(JMB 1983)

*'O'-Level question

Wordsearch

Copy this grid into your workbook. In the grid you will find 9 words all to do with storing data on a computer. The clues will help you.
1. This could also open a door.
2. With this type of access method you always start at the beginning.
3. With this type you get straight at the data.
4. There are several of these in each record.
5. There are several of these in each file.
6. This type of storage media allows only sequential access methods.
7. With this type, any access method is used.
8. Keeping data safe from damage and illegal access.
9. You could trim your nails with this, or keep records in it.

COMPUTER FILES WORDSEARCH

```
S Q V R E X Q T I R I N D N V
T E D X C G O E K T K T D C I
A V Z D O S E Q U E N T I A L
P S Q F F M C C X G P X C A L
E I U V E J V N N D N P F X L
U G W Z L P A M J E I D I A D
D K U E N K K M A J R R L L H
R I Z H B Z U M R O K V E G O
O I S I Q U N K C D B I P C M
W C O C T A H E N P F D S K T
M J C K C F R E Y M Q M I H Y
Q D H I E N W C J H R I R S N
M C W X A Y S H D J S A D W O
M N T V N R H I M P Q B C Y V
C N E X X L H S E C U R I T Y
```

Case Study
— Hospital in-patient system

Computers are used in hospitals to provide information for administrators, doctors and nurses. This information may be broken down into two types:
- information about the patient—personal data
- information about how the hospital is being used—service data.

A computer system for recording and using this data is very useful in the running of a hospital.

Personal data

When a patient is admitted to hospital a lot of data about their personal details are recorded, for example: name, address, date of birth, sex, religion, etc. A patient is also allocated a 'unit number'. This is a code number which is unique to each patient. This code number is used as the *key* to *records* about the patient. It is used because a name and address is too long and may not be unique. The new patient record is added to a *patient file*. This file is accessed to provide information about the patient.

Validation of the personal data The personal details data must be checked for being reasonable. For instance, the date of birth should be a valid date (e.g. 32.12.84 is impossible, 31.12.84 is possible) and it must be before today's date.

Some of the data may be *coded*, e.g. M for Male, 1 for Church of England, etc. The codes may be checked for being valid.

Once the data is proved to be valid, the record may be added to the patient file.

Other files in the system (service data)

The system might also contain a *bed file*. This would consist of a record for each bed in the hospital with data about which ward it is on, and whether it is occupied. Other files might include data about drugs available, etc. Using data from these files the system could provide information about the number of beds in use, amounts of drugs being used, etc.

Outputs from the system

Examples of outputs from the system are:
- daily admissions—in patient name order for ward sisters and hospital reception
- labels—used for attaching to patient, patient's bed, case-notes folder, etc.
- list of patients in hospital in name order—for telephone enquiries, etc.
- list of empty beds—used when admitting a new patient.

All these outputs are extremely useful in a hospital. They could all be produced manually, but using a computer makes the task much easier.

Recording the data

Each item of input data has to be entered into the computer. If this is done *off-line*, the data is recorded on an input document to be entered into the computer later. With an *on-line* system the data would be entered direct to the computer by means of a keyboard and VDU. The advantages of entering the data on-line are that the data is recorded immediately and any errors are notified straight away.

On-line or off-line—micro, mini or mainframe?

Hospitals have always kept records about patients and beds. Using a computer should make the job easier. The systems designer has to decide on the 'best' way of computerizing the system. An on-line data entry system seems best because data is kept up to date and more accurate. However, this may be more expensive because the hospital has to buy its own computer, or send data over telephone lines to a central computer. A microcomputer would be cheaper but may not have the facilities for producing all the outputs. It may also be short of storage capacity for all the data.

A solution to the problem

One solution could be as follows:
- purchase a medium-sized computer to be sited in the hospital
- provide terminals at reception and on each ward
- provide the computer with a printer and disk storage devices
- provide all inputs and answers to queries through the terminals on-line
- produce all lists of patients, labels and note files, using the printer.

Some hospitals have this sort of system installed. If you need to visit a hospital perhaps you could ask whether they use computers, and if so, how.

Fig. 6.33 The patient enters hospital and the data enters the computer. When the hospital staff require information on the patient the computer can supply it 'instantly'

Case Study
— Monitoring and controlling river levels

Introduction

Computers are often used to *monitor* and *control* activities in systems. These systems may be industrial processes such as a large chemical plant or steel rolling mill. In this type of application data about the system is passed to the computer. The computer then processes the data and produces various outputs. The outputs may be signals to devices, (e.g. to close a valve) or messages to people operating the system. The system operates as a 'closed-loop' as shown below.

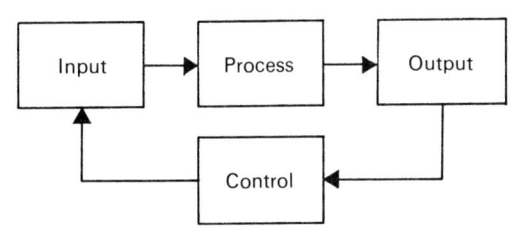

Fig. 6.34

This case study describes how computers, data collection and data transmission are used to monitor and control water levels in a system of reservoirs, a lake and a river. Monitoring is done by collecting data about rainfall and water levels. Control is achieved by opening and closing sluice gates.

Description of the system

Bala Lake and the man-made reservoirs Llyn Celyn, Alwen and Llyn Brenig are all used by The Dee and Clwyd River Authority to regulate water flows in the River Dee (see map). The river is used to supply water for domestic and industrial use in the area below Llangollen and the city of Chester. The flow of water in the river has to be enough to provide for domestic and industrial users and to maintain fish stocks below Chester. However, the flow

Bala Lake

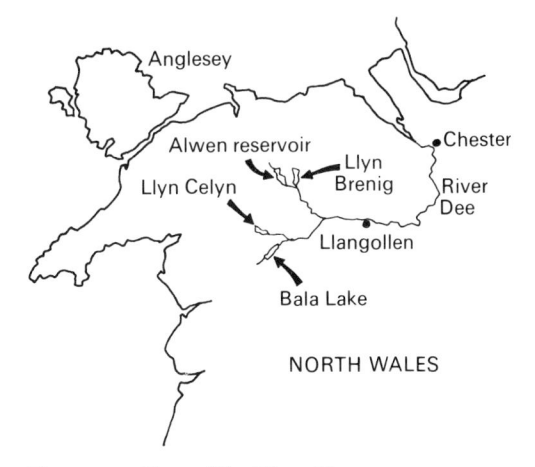

Fig. 6.35 Map of the River Dee

has to be regulated so that flooding doesn't occur around Chester in times of high rainfall. To maintain the correct water levels in the lakes and river the authority needs to measure:

- lake levels
- river levels
- rainfall in the area.

This data needs to be accurate and up to date. It is used by the authority to control water flows at the lake and reservoir outlets by means of sluice gates.

Collecting the data

Previously, the measurements were collected by people at various points along the river and in the valley. This was a very unpleasant and expensive task especially in winter when a round-the-clock watch is needed. An automatic data collection system has now been installed which collects measurements at 35 points. The measurements are transmitted for processing at a central computer near Bala. The computer processes the data received and outputs the results, which are used by water engineers to control the outlets at the lakes.

Input data

All the input data measurements are in *analogue* form, i.e. they take any value along a continuous scale. These have to be converted to *digital* form before being transmitted.

Rainfall This is collected when it falls through a funnel into one of a pair of tiny buckets. These are arranged on a see-saw mechanism. As one bucket fills it tips, emptying its contents and the second bucket takes its place. As each bucket fills and empties, a digital signal can be transmitted. Each bucket holds the equivalent of 2 mm of rain so, the number of buckets tipped, times 2 mm gives the measurement of rainfall.

River and lake levels These are measured by having a float on the surface of the water. Attached to this float is a tape which runs over a pulley. The float rises and falls with the level of the water. As the float rises and falls it rotates the disk. This disk is marked off into sectors, each sector having a different value. A sensor is positioned so that it can detect which sector is opposite it. The value represented by the sector of the disk is then transmitted. In this way, an analogue value is converted into a digital value before being transmitted.

Transmission of data

The data is transmitted from the measuring stations in three different ways. These are:
- direct line
- telephone lines
- radio signals.

The central computer sends a signal to the outstation which causes it to transmit a reading. The readings are transmitted as binary values. The system operates in *real-time*, using the real-time clock to measure the time between each transmission.

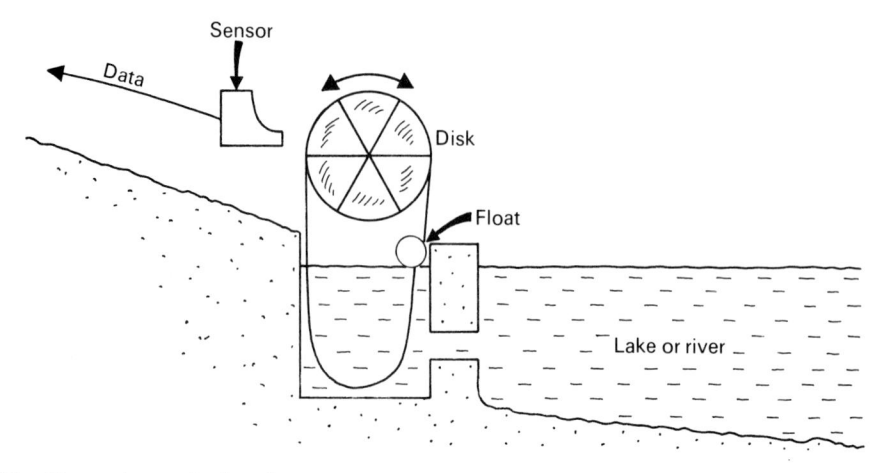

Fig. 6.36 *Measuring water levels*

Outputs from the system

The data collected from the outstations is stored in the computer and processed to produce various outputs. These are:
- forecasts of flood flows based on the rate of rainfall displayed on VDU screens
- a graphical record of the measurements on a chart recorder
- river levels and rainfall summaries—printed on a line printer for permanent records.

The flood forecast output is important since it allows engineers to take action before flooding occurs.

In this case study the computer is being used to *monitor* and provide information for people to make *control* decisions. The system makes use of *data transmission* and *real-time* computing. It would be possible to extend the system to make it control the sluice gates directly. The system would then be collecting data and acting on the information this provides.

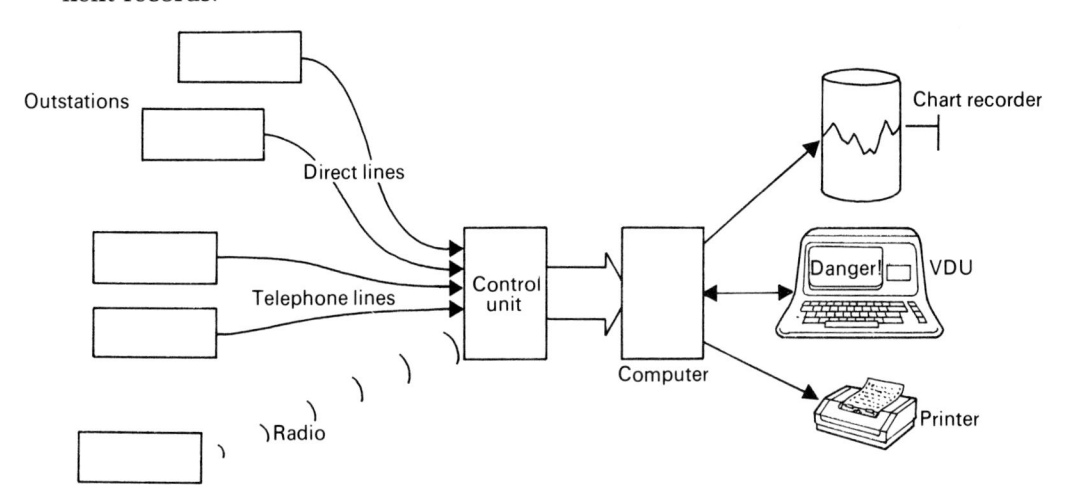

Fig. 6.37 *Data transmission from measuring stations to the water authority's computer.*

Part 7

Information Technology

7.1 What is information technology?

Information technology is often said to be 'the technology of the future'. But it's hard to define exactly what information technology is. It is sometimes called the 'science of information handling', but what does this mean?

Information Technology (IT) arrived with the coming together of three technologies: microelectronics, computing and communications. This unit looks at each of these technologies in turn.

Microelectronics

There are three main electronic devices: transistors, capacitors and resistors. All have been used for the last thirty years. Until quite recently (about 1964) each of these devices was made separately and then wired together to make an electronic circuit. This can still be done, but nowadays electronic circuits are commercially produced by making and connecting all the devices on a tiny wafer of silicon in one continuous process. These tiny circuits on thin silicon wafers are called **'chips'**. The science of designing, making and using these chips is called **microelectronics**.

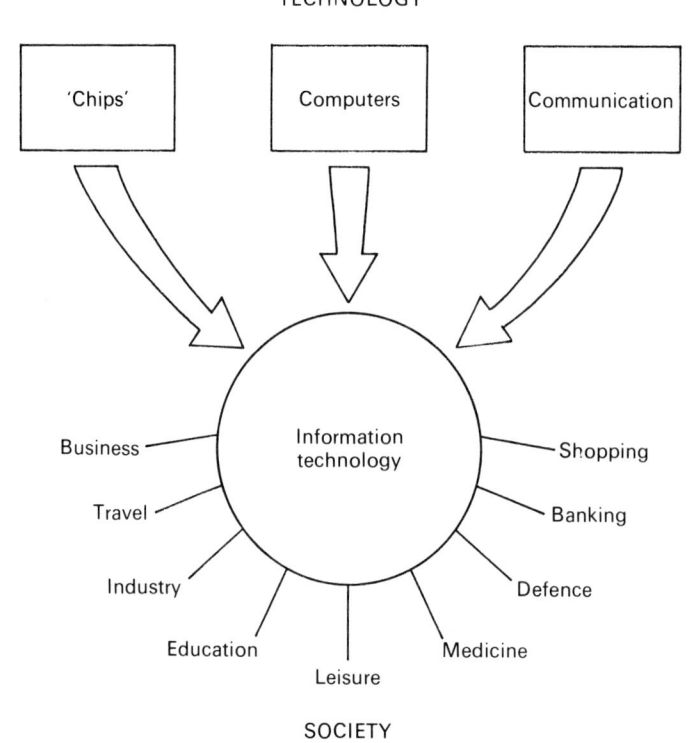

Fig. 7.1 *The convergence of the three "C's"*

Devices which use 'chips'

There are two main types of chip: **processing chips** and **memory chips**.

Microprocessors Chips used for processing data are called **microprocessors**. They can be designed to carry out arithmetic and logic processes, or to *control* the flow of data. Microprocessors may be used in microcomputers—but they are also used in washing machines, calculators, robots, cameras, watches, sewing machines, and so on. The list is always growing.

Memory chips Memory chips are designed to store data, including computer programs. Some have their data 'etched' into them. These are **ROM** (Read-Only Memory) chips. Some are like an empty sheet or a blank notepad. These can have data *written to* them or *read from* them, i.e. write-or-read memory. These are called **RAM** (Random Access Memory) chips (though WORM—Write-Or-Read Memory—might be a better name). Between the two extremes of ROM and RAM are **PROM** (Programmable Read-Only Memory) and **EPROM** (Erasable Programmable Read-Only Memory). PROM chips can have data recorded on them using a special process—but once it is there it cannot be changed. EPROM chips *can* have their contents changed or *erased*, by exposing them to ultra-violet light.

Chips have many advantages over old-fashioned electronic circuits:
- *size:* Computing power that would have occupied a large room in 1950 can now be achieved on one chip. This helps to make them faster. It also means that they can be used in many devices and their size is hardly noticed.
- *cheapness:* Chips are cheap to make. Once designed, thousands can be mass produced, often for only a few pence. They are cheap to run, using very little energy.
- *reliability:* Chips have no moving or detachable parts. This makes them robust and reliable, in all kinds of conditions.

Microelectronics, the technology of chips, is the most recent element of information technology.

Computing

The second of the triplet technologies is computing. Computing involves microelectronics as one of its parts or foundations—but the computing industry involves much more. The technology of computing involves: designing and analysing systems, producing software, collecting and coding data, producing clear and readable information, developing new hardware, and so on.

ICL's computer hall, West Gorton, Manchester

Computing is a slightly older technology than microelectronics. Today's computers, from micro to mainframe, contain one or more microprocessors (e.g. the BBC micro has a processing chip called the Motorola 6502, and ROM and RAM chips). But computing did exist well before the first chip was ever made.

Communications

The oldest technology of the three is communications. People have been communicating with each other for centuries: with smoke signals, bonfires, beacons, semaphore, morse code and now telephones and satellites. Modern forms of communication are often called **telecommunications**. This is likely to involve at least three parts: telephones, television and radio waves, and fibre-optic cables.

Telephones One French expert estimated that in 1970 there were about 200 million telephones in the world; by the year 2000 there may be 2 billion. By AD 2020 he forecast a total of 10 billion telephones worldwide—more phones than people. If the telephone network does spread this widely, computer terminals will be linked by telephone throughout the world to form global computer networks. The number of computer terminals may one day equal the number of telephones.

Satellite communications dish on a North Sea oil rig

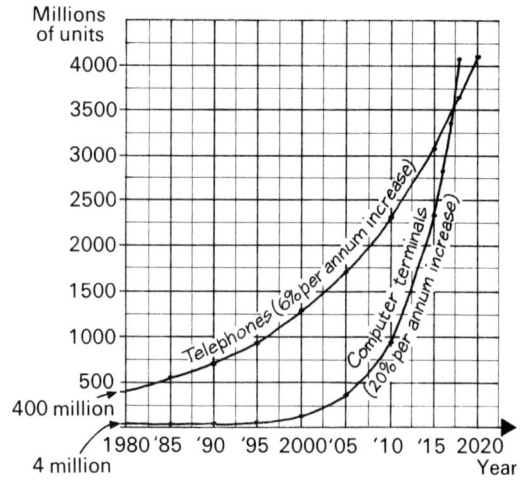

Fig. 7.2 When will the number of computer terminals catch up with the number of telephones?

Radio waves Radio waves travel through air, or empty space, at the speed of light (television waves are simply shorter wavelength radio waves). They are ideal for sending messages, including messages from one computer to another. Satellites are now used to help the passage of radio waves from one part of the globe to another.

Fibre optics The latest development in communications is the **optical fibre**. This is a strand of glass only as wide as a human hair, but often several kilometres long. Light or laser messages can be transmitted along these fibres. The message is first *coded* into binary form. A pulse of light represents 1—no pulse represents 0. At the receiving end the pulses are decoded. Optical fibres can carry over 40 million bits of data every second—at the speed of light. The fibres are collected together (perhaps 24 in all) into a narrow cable. These cables can join one person, business or industry to another to form a **cable network**.

Optical fibres

Telephones, radio waves and satellites, and fibre-optic cables will form the communications systems of the future. Each system has the same basic parts.

The three industries of microelectronics, computing and communications will form a 'tripod' for the 'information technology' age. The three technologies will vastly improve the *storage*, *processing* and *communication* of information. But what about information itself? Why should information be so important?

Good and bad information

Suppose you telephone your local railway station to inquire about trains to London. Your reply comes back: 'A train will probably be leaving some time today'. This is poor quality information—it is vague, uncertain, and inexact. A more helpful reply would be something like: 'A non-stop train is leaving at 10.12 a.m. from platform 2, reaching King's Cross at 12.24 p.m.' The table below summarizes the differences between high- and low-quality information.

HIGH QUALITY	LOW QUALITY
Reliable	Misleading
Accurate	Inaccurate
Up to date	Out of date
Complete	Incomplete
Precise	Vague
Clear	Unclear
Well presented	Poorly presented

High- and low-quality information

In other words, the more the uncertainty the worse the information.

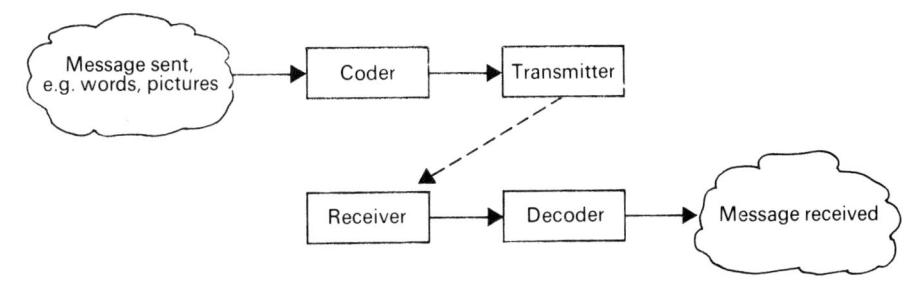

Fig. 7.3 The basic parts of a communications system

As information technology spreads, the *quality* of information will become more and more important. High-quality information about banks and money supply, current prices, world markets and trends, crops and agriculture, the weather, in fact almost anything, will become a valuable commodity. It will be the key *resource* in the society of the future—a resource which can be bought and sold, imported and exported. This is why people talk about the 'information industry'.

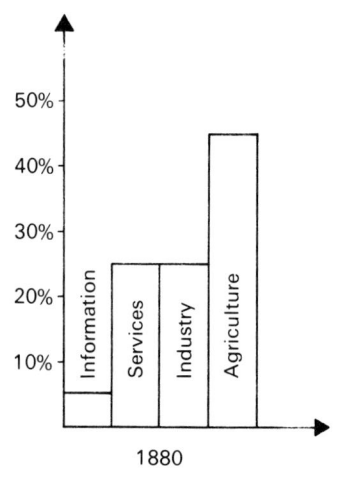

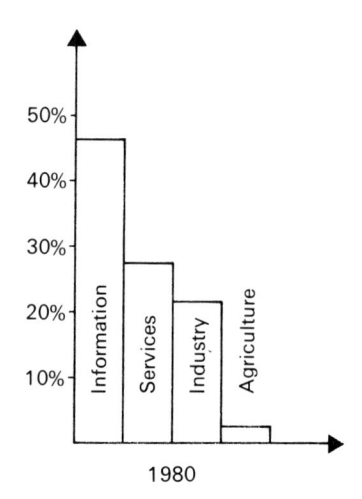

Fig. 7.4 How the pattern of employment has changed in the last 100 years in the USA

Questions

1. Copy out this passage and fill in the blanks.
   Information technology involves three technologies: _____, _____, and _____. Chips used for processing data are called _____. These may be used in _____, _____, _____ and many other devices.
2. Design and draw a clear and attractive chart or poster to show the main landmarks in the history of communications. You could call it 'From Smoke Signals to Satellites', or you could choose your own title.
3. It has been suggested that through the use of computers we shall all have far greater access to information. Give one reason, with an example, to show why you agree or disagree with this view. (SREB)
4. 'More and more people are being employed in the information industry.' Try to explain what each part of this statement means.
5. Explain, in your own words, the meaning of each of these terms:
   chip   RAM
   ROM   optical fibre
   microprocessor   microelectronics
6. What is the difference between high- and low-quality information? Make up one example of each type.

Some landmarks in the history of information technology

COMPUTERS	ELECTRONICS	COMMUNICATIONS
1642: Blaise Pascal's mechanical calculator, France	1919: Flip-flop binary device, USA	dates unknown: Smoke signals, e.g. Red Indians
1833: Babbage's analytical engine, Britain	1948: Transistor (Brattan & Shockley, USA)	1588: Spanish armada: bonfires and beacons used as signals
1889: Hollerith's punched card machine, USA	1952: The idea of the integrated circuit: G. W. Dummer, Britain	1816: Semaphore signalling using moving 'arms'
1946: ENIAC computer, Pennsylvania, USA	1958: LASER invented, USA	1821: Flag-signalling, e.g. between ships
1948: EDSAC, Cambridge, UK	1962: The silicon chip, USA	1837: Morse code telegraph system, Samuel Morse, USA
1951: First general-purpose computer, Ferranti, USA	1963: Electronic calculator, Britain	1847: Underwater telephone cable, W. Siemens, Germany
1960: First solid-state computer, USA	1970: Floppy disk, IBM, USA	1858: Trans-Atlantic cable laid
1961: First minicomputer, USA		1876: Telephone, Alexander Graham Bell, USA
1972: The microcomputer, USA		1881: First Post Office telephone exchange opened
		1888: Successful transmission of radio waves, Heinrich Hertz, Germany
		1896: Wireless telegraphy, G. Marconi, Italy
		1925: Television, John Logie Baird, Britain
		1950: MODEM for data transmission, USA
		1957: SPUTNIK—first satellite launched, USSR
		1966: Optical fibres communication, USA
		1960's and 1970's: Private and public data networks

Information technology

7.2 Information technology in action

Information technology involves storing, processing and communicating vast amounts of data. This unit tells you how IT is being used already, and how it might be used in the future.

Videotex

You can receive data either through your television aerial or down your telephone line, then display this data on your television screen. The general name given to this is **videotex** (text on video). There are two different types of videotex.

Viewdata With this system information can be called up from a large computer by *telephone*, and displayed on your TV screen. (The best example is Prestel, British Telecom's version, which is explained fully later.) Viewdata is a two-way or *interactive* system. All the information stored in the central computer is called a **database**. A viewdata user can interrogate this database to get to, or *access*, the exact information he wants.

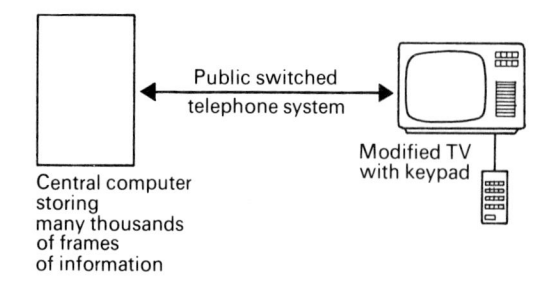

Fig. 7.5 Viewdata

Teletext This is the name given to information which is sent from a TV transmitter, received by your television aerial, and displayed on your television screen. Two examples are Ceefax ('see facts') on BBC, and Oracle on ITV. These are both one-way or non-interactive types of videotex. You can receive information, but you cannot send it back. You can call for a particular 'page' of information using a keypad.

The main advantage of teletext is that it is free—once you have a proper keypad and television. On the other hand, Prestel can be quite expensive to use.

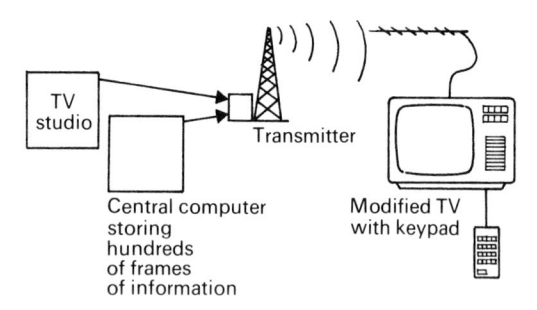

Fig. 7.6 Teletext

More about Prestel

Using Prestel Prestel was invented and developed in Britain, through the British Post Office. It is simply a *computer-based information service*. To use it you need three things:
- a special Prestel television set, or an adaptor on your present television
- a telephone, and a jack-plug to connect it to your television
- a keypad, which looks a bit like a pocket calculator.

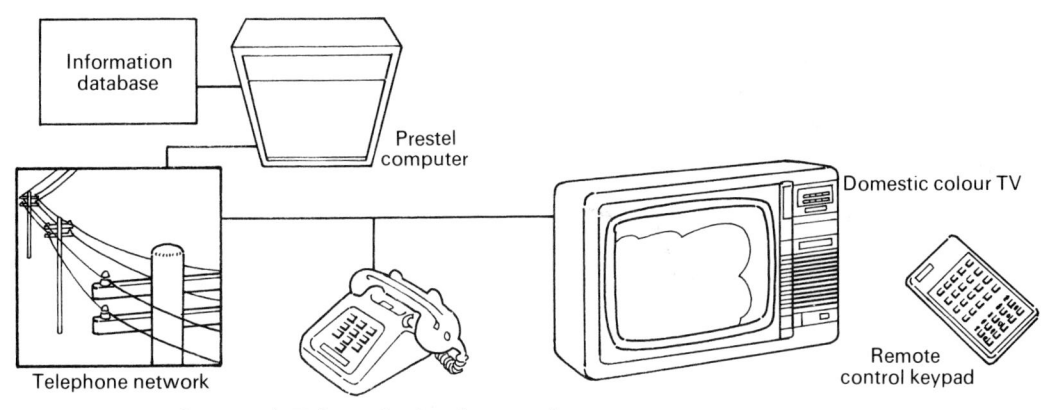

Fig. 7.7 Prestel—British Telecom's viewdata service

By pressing the right buttons on your keypad you get in touch with the central Prestel computer via your telephone line. Pressing another button will give you an index of all the information available. Hundreds of thousands of pages of information are stored on Prestel. To help find the page you want a free directory is supplied to Prestel users. A user can then access any Prestel page by keying-in the full number, or he can browse through various pages, pressing a single key each time. Every Prestel user has to pay a rental charge *and* the cost of the telephone calls. This means that many users make a note of the page numbers they use most, just to save time and their phone bill! Some pages actually cost extra money if you use them (they have a 'frame charge')

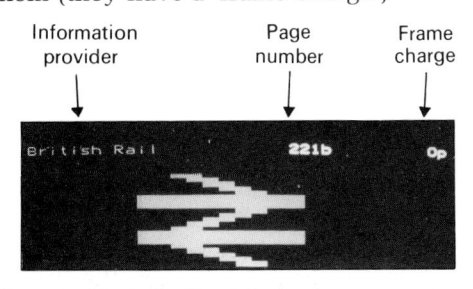

Fig. 7.8 Part of a Prestel page

What's on Prestel? Information is supplied to Prestel by **information providers**. These people rent pages from British Telecom and display their information on those pages. Information is provided about: travel, farming, imports and exports, hotels, the law, houses, business

Fig. 7.9 Some Prestel pages

183

news, the world's economies, theatres, cinemas, currency exchange rates, share prices, even the weather.

Computer programs are now being sent via Prestel. You can receive them in your home and record them on tape or disk. This is often called **telesoftware**. Some newspaper companies now use **Prestel** to communicate the news. You receive **news** pages on your screen and pay a small charge for each page. This is called the **electronic newspaper**.

Inside Prestel there are now **closed user-groups** (e.g. Micronet 800). These are groups which only certain people belong to, and pay extra rent for. They have their own pages which only group users can get to, or access. One of these groups, 'Homelink', enables shopping and banking to be done from home.

Using 'Homelink'

Responding Prestel is interactive. Using the keypad you can send messages back to the central computer. You can book a train or an aeroplane, reserve a hotel room, book a theatre ticket, or even buy a crate of champagne. You will need to key in your user number and your secret password—otherwise somebody else could spend your money.

Databases

What is a database? Prestel is often called a national database. A database is any collection of facts, items of information or data which are related in some way. A telephone directory is a database, so is an address book. Some other examples could be:
   a collection of recipes
   a filing cabinet
   the Oxford English Dictionary
   a library of books
   a textbook

Every database should contain data which is *organized* in a sensible and systematic way, for example, by placing names in alphabetical order. This should allow anyone using a database to put in, or get out, the information they want as easily and quickly as possible.

None of the examples of databases given above are computerized, but Prestel is. The main advantages of computerized databases are:

- unlike printed guides or books they can easily and quickly be kept up to date.
- the information they store can be accessed easily, quickly and directly—and often from hundreds of miles away.

Searching a database To search for information in a database like Prestel you use an **information tree**. At the top of the tree, Page 0, you are given a choice of nine options. You choose one by keying in its number (e.g. '3') then you are given, for example, ten further choices. You might choose Option 5. You will then be sent

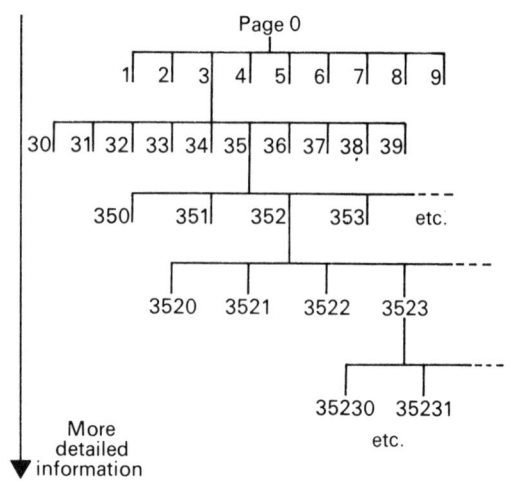

Fig. 7.10   An information tree to search a database

184

Photo 12 Inside the machine. This photograph shows the microelectronics of a single-board computer. The CPU is the large integrated circuit in the centre.

Photo 13 A magnified view of the architecture of a silicon chip. The number of components and interconnections that can be integrated onto a single chip has grown from 12 to greater than 100 000 in the past 20 years.

Photo 14 A satellite photograph of part of Nepal which has been processed by computer to give a false-colour image. Controlling the colours of the picture lets scientists see certain details more clearly. For example, the 'blue' river systems stand out extremely well against the 'red' mountains.

Photo 15   Robots being used to assemble Ford Sierra cars. Robots are ideal for many of the repetitive, dirty or dangerous jobs in industry. However, if machines take over jobs that were formerly done by humans, what will happen to the people who are affected?

Photo 16   The apron control centre at Heathrow airport uses computers to keep track of aircraft on the runways. With a plane either taking off or landing every minute — they have to get it right.

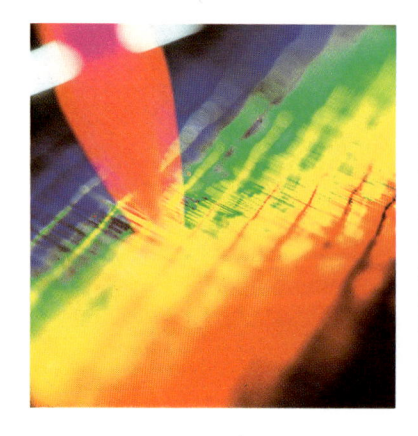

Photo 17   Data is held on the surface of a videodisk in a 2-state code. This is physically achieved by burning tiny holes with a laser so that, for example, a 'hole' or 'no hole' represents '1' or '0'. It is the tiny holes on the disk surface which break up natural light into the component colours to produce the rainbow effect seen in the picture. The pink beam of light on the left is a scanning laser beam which detects whether or not a hole is present and converts the presence or absence of a hole into an electrical signal.

Page 35. Then if you choose Option 2 the next page displayed is Page 352. As you go down the information tree the information you receive becomes more and more precise. You might stop at page Page 35231, or even go as far as 35231762.

Imagine you wanted to find out the nearest cinema to you that is showing a funny film. You might start from the 'Entertainment' page, go down to 'Cinemas', then on to your local cinemas and finally to a list of the actual films being shown. In other words you start from the *general* (e.g. 'Entertainment') and go down to the *particular* (e.g. the nearest funny film to your home). This is how any database is searched.

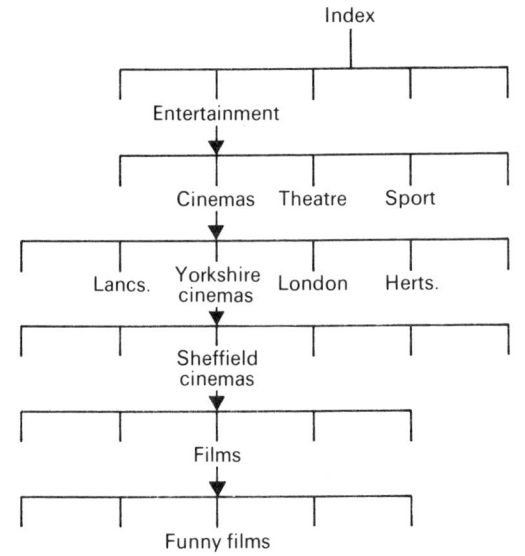

Fig. 7.11 *Searching an information tree*

Fig. 7.12 *Widening circles of networks*

A network of microcomputers can be formed in a room or a house just by linking them with wires or cables. A **local area network** (e.g. in a large school, factory or university) can be made in a similar way. A wider network can be called a **district network**, for example, a village, town or city linked by telephone lines and possibly cables. Wider still is the **national network**, and then the **international** or **global network**. On these networks data will be sent by telephone line, land or submarine cable, radiowaves and satellites.

Using networks How can these networks be used? Here are just a few examples:
- *the electronic office:* In a large office or company all the electronic devices used can be linked together to form a local data network. Microcomputers, word processors, high-speed printers, mass storage tapes and disks, can all be joined together. Another device in the network will be used to send out, and receive back, communications from other local, national and international networks.

Computer networks

You already know that computers work with data which has been coded into a string of 1's and 0's (a binary code). Computers, and other devices which use computer-coded data, can be connected together to form **networks**. Using a network, coded data can be sent from one device to another. The signals are digital signals, or on/off pulses. These signals can be sent along wires, telephone lines, via television transmitters, or along optical fibres.

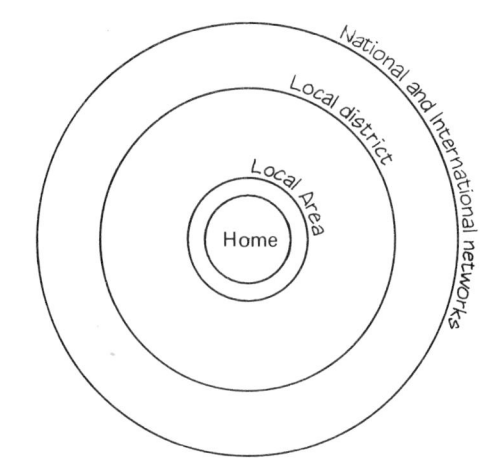

185

- *electronic mail:* Using a data network, messages can be sent from one computer terminal to another. The message to be sent is *converted* to an electronic digital signal, *transmitted* via a cable, telephone or satellite, and then *converted back* again at the receiving end. It may be displayed on a television screen for the receiver to read, and then perhaps stored on file or disk. No paper is necessary. This system for sending messages is one type of electronic mail.
- *teleconferencing:* Business meetings and conferences can be held by linking people through a computer network. Business men can send information to and from each other, discuss it and display it on a screen. They may even be able to see each other. This is called **teleconferencing**.

(The use of networks and they way they have affected, and will affect, society is discussed fully in Part 8.)

Linking up with lasers

Laser beams are now being used to send, receive, store and process information. They have become an essential part of information technology. You will hear more and more about their uses. But first of all, what is a laser? The initials LASER stand for 'Light Amplification by Stimulated Emission of Radiation'. A laser beam is a light beam—but its light is very *pure* (all rays are exactly the same colour), very *intense*, and very *concentrated*.

Sending information Lasers are now widely used to transmit information. Flashes of light have been used to send messages for many years (e.g. with an Aldis lamp on ships at sea). Lasers work in a similar way, but their higher power means that they can travel over huge distances. They can now be carried along glass fibres or optical fibres which can be used to carry several messages at once.

The coming of cable Glass is cheap, plentiful and light. Glass fibres can be tightly packed together into cables which can carry many messages separately. This means that cables of optical fibres will be the message carriers of the future. They are likely to be used in:
- *banking:* sending messages from one bank to another
- *publishing:* electronic magazines and newspapers, newsletters and advertising could be sent via cable
- *information services, similar to Prestel:* information could be asked for, and received, from a database using optical cable instead of a telephone line
- *electronic shopping:* goods could be advertised using a cable network, and the chosen article could be ordered via optical cable.

These are just a few uses for cable networks. They already bring cable television to millions of viewers in the United States who have twenty or thirty channels to choose from. But their main use will be in *two-way* communications—between people, groups, offices, companies, and from a viewer *back* to the television centre!

Writing and reading with lasers

As well as sending information, lasers can be used to *record* information. Lasers can write information onto special disks. A high-power laser burns tiny holes onto the surface of the disk. The information, or rather data, is stored in a two-state code—a 'hole' or 'no-hole', to represent say '1' or '0'. Information can be read from the disk by scanning it with a low-power laser beam.

Video disks The picture and sound of a television video can be stored on laser video disk. Inside a video disk player a laser reads the information. This is converted into a television signal and carried into the aerial socket of the TV set.

Laser disks have three big advantages:
- there is no contact between the playing head and the disk—this means

that they should never wear out
- they can store huge amounts of information—as much as 30 encyclopaedias on a single disk
- they can be easily and precisely controlled.

Disks that can be controlled are called **interactive video disks**. They could be tremendously useful in education. A person using an interactive video disk system could show himself the same picture over and over again. A particular frame could be frozen and studied for a few minutes, or a user could go through the whole disk at once, then go back over the parts of it which were interesting, or too difficult to understand first time. The disk could easily be controlled by a computer program. A program could, for example, ask the user a few questions then show some pictures from the disks, ask more questions, then go to a different part of the disk, and so on.

Lasers are only 25 years old, but already they play a leading part in communications, alongside telephones and television broadcasting.

Skills for information technology

Have you heard of the 'information explosion'? The amount of knowledge that mankind possesses is said to be *doubling* every five years. This may, or may not, be true, but one thing is certain—in future, more and more time and effort will be used in the information industry. Some useful skills for people involved in this industry will include the ability to:
- collect useful data (e.g. by designing forms)
- code data so that it can be processed by computer
- organize data in a logical and systematic way (e.g. by good indexing)
- handle data, and know how to get to it and retrieve it
- present information, results and statistics in a clear and readable way.

These are some of the skills that will be useful to you in the information era: data collection, data organization, data retrieval, and data presentation. Exactly how information technology might affect you, your life-style and your job prospects is the subject of Part 8.

Questions

1. Try to explain the difference between teletext and viewdata. Make a simple table showing the advantages and disadvantages of each.
2. a) What is a database?
   b) Give some examples of common databases that you use which are not computerized.
   c) What are the advantages of computerized databases?
3. Give an example of information that may be obtained using Prestel.
4. Read this passage carefully:
   'A survey carried out by the British Post Office came to the conclusion that about forty-five per cent of business meetings in the United Kingdom could be held using an audio conference system together with a document transmission system. Two people travelling about 600 kilometres by air for a meeting which will last three hours will use an average of 2500 kWh of energy. The same meeting organized as an audio conference represents an energy output of 2 kWh. The saving is therefore substantial. In a roughly similar way, the journey from home to work could be replaced by electronic communications.'
   (Note: '2 kWh' is short for two kilowatt-hours. It is roughly the same as the energy used by an electric fire left on for 1 hour.)
   a) Explain how an audio conference can save energy. How much energy is saved in the example above?
   b) How could a journey from and to work be 'replaced by electronic communications'? Give some examples.
5.* 'The laborious process of moving a letter from one part of the world to another shows the limitations of traditional methods of coding and transmitting information.' (The Mighty Micro, Dr C. Evans.)
   a) (i) Describe the traditional methods referred to by Dr Evans.
      (ii) Give four different limitations of these methods.
   b) The traditional methods may be replaced by 'electronic mail'
      (i) Show how this might operate.
      (ii) Explain two advantages and one disadvantage it would have over the traditional methods for a large company.
   (AEB 1982)
6. Find out more about Prestel and how it works. You can either write to:
   Prestel Enquiries
   Temple Avenue
   London EC4 4PP
   or telephone:
   '100' and ask for 'Freefone 2043.'

*'O'-Level question

Wordsearch

Copy this grid into your workbook. In the grid you will find 7 words to do with information technology. Use the clues to help you.

1. A set of computers connected together.
2. This device may be used to transmit conversations or data.
3. _____ fibres may be used to transmit data.
4. An abbreviation of 'modulator–demodulator'.
5. A large collection of data items which are stored in a computer and may be accessed via computer terminals.
6. The world's first public videotex service.
7. A system which transmits data with television picture signals.

I.T. WORDSEARCH

```
V V M X A P R E S T E L S P C
I P O F Y P A O H Z Z A J D A
N Z D F E M L X Z U M I L O W
J D E C P Y N A K L C R E P R
T D M B E J X B K Z V X F T D
E A Z Z F E T R X F E N Z I W
L T P F Y I O N F B G M L C F
E A U M I W O P A T Z V F A C
T B R E T O I N T B U R F L G
E A L E B T E R V A K J V D X
X S N Y J T G H D C L W N T A
T E L E P H O N E N F X A S N
F A I H V Y S S K L W P C L E
G O O M L Z T G L Y Q J A R E
G N V X U Q N W K S K P A M R
```

Part 8

Into the Information Era

8.1 A changing society

'Constant change is here to stay.'—
Anon

Two men were watching a mechanical excavator on a building site. "If it wasn't for that machine," said one, "twelve men with shovels could be doing that job." "Yes," replied the other, "and if it wasn't for your twelve shovels, two hundred men with teaspoons could be doing that job."

There are two ways to regard technological development. As a threat. Or as a promise. Every invention from the wheel to the steam engine created the same dilemma.

But it's only by exploiting the promise of each that man has managed to improve his lot. Information technology has given man more time to create, and released him from the day-to-day tasks that limit his self-fulfilment.

We ourselves are very heavy users of this technology, ranging from golf-ball typewriters to laser printers to small and large computers, so we're more aware than most of that age-old dilemma: threat or promise.

Yet during 32 years in the UK our work-force has increased to 15,000. And during those 32 years not a single person has been laid off, not a single day has been lost through strikes. Throughout the UK information technology has shortened queues. Streamlined efficiency. Boosted exports. And kept British products competitive in an international market.

To treat information technology as a threat would halt progress. As a promise, it makes tomorrow look a lot brighter.

IBM

Fig. 8.1

This part looks at how new technology might affect people in the next 10 or 20 years. It considers not only the effects of *computers* on society but also *communications*—the way information will be transmitted from one person, place, office or country to another, and *microelectronics*—the use of integrated circuits (chips) in more and more ways, from washing machines to robots and nuclear missiles. These three connected areas will form the basis of the so-called 'information society'. How these areas affect your life, for better or worse, will depend on the way people make use of them.

At home

New information technology could affect you at home in at least 3 different ways.

Entertainment and education Computer programs and games can be sent to you either down your telephone line or through your television aerial. This telesoftware can be used to provide you with up-to-date information (Prestel, for example) to help your own education, or simply as a supply of video games.

Communication Home computers are already being used to communicate with other people. They can be linked together to form networks, either local or worldwide. Information can be sent by satellite, cable or telephone from one user to another. More and more people will be able to work at home.

Control Computers, or microprocessors, are being used at home to control different systems, ranging from washing and sewing machines to the house central heating system or even the lights. This 'chip control' could save a lot of household energy in the future.

At work

Although several million people in Britain are unemployed a large number still work. How will work be affected by new information technology?

The factory Most factories make or manufacture things. This can be helped by computers and chips in three ways: in *designing* the finished product—**Computer-Aided Design** (CAD); in actually *making it* by using robots or computer-controlled machines; and in *inspecting*

Spray-painting cars by robot

Sea-dart. A radar-seeking missile

A neurosurgeon working from home. The brain scan he is studying has been transmitted over the telephone network

the finished product to check that it meets certain standards. As more computers are used in factories, fewer humans will be employed. Some experts believe that by the year 2000, only 10% of our labour force will be needed to produce *all* our material goods.

This problem of employment is discussed in the unit: More Jobs or Less?

The office In most big cities a lot of people work in offices. Many are involved in sorting out information, filing it away and storing it, or simply sending it from one place to another. Computers are ideal for sorting and storing information while the new communications will send it anywhere in the world in seconds. The office of the future, and the idea that paper messages will be a thing of the past, are looked at in: Can the Computer Save the Woolly Monkey?

In politics

The way the country is ruled, governed and controlled could be affected by new technology.

Voting People in the future could vote in an election by using their own home computer terminal. If it is connected to a central computer they could send a message *electronically* saying who they wished to vote for. This has been called the **electronic vote**. This form of voting could be used more often, for example, in voting on certain issues between elections: should hanging come back; should Britain leave the common market; should new motorways be built? Some people feel that electronic voting would give people more 'say' in their own lives—others feel that it would become impossible for governments to decide on anything.

Big brother Because of computers more and more information about people (their past history, beliefs, likes and opinions) can be stored in so-called 'data banks'. This may be useful, for example, in helping police to trace a criminal. But it may stop people from having a private life. The problem of storing information, and people's privacy, is dealt with in: Will Big Brother Be Watching You?

Machines deciding for us? This sounds like science fiction, but some experts believe that computers will one day be able to make important decisions for businessmen, doctors, and even politicians. How would you feel about a computer as Prime Minister? It seems like a joke but one or two people believe it could happen. The future of intelligent computers, or artificial intelligence, is considered in: Can Machines Have Minds?

At school

Primary school children using a microcomputer

Microcomputers are already used in schools to help people learn. This is called **Computer-Assisted Learning** (CAL). Some programs give pupils practice in certain skills, for example: spelling, arithmetic, measuring angles. Other programs provide *simulations*. These use simplified copies, or *models*, of real-life situations, for example: a pond, a traffic roundabout, an oil slick on the sea, or the raising of the 'Mary Rose'. The program user can alter different things in the simulation to see what happens (e.g. the number of fish in the pond could be varied). A third type of program, **database programs**, can be used to store information about any subject, for example: types of fruit, the population of a town, or the scores of a football team. The program user can find out, or access, items of information by asking the right questions.

Many people feel that these educational uses of computers will go much further. Much more education could take place at home. As communication by satellite and cable become common, pupils will be able to access information and computer programs from almost anywhere. The important thing will be to learn *how* to access this information and use it, not simply to memorize it. The home computer, television, telephone, and maybe a video machine could form a sort of home education centre.

At present anyone between the ages of 5 and 16 must go to school, by law. Some people believe that, with the spread of computers and communications, compulsory schooling as you know it will disappear. Schools may become places where people mix, talk, enjoy sports, discuss their own education with personal tutors.

War and peace

The first computers grew out of the Second World War. Giant machines were used to calculate bomb trajectories and to crack German secret codes (using COLOSSUS). Since then most of the money for studying and developing electronics and microelectronics has come from the military. One use of microelectronics is to guide missiles to strike a target accurately. As one person said: 'Atomic physics provided the power, microelectronics provides the direction.'

Many uses of microelectronics have nothing to do with war and weapons, but it is worth remembering that the drive to make new weapons and missiles provided most of the microelectronics that people use today.

For better, for worse...

It is dangerous to talk as if all this new technology will somehow take over our lives. You must always remember that people are involved, and people must decide how it is to be used: for better or for worse.

Likes and dislikes A lot of people like reading books and newspapers. Reading words from a television screen is not as pleasant, and it can give eyestrain. Besides, you can curl up in bed with a good book but hardly with a VDU and keyboard. Remember this when people talk about the paperless society.

Human beings are sociable animals. They like a good gossip or chinwag. If mail is delivered electronically there will be no postman to talk to (or for the dog to bite). If people do their shopping from home using a video and a computer terminal what will happen to the visit to the shops? Finally, some people working at home may find it unsuitable. Many people actually enjoy going to work, if only to meet other people and get out of the house.

People's needs There are about 4000 million (4 billion) people living on this planet. About 2 billion of them live in slums and do not have enough to eat. How will new technology help these people, in the so-called Third World? Optimists feel that computers will save energy and this energy can be used to help the Third World develop. Pessimists feel that computers will only widen the gap between the 'haves' (the developed countries) and the 'have-nots' (the Third World).

So, whenever you read about the effects of computers on society remember:
- people's likes and dislikes
- the needs of people, throughout the world.

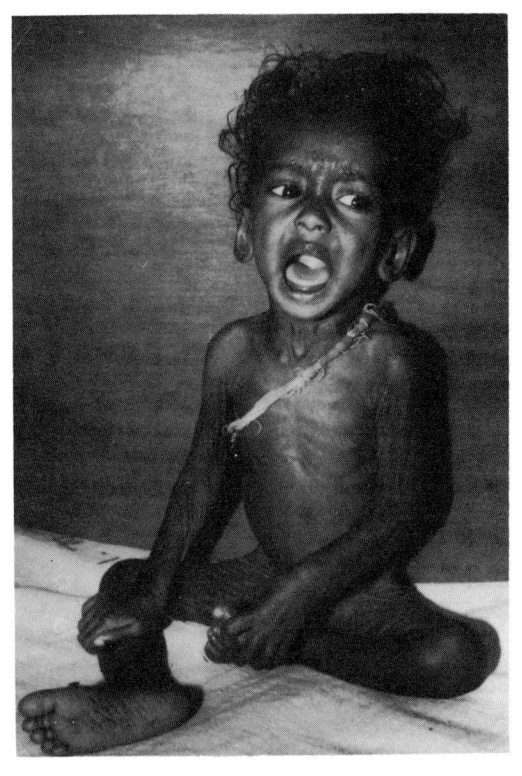

There are 2 000 000 000 people in the world who do not get enough to eat. How can computers help them?

Questions

1 One famous American computer scientist has said:
'We have seen the computer begin as a mere instrument for generating ballistic tables and grow to a force that now pervades almost every aspect of modern society.' (Joe Weizenbaum)

a) What 'instrument for generating ballistic tables' is he referring to?
b) Find out what the word pervades means.
c) Give some examples of how computers are pervading modern society.

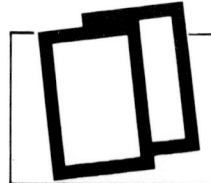

Reader
Yesterday's tomorrows

Throughout history people have tried to predict the future. Most of them got it wrong. Below are some of the forecasts which were made about computers in the 1940's and 1950's. They are just a few examples of yesterday's tomorrows.

Did you know that . . .

- IBM made less than 20 of its first model of computer. They thought that the world could not possibly cope with, or need, more.
- American experts forecast in 1955, when there were 250 computers in the USA, that the country would contain 5000 by 1965. In fact, there were 20 000. By 1975 there were 80 000, quite large machines because the microcomputer had not arrived. Twenty million microcomputers were sold in 1979.
- In the late 1940's British experts forecast that 5 of their new-fangled, giant machines would be enough for Britain's needs. Today, equally powerful computers can be carried in a plastic bag. Over a million have been sold.
- In 1948 George Orwell wrote a now world-famous novel called *1984*. He forecast that by the year 1984 everyone would be watched over by television cameras, and detailed information about everyone's beliefs, habits, likes and dislikes would be secretly stored by the ruling Party. 'Big brother' would be watching us!

Here is a short passage from the first page of Orwell's book:

> It was a bright cold day in April, and the clocks were striking thirteen. Winston Smith, his chin nuzzled into his breast in an effort to escape the vile wind, slipped quickly through the glass doors of Victory Mansions, though not quickly enough to prevent a swirl of gritty dust from entering along with him.
>
> The hallway smelt of boiled cabbage and old rag mats. At one end of it a coloured poster, too large for indoor display, had been tacked to the wall. it depicted simply an enormous face, more than a metre wide: the face of a man of about forty-five, with a heavy black moustache and ruggedly handsome features. Winston made for the stairs. It was no use trying the lift. Even at the best of times it was seldom

working, and at present the electric current was cut off during daylight hours. It was part of the economy drive in preparation for Hate Week. The flat was seven flights up, and Winston, who was thirty-nine and had a varicose ulcer above his right ankle, went slowly, resting several times on the way. On each landing, opposite the lift-shaft, the poster with the enormous face gazed from the wall. It was one of those pictures which are so contrived that the eyes follow you about when you move. BIG BROTHER IS WATCHING YOU, the caption beneath it ran.

Inside the flat a fruity voice was reading out a list of figures which had something to do with the production of pig-iron. The voice came from an oblong metal plaque like a dulled mirror which formed part of the surface of the right-hand wall. Winston turned a switch and the voice sank somewhat, though the words were still distinguishable. The instrument (the telescreen, it was called) could be dimmed, but there was no way of shutting it off completely.

The main character in 1984 is Winston Smith. Later in the story he starts to keep his own secret diary—a crime punishable by death. You will need to read the book yourself to find out what happens to Winston.

Questions

1 Do you think that a situation like this one described in the passage could ever come true?
2 The scene described in 1984 is technically possible. What could be done to prevent it happening in this country?
3 How do you know that the present Government (the 'ruling Party') does not have detailed information stored about you?

8.2 More jobs or less?

The changing world of work

In Britain in the 18th century almost everyone who did work, worked on the land. About 92 people in every 100 were working to feed themselves and the 8 others! In 1980 only 2% of all workers were employed in agriculture. These 2 in every 100 work to feed the other 98. These figures are even higher in America. One American farmer now feeds about 60 people (though the average for the whole world is about 1 to 5).

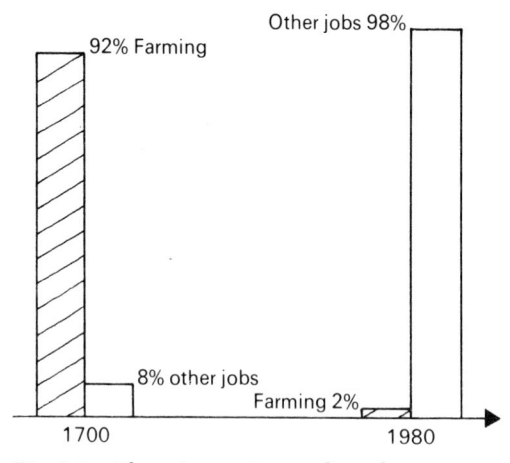

Fig. 8.2 Changing patterns of employment

These changing patterns of work have been caused by two 'revolutions' ('revolution' = total change). The first is called the **industrial revolution**. In the nineteenth century and early twentieth many *farm workers* moved to the big cities (which became even bigger) and were employed as *machine workers*. These workers were employed in the huge factories of Manchester, Leeds, Bradford, Sheffield and other cities. They were employed to manufacture goods: cloth, clothing, steel, furniture, cars and so on. But now (in the 1980's) many of these jobs are disappearing—partly because they are being done in other countries which are just starting to develop; and partly because of the next so-called revolution. This has been called the **post-industrial** or **information revolution**. Because of it some jobs have gone and new ones have arrived.

Jobs that will go

If a job can be done by a machine rather than a person, then in future it probably will be. Ticket machines are replacing car park attendants. Self-service petrol pumps with digital displays of the amount of petrol you have bought are

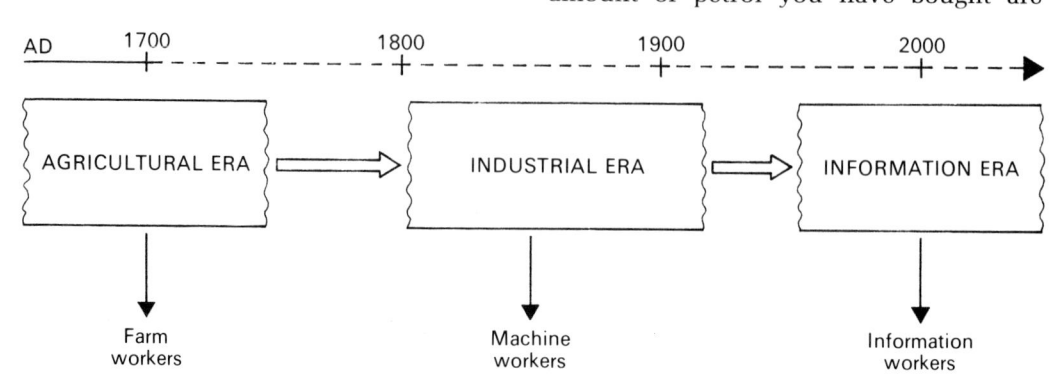

Fig. 8.3 The three eras of work

198

A driverless tractor!

Self-service petrol pumps have almost replaced petrol-pump attendants

Microprocessor-controlled coal cutter

replacing petrol-pump attendants. Much of the hard labour done by coal miners is now being done by microprocessor-controlled cutting machines.

In car factories more and more of the boring, repetitive jobs are being done by robots. A recent study in West Germany showed that four car workers could be replaced by one robot. One *new* job would be created, on average, probably to look after the robot!

The same is likely to happen in any factory where goods are made. Computers, and machines with chips inside them, will be used to *design*, *make* and *inspect* the finished product, from steel knives to a suit of clothes. This can only mean fewer jobs for people. As someone has said:
'The steel-collar workers (robots) will replace the blue-collar (factory) workers.'
But these are not the only jobs in danger . . .

Information handlers—the white collar workers

Hundreds of workers in large, commercial city centres like London or Manchester are involved in handling information. They may be office workers, secretaries, bank clerks, insurance workers, or simply messengers carrying information from one place to another. As you know, computers are excellent for handling and storing information, and the new communications will be excellent for sending it from one place to another. The new technologies of computers and communications could end the jobs of thousands of white collar workers—the so-called 'pen pushers' and 'paper handlers', administrators and clerks, messengers and telephonists, newspaper workers and printers.

If you live in London you may not yet have noticed unemployment as much as a person who lives in a manufacturing city like Coventry, Bradford or Sheffield. This may not be true for much longer. Most of Britain's information handlers travel into, and out of, London every day. The London rush hour could become a thing of the past.

What about the experts?

Some computer scientists believe that even certain experts could lose their jobs because of computers. Scientists are working to make computers which can make decisions and give advice just like an expert doctor, lawyer or accountant, for example. These are called **expert systems**. A system has already been tried which can diagnose certain illnesses by asking the right questions. Leading doctors need to be involved in programming it, of course, and giving it the right data. Some expert systems are quicker and more reliable than even the people who helped to develop them!

Computers will never replace doctors, solicitors and accountants, although they may reduce the number of expert humans that are needed—if people allow them to.

New jobs that could arrive...

One thing is certain—new jobs will be created by the new information technology. There will be a need for more engineering skills—in electronics, production and designing new systems. There will be a need for computer programmers—people who can design, and write, the software for new computer and communication systems. But there are problems:
- not enough new jobs will be created in these new areas to replace the old jobs that are disappearing
- many of these jobs need highly-skilled, well-qualified people
- many of the new jobs will not be in the same company, factory or even the same area.

For better or for worse...

Some people (the pessimists) believe that the information revolution will lead to:
- massive unemployment: millions of people condemned to a life of 'leisure'—not knowing how to use the time and no money to spend on it
- upheaval of people and communities: more people will be forced to leave their home towns and communities to seek work
- more isolation of human beings: there could be less social contact between people as communities are uprooted and communications take place via computers
- lucky people in the new jobs earning higher wages, *but* having to work longer hours or shift work to make full use of computer time
- 'more work for some, less for others': the gap between the 'haves' and 'have-nots' could widen—people on high wages in new industries, and people on the dole.

These are some of the worst things that could happen in the new information era. The optimists, on the other hand, believe that if new technology is used to benefit *people* the future looks more rosy...

An optimistic view

All the changes mentioned so far could be used to improve the *quality* of people's lives. For example:
- They could lead to a shorter working week for those who have a job. Fewer people would need to work overtime, on night shifts, or unsocial hours to produce the goods we need.
- People could retire at an earlier age.
- Many of the boring, repetitive jobs in unpleasant conditions would disappear. They could be done by machines. There might be less drudgery and boredom in the work place.
- If efficient farms and factories, helped by microelectronics and computers, produce the goods we need, more people could be employed in the *service industries*. These people could do socially useful jobs, for example: nursing, caring for elderly people, helping the handicapped, protecting and conserving our surroundings, teaching, and so on.

Service industries, that is, jobs serving and helping other people, are because of their very nature *inefficient*. They involve a lot of labour. More and more people could be employed in them if savings achieved by employing new technology are used to pay the extra wages.

There are hundreds of jobs that cannot be done by machines. These are the jobs of the craftsman—wood carving, sculpture, painting, stone masonry, and so on. The age of microelectronics could allow the return of the craftsman. Also, there would be more leisure time—for those who wanted it.

All these changes might come in the new microelectronics era: improved working conditions, more services for those who need them, a return to the craftsman, more leisure time. However, this will only happen if new technology is used to serve people—and not the other way round.

The optimists believe that the development of information technology will give us more leisure time

Questions

1 'The steel collar worker will replace the blue collar worker.'
  Can you explain what this means?
2 Write down 3 examples of jobs which require 'handling information'.
3 Many people in their everyday jobs are using computers more and more to help in their work. This has often meant that they have had to change their methods of working, and that fewer people are needed because the computers are so efficient. For each of the following jobs:
  a) petrol pump attendant
  b) shop cashier
  c) airline pilot
  describe:
  (i) One way in which the job may have, or could be, changed by the introduction of computers.
  (ii) Whether you feel that the introduction of computers will lead to fewer people being needed to do the job, and if so why?
  (iii) One advantage and one disadvantage to the public resulting from computers being used in the job.
  (SREB)
4 Write an account of the effects of computers on employment and unemployment. Consider in your answer:
  a) the creation of new jobs
  b) changes in existing jobs
  c) the loss of existing jobs
  (NWREB)

Reader
The computer revolution

Some people feel that to talk about a computer revolution is wrong. They believe that the motor car, the railways, or even bulldozers have had more effect on people's lives than computers have.

This passage is taken from an excellent story about a group of Americans building a super new minicomputer. Here, they have just left a computer exhibition, or fair, in New York. Some of their names are mentioned in the passage. Read it carefully then see if you agree with the way they see things:

> "Wallach and I retreated from the fair, to a café some distance from the Coliseum. Sitting there, observing the more familiar chaos of a New York City street, I was struck by how unnoticeable the computer revolution was. Almost every commentator has assured the public that the computer is bringing on a revolution. By the 1970's it should have been clear that revolution was the wrong word. You leave a bazaar like the NCC* expecting to find that your perceptions of the world outside will have been altered, but there was nothing commensurate in sight—no cyborgs, half-machine, half-protoplasm, tripping down the street; no armies of unemployed, carrying placards denouncing the computer; no TV cameras watching us. Computers were everywhere, of course—in the café's beeping cash registers and the microwave oven and the jukebox, in the traffic lights, under the hoods of the honking cars snarled out there on the street (despite those traffic lights), in the airplanes overhead—but the visible differences somehow seemed insignificant.
>
> (*National Computer Conference)

202

Computers had become less noticeable as they had become smaller, more reliable, more efficient, and more numerous. Surely this happened by design. Obviously, to sell the devices far and wide, manufacturers had to strive to make them easy to use and, wherever possible, invisible. Were computers a profound, unseen hand?

In The Coming of Post-Industrial Society, Daniel Bell asserted that new machines introduced in the nineteenth century, such as the railroad train, made larger changes in 'the lives of individuals' than computers have. Tom West liked to say: 'Let's talk about bulldozers. Bulldozers have had a hell of a lot bigger effect on people's lives.'

Obviously, computers have made differences. They have fostered the development of spaceships—as well as a great increase in junk mail. The computer boom has brought the marvelous but expensive diagnostic device known as the CAT scanner, as well as a host of other medical equipment; it has given rise to machines that play good but rather boring chess, and also, on a larger game board, to a proliferation of remote-controlled weapons in the arsenals of nations. Computers have changed ideas about waging war and about pursuing science, too. It is hard to see how contemporary geophysics or meteorology or plasma physics can advance very far without them now. Computers have changed the nature of research in mathematics, though not every mathematician would say it is for the better. And computers have become a part of the ordinary conduct of businesses of all sorts. They really help, in some cases.

> Not always, though. One student of the field has estimated that about forty percent of commercial applications of computers have proved uneconomical, in the sense that the job the computer was bought to perform winds up costing more to do after the computer's arrival than it did before. Most computer companies have boasted that they aren't just selling machines, they're selling productivity. ('We're not in competition with each other,' said a PR man. 'We're in competition with labor.') But that clearly isn't always true. Sometimes they're selling paper-producers that require new legions of workers to push that paper around.
>
> Coming from the fair, it seemed to me that computers have been used in ways that are salutary, in ways that are dangerous, banal and cruel, and in ways that seem harmless if a little silly. But what fun making them can be!"

(From Chapter 13: 'Going to the Fair' in *The Soul of a New Machine* by Tracy Kidder, Penguin. 1982.) © John Tracy Kidder, 1981. Reprinted by permission of Penguin Books Ltd.

Questions

1 Do you think that the new machines of the 19th century, like railway trains, have had more effect on people's lives than the computers of the 20th century?
What about motor cars and bulldozers?
2 'We're in competition with labour', one computer salesman is supposed to have said. Can you explain what this means? Do you think he is right—are computers in competition with labour?
3 Explain why the writer thinks that the 'computer revolution' is unnoticeable, even in a place like New York City.

8.3 Can computers save the woolly monkey?

In 1980 one expert estimated that the equivalent of 20 million million pages of A4 paper is stored in the offices of the USA. This is growing at the rate of 1 million pages every day. What has this got to do with woolly monkeys? Read on.

Vanishing forests

Have you ever been to the woolly monkey sanctuary near Looe in Cornwall? This sanctuary was built as a safe home for woolly monkeys where they can live, breed and above all, survive. Their natural home is in the forests of Brazil. In these, and other large forests, thousands of trees are chopped down every day *partly* to provide paper. So, the woolly monkey is an endangered species because its natural home is disappearing.

How can computers help?

Paper is used for storing *written* words. It has been used for this purpose (and others, of course) for centuries now, but the written word can now be stored and communicated in other ways which do not involve paper. This is possible because of *computer codes*.

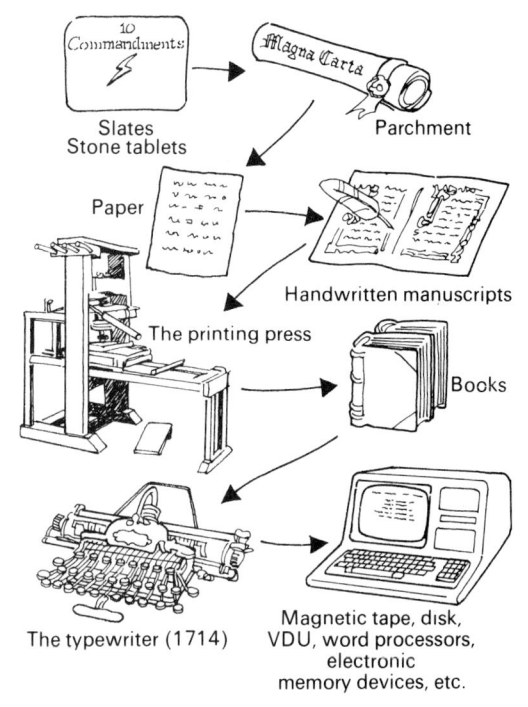

Fig. 8.4 *Storing the written word—a brief history*

Felled tropical forest, Amazon basin, Brazil

Every word on this page is made up from a string of letters and other characters. Each character can be given a code. For a computer to use it, the code must be a binary code. Examples from one widely used code are:

CHARACTER	CODE (ASCII code)
A	1000001
B	1000010
C	1000011
!	0100001

So the code for the written message

CAB!

would be:

1000011 1000001 1000010 0100001

When you type characters into a computer system, the system translates each character into its binary code. Each and every character of our written language can be changed into a binary code—the language of the computer.

Once inside the computer system all kinds of useful things can be done with this coded language.

storage: Written words can be held or stored in a computer system as binary words. If the words need to be stored permanently they can be held on long-term memory devices which use a binary code, for example: optical disks, magnetic tape or disk, magnetic bubble memory, etc.

manipulation: The words can be displayed on a screen. There, they can be moved around, altered or replaced by other words. New words, new sentences or even new paragraphs can be added. This manipulation of words is called **word processing**.

transmission and communication: Messages, papers and documents can be sent from one place to another electronically. The words of the message are converted to binary code and transmitted as a digital signal, sometimes at the speed of light. By linking computers into networks, computer-based message systems can be formed.

Some people believe that newspapers will disappear in the future. British Telecom have forecast that instant home newspapers will arrive by the early 1990's. Information will be sent to you by telephone, or by waves which your television aerial can receive. This information can be displayed on your television screen, including up-to-the-minute news. All of these uses are made possible because of character-coding which can be represented by a computer system. The next three sections tell you more about these uses and how they can help to save paper.

Storing written words: the end of books and newspapers?

Storing written words on a computer system has several advantages compared with storing them on paper:

- It is *cheaper*. One magnetic tape costs less than £10 and can hold several million characters of information which would cost hundreds of pounds to store in book form. This difference will become even greater with newer memory devices.
- It takes up less *space*. One estimate says that the words in 1 million books can be stored on only two modern mass storage devices. Figure 8.5 shows how many pages of the Concise Oxford Dictionary can be stored on different memory disks.
- It is easier to get at, or *access*, information if it is stored in a computer system. People can find the information they are looking for much more quickly than by flicking through pages of a book. Besides this, if the words of a book are stored on a computer several people can view them at once. These people could be in different parts of the world, linked by a computer network.

These advantages mean that in the future more and more written words will be stored in computer memory devices as well as books and paper—and sometimes *instead* of books.

Medium	Number of bytes stored (approx.)	Equivalent number of pages of Concise Oxford Dictionary
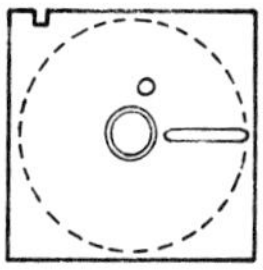 Floppy disk	0.5 M byte (500 000 bytes)	100 pages
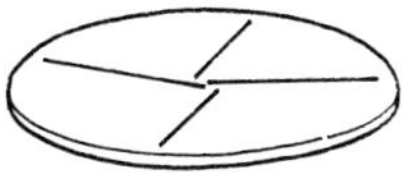 Rigid disk	10 Mb (10 000 000 bytes)	2000 dictionary pages
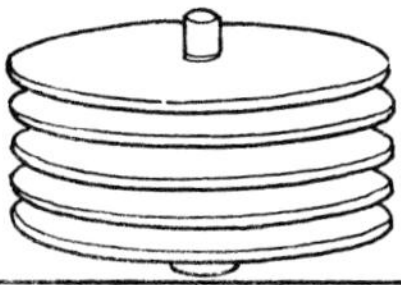 Disk pack	500 Mb (500 000 000 bytes)	200 000 dictionary pages
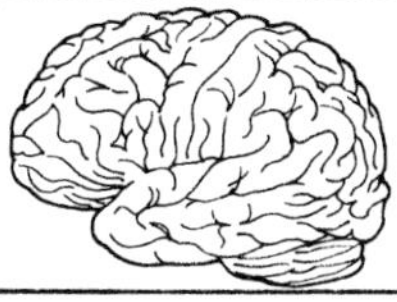 Human brain	125 terabytes (125 000 000 000 000 bytes)	But who has a perfect memory?

Fig. 8.5 *A comparison of storage devices*

If you want a paper copy, a printer attached to your Prestel television set will give you a print-out. But all this costs money. Most people will prefer to spend twenty pence on a paper—until home newspapers cost less.

So the written word stored on paper will be around for many years yet. Besides this, most people enjoy reading words from a book or a newspaper. A well-produced book often looks very pleasing, and has a pleasant feel and sometimes smell. Have you ever felt, or smelt, a VDU? Finally, many people complain that reading words from a television screen gives them eyestrain—books put far less strain on your eyes. For all these reasons, 'the end of paper' hardly seems possible.

Playing with words: the electronic office

Paper may not disappear in people's everyday lives—but there will definitely be less lying around on the desks, and in the cupboards, of offices. Most offices are involved in handling forms, bills, letters, articles, references, news bulletins, programmes and so on. These can all be called *documents*. Offices are involved in (at least) these six activities:

- *receiving* documents from outside, e.g. customers, other offices
- *storing* documents, e.g. in a filing system, record book
- *preparing* documents to send out
- *revising and changing* documents, e.g. to update them
- *printing* documents onto paper
- *sending* them out, e.g. to customers, other offices.

Computer systems can help in all six of these jobs. You have seen how they can store documents cheaply, and in a small space. Untidy mounds of paper and bulging filing cabinets can be avoided. In the next section you will see how computer systems can send out and receive documents without any need for paper in between. How can computer systems help in preparing, revising and printing documents? The main reason is the word processor.

Word processors A keyboard is linked to a computer, a VDU, a disk drive and a printer. The typist does not handle paper. Instead, the words he or she types appear on the screen. These words can be altered, underlined, removed, or replaced. Headings and footnotes can be added—or even passages or sentences from elsewhere. Some word processors can even be programmed to correct certain spelling mistakes. The word processor can be a powerful tool for preparing and revising documents.

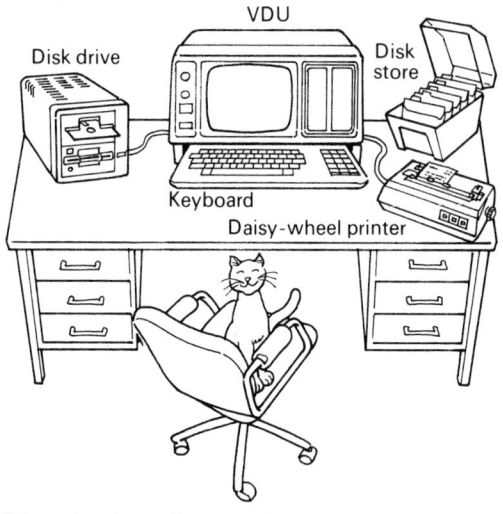

Fig. 8.6 A word processing system

Once the document has been prepared, revised or improved a printer can be used to make a paper copy of it. Standard letters can be stored on disk and the details filled in before printing the letter.

For example:

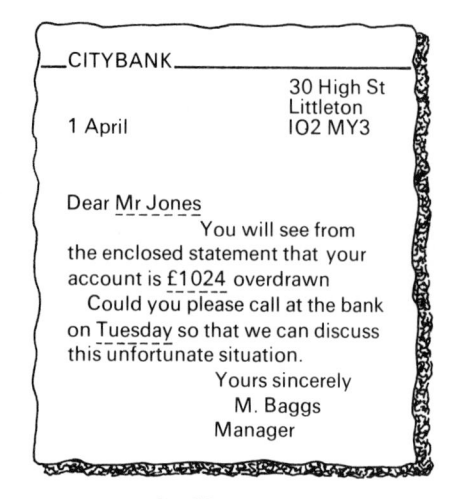

```
CITYBANK
                              30 High St
                              Littleton
1 April                       IO2 MY3

Dear Mr Jones
            You will see from
the enclosed statement that your
account is £1024 overdrawn
    Could you please call at the bank
on Tuesday so that we can discuss
this unfortunate situation.
                    Yours sincerely
                    M. Baggs
                    Manager
```

Fig. 8.7 A standard letter

It is no longer necessary to make a paper copy of a document and then to post it—it can be sent from one place to another electronically.

Sending paperless messages: electronic mail

Two ways of sending out documents without using a postman have been around for a number of years: **telex** and **facsimile**.

Telex (*teleprinter exchange*) This is like the telephone service, but instead of carrying people's speech it carries *teleprinter* signals (remember that a teleprinter is a combination of a keyboard and a printer).

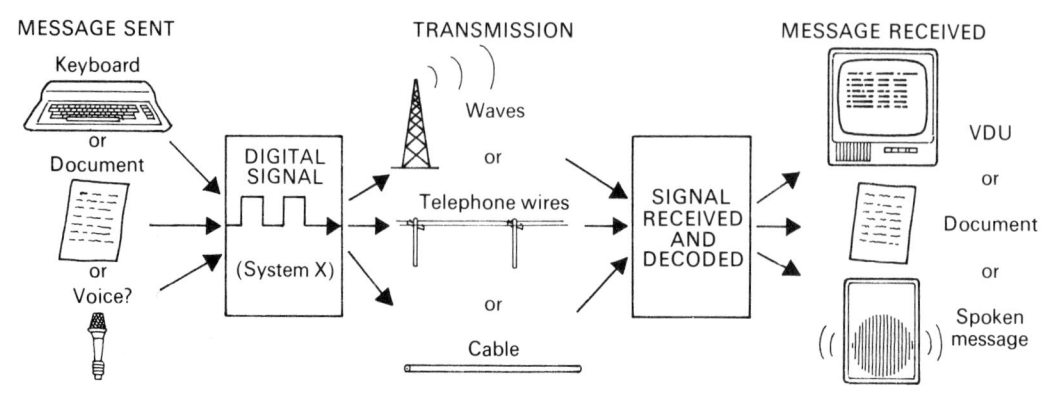

Fig. 8.8 Electronic mail

Telex

A document is typed at one end and received at the other. Both receiver and sender have a paper record of the document. There is now a worldwide telex network, used by over a million people.

Facsimile (= 'make alike', to make an exact copy) A document is copied by the sender and coded into a digital signal. This signal is sent by telephone, telex or satellite to the receiver. There, the signal is decoded and an exact copy of the original is made. An A4 page can be sent in about three minutes.

Computer networks More and more computers are being linked together to form networks. Computers in the same room can be joined together by wires while computers in different countries can be linked by radio waves and satellite.

More often, computers are linked by telephone lines. Many telephone exchanges are being modernized to cope with the digital signals of 1's and 0's that computers use.

By forming networks, electronic messages can be sent from one computer to another, for example: memos, reports, reminders, even bills. The receiver can make a paper copy if he wants to by connecting his computer to a terminal. Otherwise, he can simply read the message from a VDU, or file it on a disk. The flow of computer-coded information will gradually replace the flow of paper.

The end of the office?

Some people believe that even the idea of the electronic office is out of date. Computer networks mean that business people can now have *computer conferences*. They can discuss the same plan or document even if they are in three or four different places. In a similar way a secretary could do word processing at home to save travelling to an office. Documents could be prepared at home and sent to an office or a company along the telephone line. On reaching the office it could be checked and printed.

At the moment the centre of London is full of office blocks. A lot of them could be empty by the year 2000. The commuter hiding behind his newspaper on the morning train may disappear before his paper does.

Is the age of commuting nearly over?

Reader
The man who has given up paper

Read this extract from a magazine article, then answer the questions below.

Each weekday morning Tom Rosewall, the international director of Westinghouse Furniture Systems, sits down to an empty desk at his London office. The desk remains clear for the rest of the day. The reason: Tom has given up paper. Instead, he uses electronic mail, the latest development in the communications revolution now sweeping Britain's offices.

Using a screen and a keyboard he can send and receive electronic letters over the ordinary telephone network, the letters reach their destination in seconds. To send a message to a colleague in Hong Kong—or less, exotically, Twickenham—Tom simply dials the number of British Telecom's electronic mail computer, Telecom Gold. Once the message has been typed in, it is immediately forwarded to the recipient's own electronic mailbox.

In common with most users, Tom checks his mailbox several times a day. More impatient subscribers opt for a bleeper which warns of incoming messages. 'Now it only takes me 45 minutes to deal with my post—a lot less than when we were buried under paper,' says Tom. Like many businessmen with international interests, he finds it ideal for communicating with people in different time zones. Teletag, the game of missed telephone connections, is also largely a thing of the past.

What is really making electronic mail take off is the explosion in the number of business microcomputers, of which there are now some 300,000 in use here, with a further million machines gracing British homes. Every one of these is a potential electronic mail terminal. And indeed, from next month a new service called Micromail will give personal computer users access to the Telecom Gold system.

In the United States, electronic mail systems now claim about 2.5 million users.

(From *The Observer Magazine*.)

Questions

1. Explain the meaning of 'electronic mail'.
2. Describe how Tom Rosewall sends a message from London to Hong Kong.
3. What do you think the term 'electronic mailbox' means?
4. Explain why a microcomputer is a 'potential electronic mail terminal'.
5. How many people were estimated to be using electronic mail systems in the USA when this article was written?

8.4 Will big brother be watching you?

Sensitive information and computers

Do you like answering questions about yourself? Are you sensitive about your age, your height, or your weight? Would you become suspicious if a salesman asked you questions about your likes and dislikes, or your views about politics?

More and more information is being stored about *people*. In future, the *storage*, *processing* and *retrieval* of information will become more and more important to our society and its economy. This is what people mean by the 'information society'.

The idea of storing information about people is not new. Records of people's medical histories, or a pupil's progress at school, have been kept for many years now, although more and more information is coming out of the filing cabinet and going into the computer. Records once stored on cards or paper are now held on magnetic tape or disk. Putting information into computer systems makes three important differences.

- Larger and larger amounts of information—or rather *data*—can be stored in a smaller and smaller space. This means that more and more data about *people* can be stored if necessary.
- Information or data about people can be more easily 'got at' or *accessed*. A computer file can be searched more easily than, say, a row of filing cabinets.
- Finally, information in computer systems can easily be communicated from one system or one person to another. Systems can communicate with each other so easily that a large, comprehensive file could be made on every citizen in this country. It would be easy to compile—and easy for certain people to get at.

Dangers of an information society

One estimate suggests that between 15 and 50 computer files are kept on the average adult in Britain. Some examples, which might apply to you, are:

> bank account
> tax record
> medical history
> driving licence record
> library books
> exam results
> school records
> police record
> social security
> credit card records

What are the dangers of storing large amounts of information about people? Here are some of the fears that people have expressed:

- inaccurate and out-of-date information can be stored and still be used to make decisions affecting people's lives
- people may have no idea what information is stored about them, and have no way of checking it for mistakes
- private, confidential information could fall into the wrong hands, e.g. a burglar or a blackmailer
- information could be used for a different purpose than the one it was gathered for—especially when computer systems can be linked so easily.

However, the biggest fear is that all the separate files of information could be *merged together*. A huge data bank could be formed containing detailed information about every person in Britain.

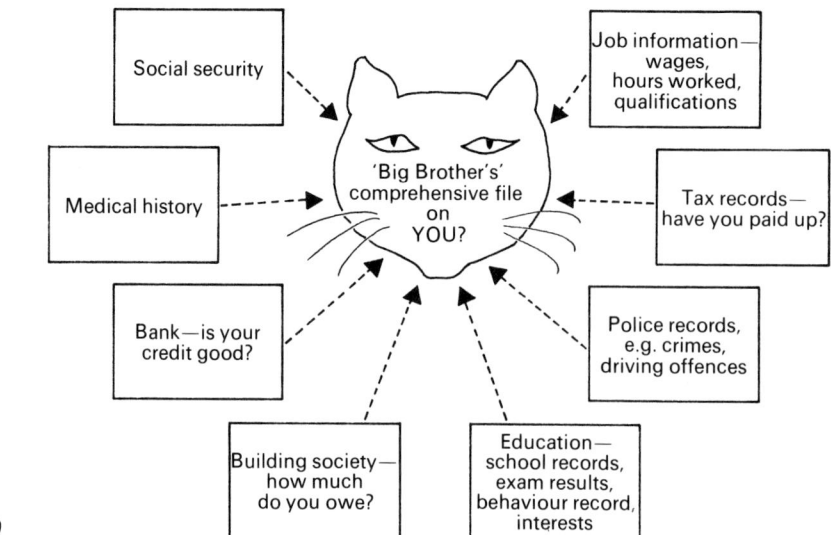

Fig. 8.9

Keeping data in safe hands: data protection

These fears have led to several government inquiries into the problems of storing information about people. Most of them suggested that data should be safeguarded or protected in some way. Britain does not have a data-protection law—although many European countries and the USA do.

The most recent government report, 'The Lindop Report', suggested several ways of safeguarding data kept about people:
- Each individual must know what data is being kept about him or her, for how long and for what purpose, i.e. what, how long and why?
- All data stored should be accurate, complete, relevant, and up to date.
- Only sufficient data should be held for the stated purpose—no more.
- Each individual should be able to check for himself that these rules are being kept.

The Lindop report suggested that a special data protection authority should be set up to make these checks, and look after people's privacy. As yet, Britain does not have such an authority. The report also suggested that the rules above should be made law—as yet, no law has been passed.

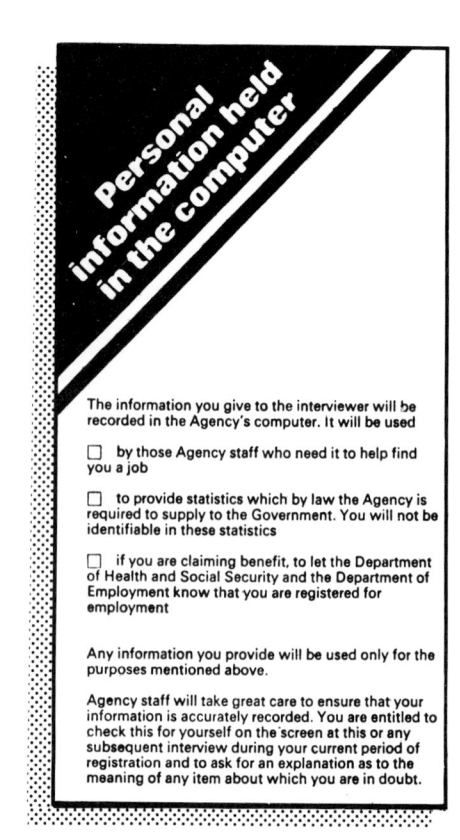

Fig. 8.10 *Safeguards are needed when collecting information about people*

LANDMARKS IN DATA PROTECTION	
1972	Younger Report. Set out certain guidelines for protecting data
1975	Government White Paper: *Computers and Privacy*. Suggested a data protection authority and a data protection law
1978	Lindop Report
1981	Britain signed the *Council of Europe Data Protection Convention*. This gives people the right to know what information is stored about them.

Keeping data private: data security

One of people's biggest fears is that information about them could get into 'the wrong hands' (e.g. a criminal or a blackmailer). Access to information is now much quicker and easier because of information technology. How can we make sure that only the right people can get certain information? How can unauthorized *access* be stopped?

One idea is to give people a **password**. The computer is programmed to ask anyone who uses one of its terminals to give the password. Without it, no-one can use the computer or get to any of its files.

Another idea is to give each user a magnetic card. The magnetic card could then be used to let the user, and no-one else, into the computer room; or a terminal could read a magnetic card and then ask the user to type in a number which agrees with the number on the card.

Unfortunately, passwords can be copied or forgotten—cards can be lost or stolen. Special terminals are now made which can recognize either: a person's signature or a person's fingerprint or handprint or even a person's voice.

An idea now becoming more popular is to put all the data in a specially coded form.

Coding the data Many computers are now programmed to scramble all the data held in them into a special code. A person can only unscramble it and use the data if he knows the secret code. Of course, codes can be cracked as they were in World War II. No code is unbreakable, but the idea of this form of data security is to make the cost of breaking the code higher than the value of the information which it protects!

One final reason for protecting data is the problem of **corruption**. This could occur if someone gained access to a computer file and changed or altered it in some way, for example, to alter the amount in their bank account from £10 to £1 million!

Fig. 8.11 Data security is important in banks!

Questions

1. In the Lindop Report of 1978, Sir Norman Lindop said that:
'We did not feel that Orwell's 1984 was just around the corner, but we did feel that some pretty frightening developments could come about quite quickly and without most people being aware of what was happening.'
a) Find out what he means by 'Orwell's 1984 was just around the corner.' Do you think this is possible?
b) Do you know what information is kept about you and who keeps it?
c) Developments could come about 'without people being aware of them'. How could this happen? How can people guard against it?

2*A critic of the Police National Computer (PNC) has said, The Criminal Names Index contains 3.8 million names of people convicted of more serious offences. This index was based on the national Criminal Records Office files at Scotland Yard, but in the process of transferring to the PNC these files grew from 2.2 million names to 3.8 million names—the more serious offences not hitherto recorded nationally included petty thefts, wasting police time and offences under the Rent Acts. The Home Office and police whimsically call this suppressed demand information retrieval. It is known that when any car is seen in the vicinity of a casino, a suspect's house or a political demonstration, information on its owner can be easily added to the records of the PNC.'
a) Give three advantages to the police of having these records on a computer.
b) Give three advantages to the public of having these records on a computer.
c) Give two reasons why members of the public who are honest might be worried about some of the information recorded on the PNC.
(AEB)

3*People are often worried about their personal information being held on a computer file. Write an article for a newspaper naming three different applications in which personal information might be held. For each application describe what information might be held and how it may be accessed, and give reasons explaining why you think it may be good, or bad, to hold that information. (Typical application areas might be: police; medical records; credit services; insurance; banks, etc.)

*'O'-Level question

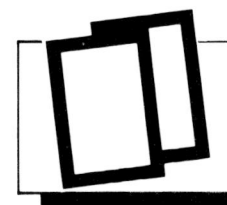

Reader
The third industrial revolution

The first industrial revolution multiplied mankind's muscle power. The bulldozer replaced the pick and shovel. The computer revolution (the second industrial revolution) multiplied mankind's ability to do routine, repetitive mental work. The computer is replacing the office clerk. Will the third revolution, with the next generation of computers, multiply mankind's ability to do real brain work? To make difficult decisions? To solve real problems? Read this passage from an American novel on the effects of the fifth generation of computers with their so-called artificial intelligence.

> 'That's very good, what you said about the second industrial revolution,' she said.
> 'Old, old stuff.'
> 'It seemed very fresh to me—I mean that part where you say how the first industrial revolution devalued muscle work, then the second one devalued routine mental work. I was fascinated.'
> 'Norbert Wiener said all that way back in the nineteen-forties. It's fresh to you because you're too young to know anything but the way things are now....'
> 'Do you suppose there will be a third industrial revolution?'
> He paused in his office doorway. 'A third one? What would that be like?'
> 'I don't know exactly. The first and second ones must have been sort of inconceivable at one time.'
> 'To the people who were going to be replaced by machines, maybe. A third one, eh? In a way, I guess the third one's been going on for some time, if you mean thinking machines. That would be the third revolution, I guess—machines that devalue human thinking. Some of the big computers like EPICAC do that all right in specialized fields.'

'Uh-huh,' she said thoughtfully. She rattled a pencil between her teeth. 'First, the muscle work, then the routine work, and then, maybe, the real brain work.'
'I hope I'm not around long enough to see that final step ...'

(From *Player Piano* by Kurt Vonnegut, Jr.)

Questions

1 '... the first industrial revolution devalued muscle work, then the second one devalued routine mental work.' Can you explain what this means?
2 Explain how the computer revolution has also helped to do some of our boring, repetitive manual work, e.g. by using robots in industry.
3 One of the people in this conversation used the phrase: 'the real brain work'. What do you think she meant?
4 'I hope I'm not around long enough to see that final step ...' was the last comment made. Why do you think he said this?
5 Norbert Weiner coined the term cybernetics. Find out what this means.

Photo 18   Optical fibres: hair-thin strands of extremely pure glass, carry information as pulses of laser light. A pair of fibres can carry 2000 simultaneous phone calls.

Photo 19   Comparing traditional copper cable with optical fibre cable. As well as the advantage of smaller size, optical cable is cheaper and can carry signals much further than metal cable before 'boosting' is required. It can carry more phone calls at any one time and is immune to electrical interference which affects the quality of calls.

Photo 20   An artist's impression of the European Space Agency's future multipurpose telecommunications satellite L-SAT (Large Satellite) scheduled for launch in 1986.

Photo 21 Satellite earth stations, like this one, transmit telephone, telex and data calls, and international TV broadcasts to satellites above the equator from where the signals can be relayed to more than 80 countries.

Photo 22 A schoolgirl does her homework with the help of Micronet 800, a Prestel facility for home computer users.

8.5 Can machines have minds?

Will you—one day—call a computer clever, wise or intelligent? Will computers be created that get angry, crack new jokes, or get fed up? Can computers be made to hold ordinary conversations with people? Will people ever say that a computer, or a robot, has a *mind*?

The race is on

During the next ten years Japan, Britain and the USA will be involved in an expensive race—not the arms race, or the space race, but the super-computer race. The race is on to build the fifth generation of computers. Nobody is exactly sure what this new generation of computers will do but they will be expected to:
- reason and draw conclusions—to work things out for themselves
- make important judgements and decisions
- make sensible guesses, estimates and forecasts
- understand things, in the same way as humans do.

In other words they will generally function in a way that people would describe as being 'intelligent'. They will have **artificial intelligence**, AI for short.

There is one other ability that these intelligent, fifth-generation computers must have. They must be able to understand human speech, so that ordinary people can communicate with them. They will be the complete opposite of the first generation—only computer experts using machine code could use them.

Problems to overcome

Many people believe that the intelligent, understanding super-computer will arrive by 1990, but there are at least four problems to overcome first:
- their memories will need to be much larger than those of present computers—much better memory chips will be needed
- they will need to handle vast amounts of data at very high speed—up to several hundred million operations in one second
- new and better programming languages will need to be developed

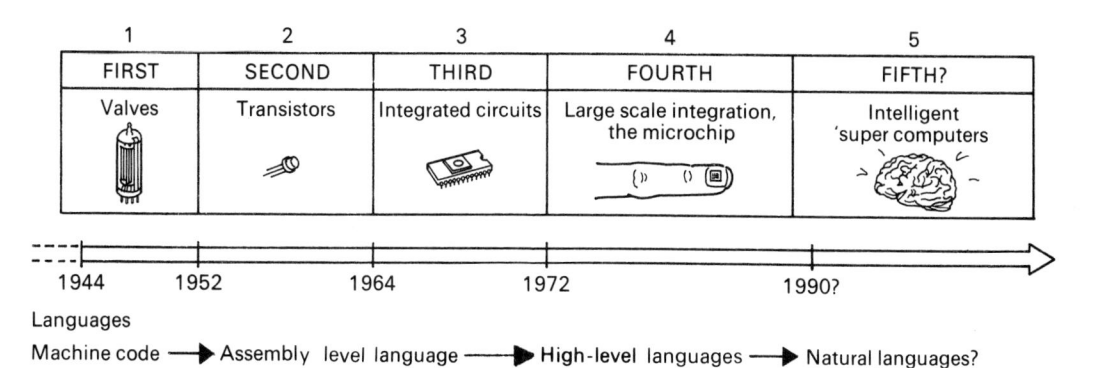

1	2	3	4	5
FIRST	SECOND	THIRD	FOURTH	FIFTH?
Valves	Transistors	Integrated circuits	Large scale integration, the microchip	Intelligent 'super computers

1944   1952   1964   1972   1990?

Languages
Machine code ⟶ Assembly level language ⟶ High-level languages ⟶ Natural languages?

Fig. 8.12 *The five generations*

- speech-understanding programs are still very limited.
  (At present, computers can only understand a very small, and well-spoken, range of commands. The machine that understands spoken English is still a long way off.)

However, billions of pounds, dollars and yen will be poured into the race to build intelligent computers. (Some of this money will come from the military who hope to build 'intelligent' weapons.)

Forecasting the future

Here are some forecasts of the jobs that fifth generation computers will do:

> robot housecleaners
> chauffeurs
> factory workers
> game players
> automatic tutors
> doctors' aides
> legal advisors
> marriage counsellors
> oil prospectors
> psychiatrists

Some of these forecasts are wild, to put it mildly! The idea of a robot driving a car is pure science fiction. Yet *some* of these ideas are already coming true. Many robots are used in factories, where a set task has to be done over and over again. Many computers have been programmed to play games, like chess. In fact, a computer has already beaten the world champion at backgammon.

A robot fitting a windscreen to a car

A robot home-help has been forecast to arrive by 1995. This will clear the floor then sweep it. It will pick up litter and put things away in the right place—if you tell it where the right place is! Future robots will be able to *learn* tasks by being *shown* how to do them first. They will be much more intelligent and flexible than the robots in factories now—like the car-spraying robot which will spray mid-air if there is no car in front of it.

Helping the experts

The most important 'intelligent' computers that are already used are the **expert systems**. These are programmed using the specialized skills, knowledge and experience of human experts (e.g. doctors, geologists). All this knowledge and expertise is stored in the computer's memory. So an expert system ends up with a very *special-purpose* kind of intelligence.

MYCIN One system already being used to help doctors is called MYCIN. This acts as an expert on infectious diseases. A doctor uses it by having a question-and-answer conversation with the computer for about twenty minutes. MYCIN can identify, or diagnose a disease—it can also give advice on the right drugs to treat it.

Prospector Another system is used for oil prospecting. The system is created by experts in geology who supply it with large amounts of up-to-date knowledge and data. This 'knowledge base' or database enables the computer to predict where oil can be found. The prospector using it supplies the computer with his *own* information. He will be asked questions by the expert system and will type in his answers. The computer system can then judge how likely he is to strike oil!

The main requirement of an expert system is that the people who use it should *trust* it. The system must be able to show its own line of reasoning and how it arrives at its conclusion. It must be able to *account for itself*. No doctor will give drugs to a patient, no oilman will spend money drilling for oil, if he does not trust the computer's advice.

Other systems Two other expert systems are forecast to arrive by 1990. The **legal adviser** will search for previous cases in the legal literature, and give advice. The **automatic tutor** will set questions to a pupil to find his or her level of understanding. It will then design an individually tailored course to suit that pupil, and to develop his understanding. The system will also have a huge collection of knowledge (on a particular topic) in its memory that a pupil can make use of.

None of these expert computer systems will *replace* human experts—but they could *help* the doctor, teacher, lawyer, oil prospector ... or even the psychiatrist. One psychiatrist has reported that a patient conversed far better with a computer than with him!

Can machines have minds: the intelligence test

How can you decide if a computer really is intelligent? A simple test was suggested by a British mathematician called Alan Turing. It involves two people, and a computer. The two people (X and Y) and the computer are placed in three separate rooms. X has to try to tell the differences between Y and the computer by making conversation (using a keyboard or a telephone) along wires to the two other rooms. If X cannot tell the difference between Y's replies and the computer's then the computer must be intelligent.

You may disagree with this test—it depends on what you mean by 'intelligent'. But one computer, in a science fiction story, did pass the test...

> The sixth member of the crew cared for none of these things, for it was not human. It was the highly advanced HAL 9000 computer, the brain and nervous system of the ship.
>
> Hal (for Heuristically programmed ALgorithmic computer, no less) was a masterwork of the third computer breakthrough. These seemed to occur at intervals of twenty years, and the thought that another one was now imminent already worried a great many people.
>
> The first generations of computers had received their inputs through glorified typewriter keyboards, and had replied through high-speed printers and visual displays. Hal could do this when necessary, but most of his communication with his shipmates was by means of the spoken word. Poole and Bowman could talk to Hal as if he were a human being, and he would reply in the perfect, idiomatic English he had learned during the fleeting weeks of his electronic childhood.
>
> Whether Hal could actually think was a question which had been settled by the British mathematician Alan Turing back in the 1940's. Turing had pointed out that, if one could carry out a prolonged conversation with a machine—whether by typewriter or microphone was immaterial—without being able to distinguish between its replies and those that a man might give, then the machine was thinking, by any sensible definition of the word. Hal could pass the Turing test with ease.
>
> The time might even come when Hal would take command of the ship. In an emergency, if no one answered his signals, he would attempt to wake the sleeping members of the crew, by electrical and chemical stimulation. If they did not respond, he would radio Earth for further orders.
>
> And then, if there was no reply from Earth, he would take what measures he deemed necessary to safeguard the ship and to continue the mission—whose real purpose he alone knew, and which his human colleagues could never have guessed.

(From *2001: A Space Odyssey* by Arthur C. Clarke.)

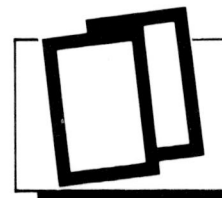

Reader
Machines with feelings

Some experts actually believe that computers and robots will one day be programmed to feel emotions: anger, sadness, pleasure, pain, happiness and so on. So far, ideas of 'machines with feelings' belong only to science fiction stories. In one story a robot called Marvin the Paranoid Android is always feeling fed up...

> In the corner, the robot's head swung up sharply, but then wobbled about imperceptibly. It pulled itself up to its feet as if it was about five pounds heavier than it actually was, and made what an outside observer would have thought was a heroic effort to cross the room. It stopped in front of Trillian and seemed to stare through her left shoulder.
>
> 'I think you ought to know I'm feeling very depressed,' it said. Its voice was low and hopeless.
>
> 'Oh God,' muttered Zaphod and slumped into a seat.
>
> 'Well,' said Trillian in a bright compassionate tone, 'here's something to occupy you and keep your mind off things.'
>
> 'It won't work,' droned Marvin, 'I have an exceptionally large mind.'
>
> 'Marvin!' warned Trillian.
>
> 'Alright,' said Marvin, 'what do you want me to do?'
>
> 'Go down to number two entry bay and bring the two aliens up here under surveillance.'
>
> With a microsecond pause, and a finely calculated micromodulation of pitch and timbre—nothing you could actually take offence at—Marvin managed to convey his utter contempt and horror of all things human.
>
> 'Just that?' he said.
>
> 'Yes,' said Trillian firmly.
>
> 'I won't enjoy it,' said Marvin.

Marvin arrives to collect the two aliens, Arthur Dent and Ford Prefect:

> 'Come on,' he droned, 'I've been ordered to take you down to the bridge. Here I am, brain the size of a planet and they ask me to take you down to the bridge. Call that job satisfaction? 'Cos I don't.'
>
> He turned and walked back to the hated door.
>
> 'Er, excuse me,' said Ford following after him, 'which government owns this ship?'
>
> Marvin ignored him.
>
> 'You watch this door,' he muttered, 'It's about to open again. I can tell by the intolerable air of smugness it suddenly generates.'
>
> With an ingratiating little whine the door slid open again and Marvin stomped through.
>
> 'Come on,' he said.
>
> The others followed quickly and the door slid back into place with pleased little clicks and whirrs.
>
> 'Thank you the marketing division of the Sirius Cybernetic Corporation,' said Marvin and trudged desolately up the gleaming curved corridor that stretched out before them. 'Let's build robots with Genuine People Personalities,' they said. So they tried it out with me. I'm a personality prototype. You can tell can't you?'

(From *The Hitch-Hiker's Guide to the Galaxy* by Douglas Adams.)

Questions

1 Do you think that machines like Marvin will one day be programmed to feel sad or miserable? How could it be done?

2 How do you think a machine could be programmed to have a sense of humour?

8.6 Towards the year 2000

Gazing into a crystal ball

The whole of Part 8 has discussed the way that modern computers and communications will affect people's lives: their jobs, their privacy and their leisure. As the year 2000 gets closer, more and more people are predicting and planning for 2001. Here are some of the changes that may arrive.

The cashless society Will people still use money in the year 2000? People have been using pieces of metal (coins), seashells, beads, or small sheets of paper for centuries now. All these things show how much the person carrying them owns. Have a look at a £1 note. It tells you that the Bank of England promises to pay you the sum of one pound. This is a piece of *information* and so could be stored in a computer. Suppose you buy something with £1 from a shop. A message can be sent from the computer holding data about your money, to take £1 from your account and add it to the shopkeeper's. This will save you giving him a piece of paper with 'One Pound' written on it. This is called direct transfer or **Electronic Funds Transfer** (EFT for short). Instead of money going from one hand to another, information will be sent from one computer to another. The flow of money may be replaced by a flow of electrons around the circuits of computer networks.

Electronic shopping To do this, a buyer will need a special card and his own personal, secret number; or he may have a home computer terminal which he can use to look at, order, and pay for, his shopping. Again, some special code number or password would have to be used. This home buying system, or electronic shopping, is already being done. Will it be common in the year 2000?

A step nearer the cashless society—payphones which will accept plastic cards instead of coins

The end of the energy crisis? The world faces a shortage of energy. Fuels like oil, coal and gas are being used up for transport, home heating and making electricity. Nuclear energy seems unable to fill the gap which they will leave. How can computers help this energy crisis? Computers themselves use very little energy—many use less than a light bulb—but they can help other energy-hungry devices to use less.

transport: Many people travel in and out of big cities every day to do office jobs. As computing and communications spread, many of these jobs will be done from home. The end of commuting would mean a huge saving on the energy used by cars, buses and trains. It could even, by the year 2000, make people ask: why do we need big cities?
control: Microprocessors, and computers, are excellent for *controlling* devices. They can switch them on and off at exactly the right time, or even *decide* if they are needed at all. A processor on

Traffic jams may soon be a thing of the past

a silicon chip can closely control a heating system and a lighting system. More than half of Britain's energy is used just to heat and light homes, offices and factories. With careful control much of this energy could be saved.
information: Accurate and up-to-date information gathered by satellites, processed and stored by computers, can be worth a fortune. Take agriculture, for example—if a farmer knows the condition and size of his crop, the layout of his land and the state of the market he can control his own business more efficiently. This can save money and *energy.* The same will be true of countries when they have accurate, easily accessed information about the food and farming they need. It should lead to the end of butter mountains and wine lakes!

What about human beings?

Isolation Electronic mail; home shopping by computer; electronically delivered newspapers; the end of commuting; working from home—all these developments could arrive before the year 2000. How will people react to these changes?

Each of these new trends would mean the loss of some human contact—the postman, the shopkeeper, the newspaper boy, the bus conductor, or friends at work. Will these contacts be replaced or will these new trends gradually *isolate* human beings from each other? The efficiency of every new change should be balanced carefully against the human isolation it brings—unless we want a highly efficient society where each person lives in their own micro-world.

The Third World Most of the world's computers are in the USA, Britain, East and West Europe, and Japan. Very few computers are used in the developing countries of Africa, South America, India and Asia. Yet over half the world's population lives in the Third World. How, and when, will computers be used widely in these countries? Nobody is quite sure. At the moment there hardly seems a use for computers in a country where most people live in slums, few are properly fed, and disease kills more than half of all children before the age of 12.

Nevertheless, computers are gradually being used in underdeveloped countries. Some are used to keep a record of the population (census work), some are used to help medical services (e.g. in keeping records), some in public administration. Computers are likely to spread through the Third World by the year 2000—partly because more than half the world's people live there. It may provide a perfect market for the large computer companies.

New developments

All kinds of new technology are likely to arrive in the computer world in the near future. There will be rapid changes in both *hardware* and *software.*

Hardware New kinds of memory device will be developed which can store huge amounts of data in a very small space, more and more cheaply! The number of components on a chip has gone up steadily since 1960. **Magnetic bubble memories** are likely to be common. These chips can

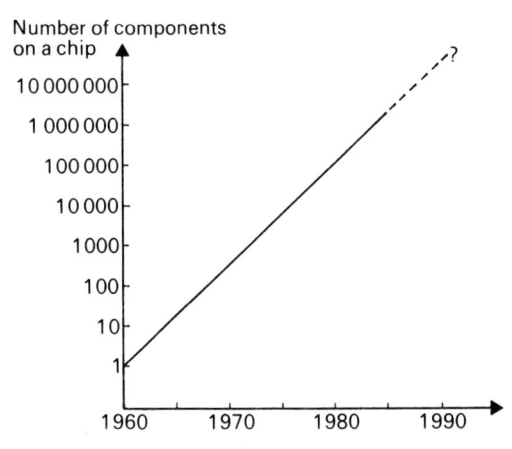

Fig. 8.13 The number of components that can be fitted on to a chip has risen dramatically since 1960

store over 1 million bits of binary information. Also they retain their data even when the power is off. One day they may replace tapes and disks, just as punched cards and paper tape have been replaced.

Another idea is the **Josephson junction**, invented by a British physicist in the 1960's. This uses **superconductors**. These are conductors of electricity that will carry an electric current forever if they are kept at a very low temperature, about −262 °C. A current flowing could stand for a '1', no current for a '0'—so they could be just right for a two-state (binary) memory device. However, there is one obvious problem—Josephson junctions need to be kept in a *very cold* refrigerator!

Many people feel that laser beams will be used more and more in the world of computers and communications. Already they are used in fibre-optics, printers, and memory storage on disk. One day they may replace the tiny electric currents at the heart of computers. They are also an important part of video disk technology and will therefore be used widely in backing storage. Video disks controlled by computer will be an important tool in education in the future.

Finally, there may well be a basic change in the whole design or *architecture* of computers. Instead of dealing with one instruction at a time (serial processing) they may be constructed to work on different instructions at the same time (*parallel processing*). A change like this could lead to new developments in computer languages: a change in *software*.

INMOS, Britain's chief manufacturing company, have developed a chip called a 'transputer'. This has several processors on one chip. To go with it there is a new programming language called OCCAM. This language can be used to write programs which use more than one processor at the same time.

Software Many experts believe that new ideas in software will have the greatest effect of all on computing in the year 2000. New, *higher-level* languages are being developed which are becoming nearer and nearer to people's language rather than a computer's. Languages will become more conversational, particularly as so-called intelligent machines arrive in the fifth generation.

All these improvements in software will mean that computers of the future can be used more easily, by more and more people. This may be the most important change of all: a computer that anyone can communicate with.

The whole theme of Part 8 has been based on two ideas: that ideas and devices in computing are constantly changing and developing; and that it is very difficult to make predictions about the future. One thing *is* certain: by the year 2000 the twin industries of computing and communications will be the largest in the world.

Glossary

A

access: to 'gain access to' or 'get to' an item of information.
acoustic coupler: a data communications device which enables a digital signal to be transmitted over the telephone network using an ordinary telephone.
address: the identification of a store location.
algorithm: a set of rules showing a sequence of operations for solving a certain type of problem.
analogue computer: a computer which represents data by a continuously variable physical quantity, e.g. voltage.
analogue-to-digital converter: a device which converts analogue signals into digital signals.
applications package: a set of specialized programs and documentation used to do a particular job.
arithmetic and logic unit (ALU): the part of the CPU where arithmetic/logic operations are carried out.
Artificial Intelligence (AI): the idea that computers can possess abilities like those of intelligent humans, e.g. the ability to learn, adapt, make decisions, etc.
assembler: a program which translates assembly language into machine code.
assembly language: a 'low-level' programming language which uses simple codes to represent machine code instructions.

B

backing store: a means of storing large amounts of data outside the immediate access store of a computer.
batch processing: a method in which computer processing does not begin until all the input data and/or programs have been collected or *batched* together.
baud: one bit per second—a unit for measuring the speed of data transmission.
Binary Coded Decimal (BCD): a coding system which uses a group of four binary digits to represent each numeral in a decimal number.
bit: binary digit (either 0 or 1).
block: a group of records treated as a complete unit during transfer to, or from, backing store.
bootstrap: a short sequence of instructions for loading a program into a computer.
buffer: a temporary data storage area between a peripheral device and the central processing unit which compensates for the difference between their working speeds.
bug: a program error, or equipment fault.
bureau: a source of computing facilities whose services may be hired.
byte: a fixed number of bits, e.g. 8 bits.

C

Ceefax: the teletext service provided by the BBC.
Central Processing Unit (CPU): the 'heart' of the computer which carries out the processing of data.
chain printer: a line printer with characters on a continuous chain.
character: one of the symbols which can be represented in a computer. (Standard character codes include: ASCII, ISO7, and EBCDIC.)

check digit: an extra digit attached to a number used to check the validity of that number.
chip: an integrated circuit.
compiler: a program which translates a complete high-level language program (e.g. in Pascal) into an independent program in machine code or other low-level language.
computer: a machine which automatically accepts and processes data and supplies the results of that processing, under the control of a stored program.
computer system: a central processing unit with its associated peripheral devices.

D

daisy-wheel printer: a printer with characters placed on the ends of the spokes of a small wheel
data: the basic building block of information.
data bank: a collection of databases.
database: an organized and structured collection of data.
data processing: the operation of collecting data, processing it, and presenting results.
digital computer: a computer in which data is represented by combinations of discrete electrical pulses, denoted by either a 1 or a 0.
direct access: the process of storing or retrieving data items without needing to read any other stored data first.
direct data entry: the input of data directly to a computer using, for example, a key-to-disk unit.
disk drive: the mechanism which makes magnetic disks rotate between reading/writing heads.
documentation: the description of a program including: helpful notes, flowcharts, program listing, test data and expected results.
document reader: an input device which reads marks or characters made in definite positions on special forms.

dot-matrix printer: a printer which forms characters from ink dots on a matrix of printing positions, e.g. 9 × 7.
dry run: the use of simple test data to check a program or flowchart without using a computer.

E

EPROM (Erasable Programmable Read Only Memory): a type of PROM memory which can be erased (e.g. by exposure to ultra-violet light) and 'written on' again.
even parity: a feature possessed by binary representation which contains an even number of 1's.

F

facsimile: a system for sending printed words, pictures or graphs to a receiver who gets an exact copy of the original.
fetch-execute cycle: the process of retrieving an instruction from store, decoding it and executing it.
fibre optics: the transmission of signals using light travelling along very thin strands of glass called optical fibres.
field: a section of a record.
file: an organized collection of related records.
floppy disk: a light, flexible magnetic disk.
flowchart: a graphical representation of a sequence of operations involved in a data processing system.
full-adder: a logic circuit which adds a pair of bits from two binary numbers and the carry bit from the previous stage. It produces a sum bit and a new carry bit (a three-input adder).

G

gate: an electronic device which controls the flow of pulses in a computer, enabling logical operations to be carried out.

graph plotter: an output device which draws lines on paper.

H

half-adder: a logic circuit which adds a pair of bits from two binary numbers (a two-input adder).
hard copy: computer output printed on paper.
hard disk: a rigid magnetic disk for data storage.
high-level language: a programming language which is designed for solving particular types of problems (e.g. business, scientific). It may be used on several different machines by using a suitable compiler.

I

immediate access store: the area of memory used to store programs and data currently being processed by the central processing unit.
information: the meaning given to data by the way in which it is interpreted by a human being.
information retrieval: the process of recovering information from stored data.
input device: a peripheral device which accepts data, decodes it and transmits it in the form of electrical pulses to the CPU of a computer.
integrated circuit: a tiny but complex electronic circuit embedded into a single wafer of silicon (usually).
intelligent terminal: a terminal able to do a certain amount of computing without contact with a central computer.
inter-block gap: a gap between two portions of data on backing store, e.g. magnetic tape.
interface: the link needed between a central processing unit and a peripheral device.
interpreter: a program which translates and executes a source program one statement at a time.

interrupt: a signal which causes a break in the execution of a current routine.

J

Job Control Language (JCL): a special language used to identify a job and describe its requirements to the operating system.

L

Large-Scale Integration (LSI): the technique of producing integrated circuits containing a huge number of components (VLSI, very large scale integration, is the next stage on).
laser: a very pure and highly concentrated light beam now important in the world of computers (e.g. in fibre optics and video disks).
laser printer: a printer which uses a laser beam to form characters on paper.
light pen: an input device used with a visual display unit, or for reading a bar chart.
line printer: a printer that prints a complete line of characters at one time.
Local Area Network (LAN): a set of computer systems linked together by wires in a small area, usually in the same building.
logic gate: (see *gate*).
low-level language: a programming language which uses code which is very close to machine code, e.g. assembly language.

M

machine code instruction: is one which directly defines a machine operation. It can be executed by the machine without any translation.
magnetic disk: a storage device consisting of a flat circular plate coated with magnetic material. Data is written to, and read from, a set of concentric circular tracks as the disk rotates.

Magnetic Ink Character Recognition (MICR): machine recognition of stylized characters printed in magnetic ink.

magnetic tape: a storage medium consisting of flexible plastic tape coated with magnetic material. Data is read, or written, as the tape passes over a read/write head.

mainframe: a large computer with many peripheral devices, a large backing store and powerful CPU.

main store: (see immediate access store).

master file: a file of data which is the main source of information for part, or the whole, of a system. It may be up-dated as necessary.

merge: is to combine two or more ordered files into a single, ordered file.

microcomputer: a small computer whose CPU is usually a microprocessor and has limited backing store and peripherals.

microelectronics: the science and technology of very small integrated circuits.

microfiche: an output medium consisting of large capacity microfilm sheets, access is by an optical reader/magnifier.

microprocessor: is a single chip which performs the functions of a CPU.

minicomputer: a computer whose size and speed lie somewhere between those of a mainframe and a microcomputer.

modem: (modulator/demodulator) device used to convert bits into analogue electrical impulses for transmission over telephone lines and vice versa.

multi-access: a computer system which allows several users to have apparently simultaneous access. Access is usually via terminals.

multi-programming: sharing the use of the CPU between several programs by allowing each program to use the CPU for short time periods in rotation. Controlled by the operating system.

N

network: a set of computer systems linked together, e.g. by wires, the telephone network, or by satellite.

O

object program: the translated version of a program that has been assembled or compiled.

odd parity: is present in any binary representation in which the number of 1's is odd.

off-line processing: is processing carried out by the computer at some time after the user has entered the job to be run.

on-line processing: is processing carried out by the computer whilst the user remains in communication with the computer.

operating system: a program which provides an easier running environment for user's programs.

Optical Character Recognition (OCR): machine recognition of stylized characters by light-sensing methods.

Optical Mark Reader (OMR): input device which reads marks from particular positions on special forms by a light-sensing method.

P

parity bit: a binary digit added to the end of a group of binary digits. The state of the bit is to ensure even or odd parity.

parity check: a test applied to binary data which involves counting the number of 1's in the data. The check is for odd or even parity.

PASCAL: a block-structured high-level programming language used in teaching programming and for general programming applications.

password: a sequence of characters

which must be presented to a computer before access to files, programs, etc. is allowed.

peripheral device: any input, output or backing device connected to the central processing unit.

pixel: a contraction of 'picture element', used in graphics to refer to the smallest element of a display screen.

point-of-sale terminal (POS terminal): an input device used to enter data about a sale directly from the point of sale to the computer, e.g. at a supermarket checkout till.

port: the point at which signals from peripheral devices enter the computer.

Prestel: the Post Office viewdata system.

process control: using a computer to monitor and control a process by programming it to respond to data fed back from a process.

program: a complete set of instructions which may be stored in a computer to cause it to carry out a required sequence of actions.

program counter: is the register containing the address of the next instruction to be executed. Also called next-instruction register, control register, sequence control register, instruction address register.

program flowchart: a graphical method of describing the sequence of operations within a computer program. Used to assist in the development of a program and to provide a permanent record of the program.

PROM (Programmable Read Only Memory): is a part of computer memory which may be written to once, but which is fixed from that time onwards.

Q

queue: is a list where new items are added at one end and items are deleted from the other, e.g. a queue of jobs in a batch system.

R

RAM (Random Access Memory): memory which may be read from and written to.

real-time system: a system which is capable of receiving data from outside sources and which is able to process that data quickly enough to be able to influence the sources of data, e.g. process control, air-traffic control.

record: a collection of related items of data, treated as a unit.

register: a memory location, which is usually very close to the CPU. Used for specific purposes, e.g. accumulator, program counter.

remote job entry: a method used in batch processing where a user's data and programs are entered to the computer from a remote terminal.

rogue value: a specified value, not normally expected in the data, which is used to terminate a list of data items. Also called terminator or sentinel value.

ROM (Read Only Memory): memory which has data stored in it by the manufacturer and which may be read but not written to.

rounding: the process of approximating a number by its nearest equivalent to a set number of significant figures.

S

sequence control register: (see program counter).

sequential (serial) access: is the process of storing or retrieving data items by first reading through all previous items to locate the one required.

sign bit: is a single bit, used to indicate the sign of a binary number, usually 0 for positive, 1 for negative.

software package: a fully documented program, or set of programs, designed to perform a particular task.

sort: is to arrange a set of data according to a particular predetermined rule, e.g. in alphabetical order.

source program: a program as written by the programmer. It must be compiled, interpreted or assembled before it can be executed.

speech recognition: is the process of analysing a spoken word and comparing it with those known by the computer.

spooling: is the temporary storage of input or output data on magnetic tape or disk. It is a means of compensating for slow operating speeds of peripheral devices.

structured programming: a programming technique which emphasizes breaking large and complex tasks into successively smaller sections.

subprogram: a set of program instructions performing a specific task, but which is not a complete program. It must be incorporated into a program in order to be used—also called subroutine, routine, procedure, function.

systems analysis: analysis of the requirements of a system and a feasibility study of potential computer involvement.

systems design: the design of an appropriate system for a job, usually based on the systems analysis.

systems software: the collection of programs used for the total control of the performance of a computer system.

T

telecommunications: the transmission of information by cable or radio waves.

telesoftware: is software which is transmitted by teletext.

teletext: a television system that displays publicly broadcast information on a TV screen (one-way only).

teletypewriter: input/output device consisting of a keyboard and typewriter-like printer. Usually used for direct communication with a computer.

terminal: the term used to describe any input/output device which is used to communicate with the computer from a remote site.

time sharing: a means of providing multi-access to a computer system. Each user is, in turn, allowed a time slice of the system's resources, although each appears to have continuous use of the system.

transaction file: is a collection of records used to update a master file. Also called update file or change-file.

truncating: the process of approximating a number by ignoring all information beyond a set of significant figures.

truth table: is a Boolean operation table in which the result is tabulated for all possible combinations of the variables.

two's complement: a means of representing negative numbers. Each 0 bit is changed to a 1 and each 1 to a 0, and then 1 is added to the result.

U

update file: (see transaction file).

V

validation: an input control technique used to detect any data which is inaccurate, incomplete or unreasonable.

verification: the process of checking input data by keying it in twice and comparing the two inputs.

very large scale integration (VLSI): the technique of producing integrated circuits of a very high density.

videotex: the general name for 'text on video'. The name covers both teletext and viewdata.

viewdata: the system first developed by British Telecom for sending computer data by telephone line and displaying information on a TV screen. It allows two-way communication between a user and the computer centre.

W

Winchester drive: a disk drive which uses hard disks in a sealed unit.
word: a collection of bits treated as one unit by the computer, usually 2 or more bytes.
word processor: a computer system designed to assist in producing, storing and editing text, e.g. typed letters.

Further Questions

Multiple choice revision questions: 1

For each of these questions select one of the options. It should take about half an hour to complete the 30 questions.

1. Which of the following 8-bit words contains the binary equivalent to the decimal number 26?
   a) 00011010
   b) 11100010
   c) 00110100
   d) 00011001
   e) 00110011
2. The person credited with the idea of using punch cards to control patterns in a weaving machine was:
   a) Hollerith
   b) Pascal
   c) Jacquard
   d) Napier
   e) Babbage
3. The special characters on bank cheques are read by:
   a) an optical character reader
   b) magnetic ink character recognition
   c) a visual display unit
   d) a document reader
   e) a teletype
4. A set of program instructions which perform a specific task as part of a complete program is:
   a) a subroutine
   b) a source program
   c) an object program
   d) a compiled program
   e) an identifier list
5. A program which translates and executes a source program one instruction at a time is known as:
   a) a compiler
   b) an interpreter
   c) a utility program
   d) an operating system
   e) an executive program
6. A computer has a 32K store. What does the letter K stand for?
   a) kilometre
   b) 10
   c) 1024
   d) core
7. Which one of the following is an example of software?
   a) line printer
   b) payroll package
   c) console
   d) paper tape reader
8. A computer has a 6-bit word with two's complements used for negative numbers. What is the decimal value represented by 101001?
   a) -22
   b) 41
   c) -23
   d) 23
9. The term used to describe what happens when the result of a calculation is too large to be stored in a register is:
   a) overwriting
   b) truncation
   c) rogue value
   d) overflow
10. A series of instructions in ordinary English or algebraic form for the solution of a given problem is:
    a) an algorithm
    b) a print-out
    c) a coding sheet
    d) an analogue
11. What is meant by the term RAM?
    a) memory which can only be read
    b) memory which can be both read and written to
    c) memory which is used for long-term storage
    d) memory which can only be written to

e) memory which does nothing at all

12 Which of the following would be used for serial access storage only?
a) magnetic disks
b) ROM
c) core store
d) magnetic tape
e) RAM

13 Which of the following is the best description of a file?
a) a general collection of data items
b) a single data item
c) an orderly collection of data items
d) a random collection of data items
e) a limited number of data items

14 What does OCR stand for?
a) Other Characters Required
b) Operational Character Recognition
c) Only Characters Read
d) Optical Character Recognition
e) Outsize Character Reader

15 Which of the following would need to use real-time computing?
a) banking
b) payroll
c) weapons guidance
d) stock control
e) information retrieval

16 What is meant by the term 'high-level language'?
a) machine code
b) an assembler
c) a language that is hard to use
d) a language which is problem orientated
e) a language special to its own computer

17 What is a microprocessor?
a) something which looks at the picture in a microscope
b) a computer
c) a small device that controls other equipment
d) a small piece of equipment
e) a way of doing something fast

18 What is a word processor?
a) a computer program for checking data
b) a device that tells us the meaning of words
c) a computer program that handles text
d) an output device
e) an input device

19 Which of the following cannot be exactly represented in binary?
a) 492
b) 0.625
e) 72183
d) 0.1
e) 0.75

20 Grandfather, father and son files are:
a) three generations of computers
b) three types of magnetic tape
c) three examples of magnetic storage
d) a program in high level, assembler and machine code languages
e) recent copies of a file, kept for security reasons

21 A payroll system, working sequentially through a file of a firm's employees to calculate the weeks wages would recall the employee's relevant details from:
a) magnetic tape
b) punched cards
c) the immediate access store
d) mark-sense cards
e) punched paper tape

22 Two alphabetic characters may be stored in a single computer location. If $X = 001101$ and $Y = 010000$, then XY would be stored in a single location as:
a) 1101010000
b) 00110101
c) 010000001101
d) 110101000000
e) 001101010000

23 Which type of output from a computer could be used to control the cutting mechanism of a steel manufacturing plant?
a) punched paper tape output
b) graphical hard copy
c) electrical output
d) temporary output on VDU
e) microfilm output

24 The logical statement X = NOT (P OR Q) could be obtained by using two inputs P and Q into:
   a) an AND gate followed by a NOT gate
   b) a NOT gate followed by an OR gate
   c) a NOT gate followed by an AND gate
   d) an OR gate followed by a NOT gate
   e) an OR gate followed by an AND gate
25 A light pen used by a design engineer would be used in conjunction with:
   a) mark-sense cards
   b) a teletypewriter
   c) an optical card reader
   d) a graphical display unit
   e) a microfilm unit
26 A 'point-of-sale' device is:
   a) used to read kimball tags in clothes shops
   b) a modern check-out found in supermarkets
   c) found in banks to read the numbers on cheques
   d) part of a computer controlled water purifying plant
   e) a section of a car manufacturing system
27 A kimball tag is:
   a) a security key
   b) an input medium
   c) a gift token
   d) part of an integrated circuit
   e) an address label
28 In a library a computer may be used to obtain information on various subjects by typing in certain keywords. This type of system is known as:
   a) a batch processing system
   b) a multi processing system
   c) an information retrieval system
   d) a real time system
   e) a process control system
29 A master file containing 15 records is updated using a transaction file containing:
   10 new records
   5 deletions 1 amendment

How many records will be contained in the new master file?
   a) 31
   b) 29
   c) 11
   d) 19
   e) 20
30 Which logic gate has the following truth table?

P	Q	OUTPUT
0	0	0
0	1	1
1	0	1
1	1	1

   a) A NOR gate
   b) An AND gate
   c) A NOT gate
   d) A NAND gate
   e) An OR gate

Acknowledgements
ALSEB 1–5); SWEB (6–10); EAEB (11–19); EMREB (20–30)

Multiple choice revision questions: 2

For each of these questions select one of the options. It should take about half an hour to complete the 30 questions.

1 Early electronic computers were used for:
   a) stock control
   b) payroll analysis
   c) solving mathematical problems
   d) controlling traffic lights
   e) aircraft seat booking
2 A non-numeric character (e.g. the letter S) held in the immediate access store would be represented by:
   a) a file
   b) a peripheral
   c) a program
   d) a number of bits
   e) a number of records
3 Before a program written in a high-level language can be processed, it has to be converted into machine

code. This can be done by:
a) an assembler
b) the operating system
c) the object program
d) a compiler
e) the input device

4 Computers are used to produce charts which are used in weather forecasting. Which of the following devices would be used to produce these charts?
a) paper-tape reader
b) graph plotter
c) line printer
d) teletypewriter
e) microfilm camera

5 The term 'operating system' means:
a) the way a computer operator works
b) a set of programs which control how the computer works
c) a high-level language being converted to machine code
d) the way a magnetic disk drive operates
e) the computer operator shift system

6 An example of an 'application package' is:
a) the operating system
b) a payroll program
c) BASIC
d) the compiler
e) a database

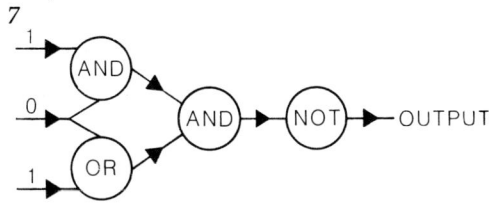

7 The output from the logic diagram shown above with the inputs as shown is:
a) logic 0
b) logic 0 and logic 1
c) logic 1
d) nothing at all
e) logic 1 or logic 0

8 A large school has details of all its pupils on a computer system. On which medium would it be best to store data for rapid random access?
a) punched cards
b) paper tape
c) magnetic tape
d) floppy disk
e) mark-sense cards

9 One of the major developments which led to the microcomputer was:
a) the teletypewriter terminal
b) magnetic disks
c) core stores
d) magnetic tape
e) integrated circuits

10 The system used when making airline bookings is:
a) real time
b) multi-access
c) random-access
d) main line
e) off line

11 The process which checks that data falls within reasonable limits is called:
a) corruption
b) verification
c) compilation
d) validation
e) documentation

12 Which one of the following is left in the accumulator when a binary number and its 2's complement are added together in a computer?
a) zero
b) one
c) two
d) the 1's complement of the binary number

13 Which one of the columns A, B, C or D of the truth table describes the output of the diagram?

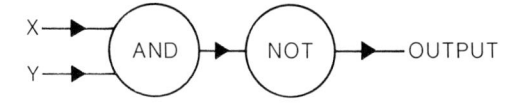

X	Y	A	B	C	D
0	0	1	0	1	0
0	1	0	0	1	1
1	0	0	0	1	1
1	1	0	1	0	1

14 Which one of the following computer personnel is most likely to work at a keyboard?
   a) a maintenance engineer
   b) a systems analyst
   c) a data preparation operator
   d) a file librarian
15 Which one of the following can be found in a record on magnetic tape?
   a) a field
   b) a file
   c) a block
   d) a reel
16 Which one of the following is a computer backing store?
   a) a visual display unit (VDU)
   b) an arithmetic unit
   d) a control unit
   d) a disk file
17 A program completes a loop twice. Nested within this loop, a second loop is performed five times. During each run of the program, how many times is the inner loop executed?
   a) twice
   b) five times
   c) seven times
   d) ten times
18 Computer output on microfiche is used directly by the public in:
   a) libraries
   b) banks
   c) supermarkets
   d) travel agencies
19 F4 is a number in hexadecimal notation. Its binary equivalent is:
   a) 000F0004
   b) 11111111
   c) 11110100
   d) 01001111
20 How many alphanumeric characters are there in PJX1982?
   a) 0
   b) 3
   c) 4
   d) 7
21 PRESTEL is a service provided by:
   a) the BBC
   b) the ITA
   c) teletext
   d) British Telecom
22 A record with a key field can be found in:
   a) a teletypewriter
   b) a console
   c) a database
   d) a key punch
23 ROM stands for:
   a) Round Off Multiples
   b) Read Onto Microprocessor
   c) Repeat Of Monitor
   d) Read Only Memory
24 Which one of the following is an example of software?
   a) a floppy disk
   b) a compiler
   c) a magnetic disk
   d) a peripheral
25 Key-to-disk operators work in:
   a) computer management
   b) program development
   c) computer maintenance
   d) data preparation
26 Overflow occurs when:
   a) a computer blows a fuse
   b) a calculation exceeds the capacity of the computer
   c) a program contains an endless loop
   d) a flowchart has to be continued on another page
27 The part of a computer used for calculating and comparing is:
   a) the console
   b) the arithmetic and logic unit
   c) the tape or disk unit
   d) the acoustic coupler
28 The output from a compiler is called which one of the following?
   a) object code
   b) source dode
   c) assembly code
   d) mnemonic code
29 Which column A, B, C or D of the truth table describes the output of the logic gate shown in the diagram?

X	Y	A	B	C	D
0	0	0	0	0	1
0	1	0	1	1	0
1	0	0	1	1	0
1	1	1	0	1	0

INPUT X → OR → OUTPUT
INPUT Y →

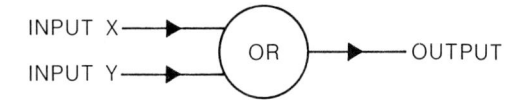

30 Which one of the following statements about the byte 00001111 is not correct?
   a) It has exactly four bits
   b) It has a binary value equal to fifteen
   c) It has even parity
   d) It could represent the two hexadecimal digits O F

Acknowledgments
EMREB (1–16); NWREB (17–30)

Revision paper 1

It should take about an hour to complete this paper.

Short questions

1 Copy out and complete these sentences with the correct word or term:
   a) A _____ check is a test applied to the number of 1's in binary data.
   b) _____ is using a series of checks or tests on input data to ensure it is reasonable.
   c) _____ is checking the accuracy of data before input for example by punching a card twice.
   d) 1024 words of storage is usually referred to as _____ of store.
   (ALSEB)

2 The diagram below shows two computers moving data from one to the other through the telephone network. What is the name of the device labelled A?

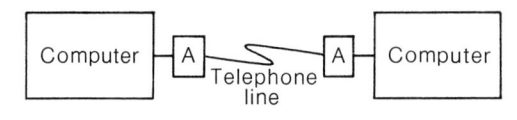

Computer —[A]— Telephone line —[A]— Computer

(SWEB)

3 a) What decimal number is represented by the binary number 001010011?
   b) How would you represent the decimal number 54 as a binary number?
   c) What is the largest decimal number that can be represented by 8 binary bits?
   (WJEC)

4 Why is a buffer store used when transmitting data between CPU and peripheral devices?
   (AEB 1982)

5 For each of the following devices give an example of a typical application and explain why the device is particularly suitable.
   a) optical character reader
   b) magnetic ink character reader
   c) visual display unit
   d) terminal—teleprinter

Longer Questions

1 Read the following passage and then answer the questions which follow.

'The standard model of the BBC microcomputer uses a 6502 microprocessor, has 16K RAM, 32K ROM, high resolution graphics and uses a keyboard, a domestic TV receiver and a cassette recorder. The 32K ROM includes a 16K BASIC and a 16K operating system.'

   a) What input devices are used?
   b) What is meant by 'high resolution graphics'?
   c) What is meant by 'RAM'?
   d) Explain the meaning of the final sentence to someone who has never met the terms 'ROM', 'BASIC' and 'operating system', and this particular use of the letter K.
   (SUJB)

2 a) Draw the logic circuit for a half adder.
   b) Explain why the half adder is insufficient to cope with the addition of binary codes with more than one bit.
   (ALSEB)

3 Domestic products controlled by a microprocessor, such as washing machines, ovens and sewing

machines, have been available for some time. Robotic devices, such as welders, are controlled by microprocessors and used in making cars.
  a) What is a microprocessor?
  b) Explain how a microprocessor-based system could be used to control the heating for a house. You should identify two inputs required and outline three functions that the microprocessor system would perform.
  Suggest a benefit, for the owner of the house, of using this system.
  c) Explain one possible effect that the use of robotic devices could have upon employment. Give an example to support your explanation.
  d) Suggest a further use for microprocessors in the year 2000 and give an advantage of this application.
  (SREB)
4 Acoustic coupler; graphics tablet/digitizer; point of sale terminal; information retrieval; viewdata. Choose four of the above and for each one:
  a) outline what it is,
  b) give a brief description of a way in which it can be used.
  (OLU)

Revision paper 2

It should take about an hour to complete this paper.

Short questions

1 By using an example, show how two's complementation is used to represent a negative number in the binary system.
2 Explain one advantage of using a word processor, instead of an ordinary typewriter, to correct a letter. Suggest a disadvantage of introducing word processing.
  (SREB)
3 Magnetic tape in the form of cassettes is a popular type of backing store for use with microprocessors. Give TWO possible reasons for this.
  (YREB)
4 In each of the 'three generations' of computers what was the major electronic component used?
5 a) Name an application which would use COM.
  b) Name an application which would use an OCR.
  (WJEC)
6 One of the problems with storing large amounts of information is in making sure that the information does not fall into the wrong hands. Give two methods of ensuring that terminals are not used by the wrong people to access data held in computers.
7 A certain computer can obey 16 different kinds of instruction.
  a) How many bits are required for its operation code (sometimes called its op-code or its function code)?
  b) Each instruction consists of an address part and a function part. How many address bits are required in each instruction if the main store has ½K words?
  (WMEB)
8 Explain, briefly, with the aid of a diagram, how a chain printer operates.
  (AEB 1982)

Longer questions

1 Copy and complete the table for this logic circuit.

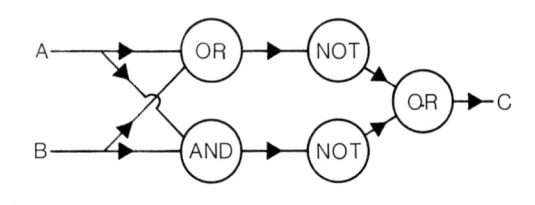

a	b	c
0	0	
0	1	
1	0	
1	1	

Draw an equivalent logic circuit which uses only 2 gates.
(SUJB)

2 Construct a table showing the contrasting abilities in general terms of magnetic tape and magnetic disk with reference to:
   a) application
   b) cost
   c) speed of transfer of information
   d) type of access
   e) complexity of equipment
   (JMB)
3 Read the article below before answering the questions.

   'Files of personal information have always been held by many people such as goverment departments and the police. Some people believe that storing this information in a computer data bank increases the threat to an individual's privacy.'

   a) Suggest one reason why using a computer to store and retrieve personal information is considered a threat to privacy. Give an example to support your reason.
   b) One view is that people should have right of access to data about themselves.
      (i) Give one reason to support this view.
      (ii) Explain in two or three sentences how a person might obtain this information.
   c) In certain cases it might be better if a person was prevented from seeing some information held in his record. Give an example of such information and an explanation for your choice.
   d) Suggest one way in which personal data held on a computer could be misused and give an example to illustrate your answer.
      Explain briefly how this misuse could be prevented.
   (SREB)

Revision paper 3

It should take about an hour to complete this paper.

Short questions
1 What do you understand by the term 'peripheral'? Why are peripherals necessary?
2 A word processor consists of a keyboard, visual display, floppy disk drive, a limited amount of main store and a printer. It is used to process and output information.
   a) What form of backing store is used?
   b) How is the information input?
   c) Give a specific example of information that is stored on a word processor.
   (SREB)
3 a) Change the octal number 24 to a binary number.
   b) Change the decimal number -7 to an 8-bit binary number using two's-complement representation.
   c) How many bits are needed to represent all the characters possible in a two digit hexadecimal number?
   (ALSEB)
4 What is a large file of related information which can be used for several different applications, e.g. vehicle records, called?
5 'A computer has a store of 64K.' What is being referred to? What does '64K' mean?
6 What is the output, X, from each of the following logic gates?

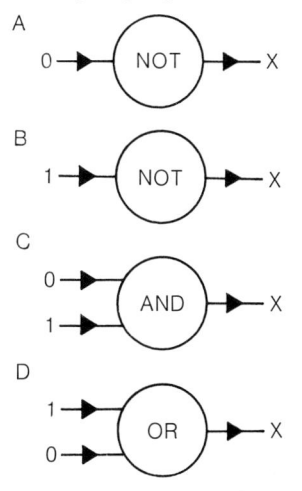

A
$0 \rightarrow$ NOT $\rightarrow X$

B
$1 \rightarrow$ NOT $\rightarrow X$

C
$0 \rightarrow$
$1 \rightarrow$ AND $\rightarrow X$

D
$1 \rightarrow$
$0 \rightarrow$ OR $\rightarrow X$

(NREB)

Longer Questions

1 Computers are being used increasingly in the field of medicine.
   a) Name THREE tasks for which computers are likely to be used for either medical or administration work in hospitals.
   b) State TWO advantages of the use of computers in medicine.
   c) Suggest TWO reasons why people may object to the use of computers in hospitals.
   (YREB)

2 A particular computer stores whole numbers in a five-bit register. The left-most bit is the sign bit and negative numbers are held in the two's complement form.
   a) How would −6 be represented in this register?

   b) What denary (base ten) number would be held in this register as

1	0	0	0	1	?

   c) Add together the following binary numbers and show the answer as it would be held in this register.

	1	1	0	0	1
+	0	1	1	0	1

   (NREB)

3 a) Using the logic system below, make a truth table showing the results Z for all possible combinations of inputs at A and B. Include V, W, X and Y in your table.
   b) Sketch a simpler logic system which gives an identical set of outputs at Z.
   (NWREB)

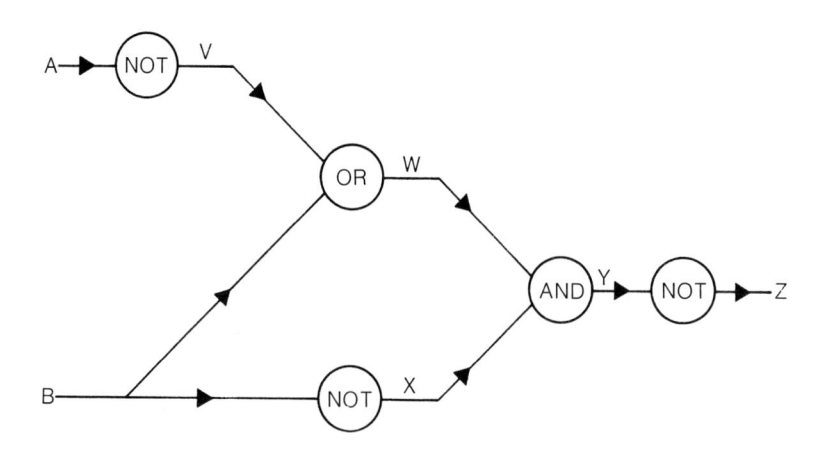

Acknowledgments

The authors and publishers would like to thank the following for permission to reproduce copyright material:

Colour photographs

Paul Brierley: photos 1, 12 and 17
IBM (UK) Ltd: photos 2 and 3
British Telecom plc: photos 4, 13, 18, 19, 21, 22
Apple Computers (UK) Ltd: photo 5
NCR Ltd: photo 6
Dept of Trade and Industry: photos 7 and 8
Tektronix (UK) Ltd: photo 9
Honeywell Information Systems Ltd: photo 10
Acornsoft Ltd: photo 11
T J M Kennie, University of Surrey: photo 14
Ford Motor Company Ltd: photo 15
British Airports Authority: photo 16
European Space Agency: photo 20

Black and white photographs

Honeywell Information Systems Limited: page 4, left
Digital Equipment Co. Limited: page 4, top right
Acorn Computers Limited: page 4, bottom right
Science Museum, London: page 11; page 12, left and right; page 13
Moore School of Electrical Engineering, University of Pennsylvania: page 14
Mullard Ltd: page 15
Texas Instruments: page 16
Tektronix (UK) Ltd: page 23; page 27, right; page 32, left and right
IBM (UK) Ltd: page 24, left; page 38, bottom
UniChem Ltd: page 24, right
Midland Bank plc: page 26
NCR Limited: page 27, left; page 177, top right
Pertec International Ltd: page 38, top
TI Creda Ltd: page 136
South of Scotland Electricity Board: page 155
Wales Tourist Board: page 171
Seiko Time: page 177, bottom left
Olympus Optical Co. (UK) Ltd: page 177, top left
Austin Rover Group Ltd: page 177, bottom right; page 218
International Computers Limited: page 178, left
British Telecom plc: page 178, right; page 183, left and right; page 184; page 209, top; page 222
Ford Motor Company: page 193, top left
Marconi Space and Defence Systems Ltd: page 193, right
Central Office of Information: page 193, bottom left

World Health Organization: page 195
National Institute of Agricultural Engineering: Page 199, top left
National Coal Board: page 199, bottom left
Ferranti Autocourt plc: page 199, right
Camera Press: page 201; page 205; page 209, bottom; page 223

Exam questions

The Associated Examining Board (AEB)
Associated Lancashire Schools Examining Board (ALSEB)
East Anglian Examinations Board (EAEB)
East Midland Regional Examinations Board (EMREB)
Joint Matriculation Board (JMB)
London Regional Examining Board (LREB)
North West Regional Examinations Board (NWREB)
The South-East Regional Examinations Board (SEREB)
South Western Examinations Board (SWEB)
Southern Regional Examinations Board (SREB)
Southern Universities' Joint Board (SUJB)
University of Cambridge Local Examinations Syndicate (Cambridge)
University of London School Examinations Department (London)
University of Oxford Delegacy of Local Examinations (OLE)
Welsh Joint Education Committee (WJEC)
The West Midlands Examinations Board (WMEB)
Yorkshire and Humberside Regional Examinations Board (YHREB)

Other copyright material

Control Dataset Ltd: punched card, page 13
Sinclair Scientific Ltd: extract from Sinclair Spectrum handbook, page 19
British Standards Institution: extracts from BS 5464 Parts 1 and 2 (OCR font) and BS 4810 (MICR font), page 25
Midland Bank plc: specimen cheque, page 25
Marks and Spencer plc: Kimball tag, page 26
The Guardian: Computer, watch your language by Douglas Bell, page 68; Extract from Review by Peter Large, page 134
National Computing Centre: flowchart graph papers, pages 151–153
Pharos Ltd: sample invoice, page 156
IBM (UK) Ltd: advertisement, page 192
The late Sonia Brownwell Orwell and Martin, Secker and Warburg Ltd: extract from 1984 by George Orwell, pages 196–7
Penguin Books Ltd: extract from The Soul of a New Machine by Tracy Kidder, pages 202–4
The Observer Magazine; extract from The Man Who Has Given Up Paper by Julian Allason, page 210
Manpower Services Commission: data protection leaflet, page 212
Macmillan Ltd, London and Basingstoke: extract from Player Piano by Kurt Vonnegut Jr, pages 215–16
Inner Circle Books: extract from 2001: A Space Odyssey by Arthur C Clarke, page 219
Pan Books Ltd: extract from Hitch-hiker's Guide to the Galaxy by Douglas Adams, pages 220–1

Index

A

abacus 11
accumulators 119
acoustic coupler 132
address 8, 118
ALGOL 63, 64
algorithm 44, 46–50
analogue 2, 172
analogue-to-digital converter 2, 127
applications software 9
arithmetic unit 9, 118
artificial intelligence 16, 217–20
ASCII code 88, 206
assembler 62
assembly language 61, 62, 66

B

Babbage, Charles 12, 14
backing store 9, 35
BASIC 55, 56, 58, 63, 64
batch processing 75, 79
binary code 86–95
binary coded decimal 93
binary numbers 91–9
binary word 87
bits 8, 86
bootstrapping 74
branch instructions 122
bubble memory 38, 206, 223
buffer 128
bytes 87, 119, 207

C

carry bit 109–11
central processing unit (CPU) 9, 118, 122, 125
character code 87–8
check digit 157–8
chip 15, 176
clock pulses 123
COBOL 55, 57, 59, 63, 64
command language 73
compiler 63–6
computer-aided design (CAD) 192
computer-assisted learning (CAL) 194
computer bureau 148
computer networks 185, 209
computer output microfilm (COM) 31
control 128, 136–7, 140
control unit 9, 119
CP/M 82–3

D

data 3
database 78, 182, 184, 194
data processing 141
data protection 212–13
data transmission 172, 173, 206
denary 91
digital 2, 172
digital-to-analogue conversion 127
direct access 37, 161, 162
direct data entry 144, 155
disks 35, 36–9, 162, 187, 207
document readers 24–5

E

electronic funds transfer (EFT) 222
electronic mail 208
ENIAC 15, 17
EPROM 177
execute cycle 121–2
expert systems 200, 218–19
exponent 102–4

F

facsimile 208, 209
feasibility 147
fetch cycle 121, 122
fibre optics 179
files 160–6
fixed-point representation 101–2

243

flag register   111
floating-point representation   102–4
flowcharts   46–50
FORTRAN   45, 55, 56, 63, 64
full adder   110–11

G

gates   106–14
generations, first to fifth   14–16, 217
generations, of files   165

H

half-adder   109
hexadecimal   93–4
high-level languages   63–6
Hollerith   13

I

immediate access store   9
information   3
information technology   176–87
input devices   22–8
instructions   119
integrated circuit   15
interactive processing   77
interface   136
interpreter   63–5
interrupts   127–8

J

job control language (JCL)   75, 79

K

keys   161
key-to-disk/tape   24

L

lasers   186, 224
Lindop report   213
local area network (LAN)   83, 130, 185, 209
logic circuits   109–14
logic unit   9
Lovelace, Lady   13
low-level language   61–2

M

machine code   61, 120
magnetic disk   35, 36–9, 162, 207
magnetic tape   35–6, 162
mainframe computer   4, 78
mantissa   102, 104
mass storage   9
master file   164–5
memory   8
merging   163
microcomputer   4, 78
microelectronics   176, 192, 200
microprocessor   15, 136, 138, 177, 192
minicomputer   4
modem   131, 132
multi-access   78
multiprogramming   76
multitasking   83

N

Napier's bones   11
networks   130–3, 185–6, 209

O

object code   62, 63
octal numbers   94
off-line processing   76, 155, 156
on-line processing   77, 154, 156
operating system   72–9
operation codes   119, 120
optical disks   38, 206
optical fibre   179
output devices   29–34
overflow   96, 111

P

parallel input/output   126
parity bits   88–9
PASCAL   55, 56, 57, 59, 63, 64
Pascal, Blaise   11
peripherals   9
ports   125, 136
PRESTEL   182–4, 192
printers   29–31
program   3, 44
programming language(s)   9, 55–66
PROM   138, 177
punched cards   13
pure binary representation   92

R

RAM   82, 177
random access   37
real-time computing   78, 172, 173
records   160–1
registers   119
ROM   73, 177
round-robin   77
rounding   101, 112

S

scheduling   76
security   165
sequential access   161–2
serial access   161–2
serial input/output   126
sign bit   96
software package   147
sorting   163
source code   62, 63
structured programming   52–3
sub-tasks   52–3
systems analysis   146–9
systems analyst   143, 144
systems designs   143–5, 150–9, 169
systems flowcharts   144, 150–4

T

tape, magnetic   35–6, 162
Teletext   182
transaction file   164
transistor   15
truncation   101, 112
truth table   106
two's complement   96–9

U

underflow   111, 112
updating files   164, 165

V

validation   157, 158, 169
verification   157
video disk   187
Videotex   182
Viewdata   182
visual display unit (VDU)   23, 32
VLSI   16

W

wide area network (WAN)   130, 185, 209
Winchester disks   38, 165
word processing   206, 208